Memories *From My* **AIDS** *Years*

Memories From My AIDS Years

MARGARET LEMBERG

To order additional copies of this book, contact:
Xlibris
1-888-795-4274
www.Xlibris.com
Orders@Xlibris.com
803373

CONTENTS

Dedication

My writing is always for my children, and now for my grandchildren. And for all others in my life, who love me and trust me to love them.

Introduction

I remember people, places, organizations, and relationships from those years (1990–2000) when I was part of the Seattle AIDS community. I was a massage therapist. I was a friend. I was interested in learning about the disease and hoping to bring some comfort to people I met during those years.

I was in transition in 1990. I had been working for my husband's wholesale clothing business. I wanted something different and ended up going to massage school (1992–1992). I wanted to participate in the LGBT community. AIDS seemed like an important way to do this. I eventually left my marriage and moved to my own house (fall 1993).

It is now twenty-five years since my friend John died of AIDS, having never dictated or written the story of his own life. I wish he had. He often said that he planned to tell his story. All I can do now is tell part of his story from the years I knew him. When I began thinking about writing his story, I also began to remember other people. I began to think about all I learned from those years. And I began writing.

As I wrote, I remembered people living with AIDS and caregivers. I remembered theories and treatments. I would like to share these memories with others who provide medical care for sick people (whether with AIDS or dying from other causes). I would also like to share with therapists and social workers who help with practical solutions and emotional support.

Putting Together Memories of AIDS

I began writing essays about my experiences in the AIDS community (1990–2000) just over two years ago. I made numerous notes about various memories. I drew on journal entries and poems written before. All along, I wanted to write about my life during those years and even more about the remarkable people I met during that time.

I know very well as I write the essays that I am forgetting some details and getting others completely wrong. Yet I think it's better to write it than not. No one else had the same experiences and knew all the same people as I did. Perhaps others could write pieces of these memories better than I have, but not all of it. Sometimes I feel frustrated when I write about individuals. I know some very well in a small segment of their lives but know little or nothing about their lives before they had AIDS. I didn't always ask. Being in the moment with each person was most important.

My years in the AIDS community began in 1990 and continued through 2000. At first, I was a volunteer for Chicken Soup Brigade (1990), giving rides and preparing food. I later volunteered at Madison Clinic and the AIDS Clinical Trial Unit, doing massage. People who worked at those places introduced me to people who worked at Northwest AIDS Foundation, and some became massage clients. The AIDS community was a small world and interconnected.

Over time, I visited people who were living (and dying) at Rosehedge and Bailey-Boushay. Both offered intensive nursing care and hospice for people with AIDS. I also visited people at area hospitals. I heard about and sometimes interacted with other helping organizations.

By 2000, fewer people were dying of AIDS, and some of the organizations were closing down. At the end of that year, I had to stop doing massage because of arthritis in my hands. This was mostly the end of my connection with the AIDS community although I still know a few people. Much of the community no longer exists—good news if it is no longer needed and a loss if those who still live with AIDS don't have as much support.

Not long ago, a friend asked me how I began writing these essays so long after the events described and many years after most of the people described died. How did I remember?

Many of the people are still as vivid to me as they were then. I made quick and deep connections with people in that community. I guess people who know they are dying are often open to talking about things that would have otherwise seemed too private for a new acquaintance. When the person was dying of AIDS, there seemed to be even less reason to be careful about what was said. Someone who dared to be close to the dreaded disease (which was mostly a shameful secret at the time) was a person to be trusted, whether caregiver or friend. I was sometimes caregiver (giving massage), sometimes helper (offering rides and other assistance), and sometimes simply a friend.

I also thought that people who worked within the AIDS community easily felt connections with others in that community. I thought we trusted each other as people with integrity and loving hearts.

I met some remarkable, interesting, and lovable people during those years. Several of those who were living with AIDS mentioned that they wanted to be remembered or wished to write about their experiences. So many were dying. They wanted to matter.

I wanted to remember. I kept lists, documents, and some photos. I kept obituaries and notes. I have some of Shawn's writings and Eric's. I have read over some of those pieces recently. They make my heart hurt and make me miss my friends even more.

Perhaps there is an organization that would like to have Shawn's papers and Eric's. I see that there is a possibility in San Francisco. I thought about getting in touch with them. Maybe even to find a home for photos and other items. I haven't seen a similar collection in Seattle even though I thought I had heard of it. Maybe it's a special collection at the University of Washington.

Other people had the same impulse for remembering. Rosehedge and Bailey-Boushay had walls with photos of those who had died. Bailey-Boushay also had a wall where people could write memories after someone died. I wonder if all their photos and other records have been archived. Other organizations were more careful about privacy. They didn't post photos and didn't post names. This was especially true of clinics. The AIDS Memorial Quilt is another way of remembering.

People in the community mourned both publicly and privately. The AIDS Memorial Vigil included photos and names as well as many tears. The *Seattle Gay News* published a list of those who were known to have died of AIDS each year before the vigil.

John asked me (and others) to provide him with tape recorders and tapes so he could begin to tell his story. He had two or three tape recorders, and many tapes stored on a shelf in his apartment. However, as far as I know, this never got beyond the planning stage.

Shawn also wanted to tell his story, mostly about the abuse he endured during his childhood. He wrote pages and pages in longhand. Much of it is almost impossible to decipher. Spelling, handwriting, and grammar are on about the third-grade level since that's all the schooling he had. He repeated himself and never got far beyond a few pages of description.

Eric wrote at length in longhand. Much of what he wrote was philosophical conjectures. He was greatly influenced by Ken Wilber.

Jack spoke about his life to nursing students and others. I have a videotape of one of those speeches. (At least one other person I knew also made speeches, but I don't have a record of what he said). Jack made sure I took a photo of him toward the end so he could send it to friends and relatives.

From the time I first volunteered in the AIDs community and saw people dying alone, I felt sad that they were disappearing without a trace. I wanted them to be remembered and especially those I loved the most. I began writing poems years ago, back when I was part of the community. I also kept a list of people I knew with AIDS (whether or not they had died or if I knew what had happened to them) written in pencil in the front of a prayer book. Some of those names are blurred now. Others mean nothing to me after all these years. I kept obituaries and other odds and ends.

Poetry began to feel like a burden, and I mostly stopped trying to write this way. When I began writing small essays about people with AIDS, I focused on people, organizations, and issues around illness and death. I made notes about topics that interested me and seemed to illuminate that time. Over time, I have expanded most of them although a few of those thoughts didn't seem to lead anywhere.

I realized somewhere along the line that this could become a book. I didn't think about it a lot at first since the idea of a whole book was kind of overwhelming. As I wrote more and more essays, it seemed more possible.

I began to think about how to order the pieces into a book. I decided to order the essays chronologically as much as possible. I made a timeline with names of people and organizations written in along the line. Some people and groups were easy and rested in one year or another. Some (for instance, Kelly and Shawn) stretched over many years.

Next, I went through my essays and decided where they belonged on the timeline. In order to be able to track them, I used letters of the alphabet to place them in order (*AA*, *AB*, BA, *BB*, etc.). I decided I could use those letters to place any additional pieces where I wanted them. I put all the essays into their own folder on my computer. The lettering scheme automatically put them into order in the folder.

I also pulled out the poetry I liked best from all the ones I wrote about people with AIDS. I ended up with fifty-three pages (two or three poems to a page). I attached individual poems to essays that seem related. Some of the poems are general reflections about these years. The friendship with one person or another inspired most of the poems. I hope the poems will carry the emotions. Some essays have many poems attached (mostly those where Michael, Jack, or John is discussed in the essay). Others have none or few.

I've realized as I was writing this that my friend Julene inspired me to write. Her most recent book was filled with poems about her years working at the Northwest AIDS Foundation. Her poems are vivid and bring back small details of those years. She inspired me to want to write my experiences. Her book took me back twenty years and more. I read it twice and wanted more. I wanted to write.

I realized also that Sherman Alexie also had an influence on my AIDS book. His book about his mother was the first time I saw a book mixing prose and poetry (and photos). I realized from reading his book that I could do the same thing.

I decided to change the names of people who are still alive. For those who died (mostly twenty-plus years ago), I feel comfortable with first names. I don't think the real first names matter with people who died so many years ago. Those who talked about it wanted to be remembered.

I decided to paraphrase information from online sources.

As I wrote about all these people, I also wrote about my life during those years. I wrote about myself. I wanted to portray the people involved and to include my thoughts and emotions.

==========

Inside the Cover

This prayer book carries memories
of services once attended.

Within a list of people, the first met in 1990
when I learned the AIDS community
people I gave rides to
people I met in the hospice
people I met at the AIDS clinic
at the support group
or friends of friends

So many names, more than one hundred
I stopped writing after the first few years

Some only first names
many no more than names to me
most are dead but not all
many I do not know for sure
I grieve about not knowing
about not remembering
all their friends may be dead

==========

c. 1995

packed in a box, yellowed from the years
a page of a newspaper, columns of names
in memorial, from
when we gathered each year
all dead of AIDS
many have quietly died since then
known to none but the closest few
no more public mourning
no opportunity to read all those names

==========

In the Obituary Column

A young face, a young man, I stop to read, and consider.

Choir director at a church, known for accepting all,
cared for his partner until the other died of AIDS.

The virus is alive and well, preying on handsome young men,
stealing life and spirit. I did not know him but now I grieve.

==========

Coming Out

courage grew in the alternative bookstore
before the display of shiny bumper stickers
to a moment of exhilaration and daring
a simple statement, hardly a secret

Fight AIDS not people with AIDS

smoothed on to the car, a frisson of fear
too late to undo, no surprise the next day
finding the car with a broken headlight
done now, worries subside

==========

A Portrait (Aryan Woman)

Fires dance behind her as she stands and speaks on TV

Her children carry signs
Condemning all others
Alien to them
She speaks of Matthew Shepherd

A tragedy she says
Not that he died
But that he went straight to hell
If her child were gay
Or in love with a black
She would cry
Never speak to him again

She speaks to us from hell as fires dance behind her

==========

Too Soon

Damn
he's dead

>That can't be
>I see him
>greeting me
>leading the way
>I could walk
>to his home
>He'd be there
>wouldn't he

He's dead

>He's not there
>no more messages
>on my machine
>I can't believe
>won't accept
>Perhaps if I saw
>his obituary
>then I'd know

Damn
he's dead

==========

In Writing

King County Deaths
just a list
Name
Age
Date
in writing
Now it's real

Disarming Death

Following a passion is one thing. Finding an alternative to something that has become boring or difficult is another thing. For me, the boredom seems to come first. But after I realized I was bored, I followed up on my earlier realization that I needed to become more comfortable with death. In addition, I wanted to help people. And I wanted to get to know people in the Seattle gay community.

I've been thinking about how and why I ended up volunteering in the AIDS community in 1990. I've always been interested in medical matters and wanted to know more about this disease. AIDS got my attention initially because it was a new and mysterious disease. The disease seemed to attack gay men, rich or poor. I wanted to know more about the LGBT community. AIDS was devastating and quick with no good treatment. This added a special horror to the situation.

I was not having a lot of fun with my life at that point. I was chauffeur for my teenage son. I worked in my husband's business (with less and less to do). We went as a family on business trips. My closest friend had a couple of years of bad health and then died in 1988. I still took care of family needs (including cooking, cleaning, and laundry), and that didn't fill my time. I didn't especially enjoy those tasks. I was passive in my own life.

The work I did at my husband's business was routine and not interesting. I took in returns and entered credits into the computer. I wanted something where I could feel like I was helping people. I wanted to bring my heart into the work I was doing (as I had when I was teaching).

I looked into opportunities to volunteer in the AIDS community and decided to get trained for Chicken Soup Brigade. Not long before that, I also found out about CTC, the local LGBT Jewish congregation. I felt like an appendage to my husband and the kids at our synagogue, so joining my own Jewish group seemed like a way to find my own identity. Starting massage school (in 1991) was also a way to claim my own life. I wanted work other than in my husband's business. Massage seemed like an opportunity to do work that would help people toward wellness.

In 1990, my work at my husband's business took only a couple of hours in the morning. There was so little to do that it didn't make much difference if I were sick or had something else to do. Once I became a volunteer, I filled empty afternoon hours (before going to pick up my son from school). This was much better than reading or sleeping for hours every day.

Recently, a woman who advocates facing fears got me thinking (again) about my own decision to face my fear of death. That was a part of why I began hanging out with people who had AIDS.

The woman (Michelle Poler) who did the TED talk about facing fears went straight into each of her fears, including public speaking. She realized that her one hundred fears really were different variations on seven fears. For instance many things (public speaking, dancing in public, wearing a bikini downtown) were all related to the fear of embarrassment. She seems to believe that one shot at each fear is an answer. Maybe it is for her.

My path to more comfort with death was more like a gradual desensitizing, such as is used by therapists to work with people who have phobias. I started small and kept going. Or I guess I could say that each experience was a variation on the general fear of death. At first, I was afraid just to see someone who was dying. Then I was afraid to stand close. Next, I had to deal with touching the dying person. Hugging or holding close to a dying person came next. Seeing and touching a dead body came later. One experience never took care of the fear completely. Comfort developed gradually.

The process began before I ever met a person with AIDS. This was a few years earlier (1980 actually) when my husband's mother was dying. Even being in the room with her was difficult, although it was easier for me than for my husband. He insisted that I go to see her every day. I could stand next to her and chat. However, I never touched her and didn't make eye contact often. (Oh, now I remember just standing barely inside the door when my sister was dying in 1979. The memory shames me.)

After my mother-in-law, my husband's cousin died in 1985. She was just two years younger than his mother. I was more comfortable with her. My friend Dick encouraged me to hold her hand as we talked. It was hard but easier when I realized that she liked the contact. I went to see her many times and stayed for an hour or so for each visit as long I could think of things to say. I guess I thought that I was supposed to be entertaining her and should leave when I ran out of interesting news.

Dick's coaching stayed with me when Dick himself was dying in 1988. He talked comfortably about the fact that he was dying ("going to the other side"). Hugging him and holding his hand felt good. I helped him when he couldn't walk to the bathroom on his own. We were already close friends and became closer during this process. When I went home the last time, he said that he wouldn't see me again in this life. He accepted his death and got me to accept it.

Dad died a couple of years later after having hip replacement. His death was sudden since he had been healing from the surgery. I drove over to my parents' house after I heard the news. I wailed the whole way over. When I got to the house, his body was on the couch covered by a blanket. I went over and uncovered his body, touched his arm, and said goodbye.

The day Dad died was at the end of the day I attended training to volunteer for Chicken Soup Brigade, adding to an already-emotional day.

The trainers explained that they had different uses for volunteers, depending on the comfort level of the volunteers. Some people worked preparing food for people living with AIDS and might never meet a person with AIDS. Others packaged the food and also might not meet anyone living with AIDS. Some volunteers delivered food. They met people with AIDS but only for a few minutes each time. People who gave rides might get to know those living with AIDS much better. They might have to assist people getting in and out of cars. They likely would converse in the cars.

The trainers made it completely clear that any level of volunteering was perfectly okay. They wanted volunteers to feel comfortable with what they were doing. I wanted to give rides so I could get to know people. I also wanted to help with the food, so I signed up for both. We were cautioned to keep relationships professional, and we were told how much people with AIDS appreciated hugs since so many people were afraid of them (including family and friends).

As it happened, a couple of people who packed food with me were HIV positive. One of them (and I don't recall his name) was not well and only came once or twice. The other was my good friend Kelly. He had resistance to HIV and never had an AIDS diagnosis. All he had, and it was a big thing, was the shame of living with HIV. He told me about it when he felt that he could trust me. I felt honored by the trust.

Rules were flexible for those giving rides. We were allowed to sign up (in the book where ride requests were recorded) to drive people we liked and wanted to see. There was no rule against sharing our phone number. People could call us to request rides. My friend Bob, who worked for Chicken Soup Brigade at the time, encouraged my close friendship with various people, including Michael and Jack. He knew I was visiting with Michael every day after knowing him for a few weeks. And the same happened with Jack a month after Michael died.

Once I began giving rides (fall of 1990), I met many people once or twice and never again. And several of those first rides led to intense friendships, including with Michael and with Albert.

The first time I drove Michael, I realized he was expecting a hug. I guessed other Chicken Soup Brigade drivers had hugged him. We were encouraged to show to hug those who wanted hugs. Still it was a little challenging for me. I understood that hugs were not a way of transmitting HIV, but my emotions weren't so sure. I went ahead anyway. The hug turned out to be easy and a good thing. My fears about casual contact exposing me to the virus disappeared.

I faced another challenge one day when I was visiting with Albert. I needed to go to the bathroom and felt afraid of using his toilet. But I calmed myself and went ahead. Some months later, he had a lot of foot pain (neuropathy from HIV) and asked me to massage his feet. At the time, I had just started at massage school, but we talked about foot massage in one of the first classes, so I knew what to do. I was nervous about skin-to-skin touch, but his pleasure in the process calmed me and made me comfortable.

Over time, I spent many hours with Michael sitting close as his health declined. I read psalms to him (something a Jew and an Episcopalian could share). We expressed love for each other. I had a strong sense of our connection as something that would last after he died and after I would die as well. I also had decided (which I've continued to believe) that this connection is how I understand God.

I kept learning about death and having less fear of death as friendships progressed. Michael was the first person I sat with quietly after he died. I felt the change in him. His spirit was gone from his body. I wasn't afraid, and it felt odd that I could touch his body and know that pain was gone. I didn't need to get away from his body. In a way, he was still there, but not in the body.

My experience of Albert's death was very different. I heard he had died from his mother. I hadn't seen him for days before he died. He was bedridden but refused to consider going to Rosehedge (AIDS hospice). He didn't want his family to know he had AIDS. I don't know whether they figured it out. His mother called to tell me about the "viewing" and funeral. I attended both. At the viewing, the body was so enhanced with makeup that it didn't seem to have any connection with the person I had known. The funeral was traditional (African-American) and didn't seem to me to have a lot to do with this person who had died so young (twenty-five years old), but I was glad to be there.

When Michael was near death and in a coma, a nurse at Rosehedge asked me to talk to his sister when she came in. He said to tell her that Michael was worried about her and didn't want to die and leave her alone. He asked me to tell the sister to reassure Michael. She needed to tell him she would be okay, and it was okay for him to die. Even though Michael's eyes were closed and he didn't talk, he reacted to her words by shaking all over. Then he died. It seemed he used his last bit of energy in response to her words. I was sure he was able to hear and understand what she said. I felt sure he had understood my words when I was sitting with him earlier, telling him I loved him and goodbye. I believe he chose to let go after his sister talked to him.

When Jack knew that he was getting weaker day by day, he decided to go into Rosehedge. He wanted to be there when he died. At that point, he seemed to will the process to go quickly. He was in Rosehedge for about a week before he died. He walked with difficulty when he went in but stopped walking and stayed in bed after the first day. It seemed he had chosen the time. He had so little quality of life by then. He didn't want to stick around. I missed him so much during that week and after he died. Even so, I was sure he had the right to decide his end.

When I was sitting with Michael, he seemed to be aging each day, rapidly progressing through his life. He was already visibly sick when we met. He was thin and unsteady while walking. He had KS on his face. Over time, his hair thinned, and his muscles were flaccid. He looked like a very sick and very old man. Even though he briefly gathered more energy (when he went Christmas shopping), the process of his body ending was very clear and rapid over the four months or so we knew each other.

Jack was in better shape than Michael when we met, but he was debilitated. As it happened, he was also coming down with his second round of pneumocystis pneumonia and ended up in the hospital.

Others were also quite sick before we met. It seemed to me knowing how sick they were when we met eased the process. It wasn't like watching someone decline over a lifetime. We all knew death was close and each day was a gift (and a hardship).

A few of the people I knew and loved looked healthy when we met. I met Lee at Terry and Dwayne's wedding. Lee looked the picture of health at the time, a tall and handsome man in his forties. The next time we met, when he called me to do massage on him, he had lost a lot of weight and had KS on his legs. He looked like he had AIDS. I think he lived for about a year after that.

I hadn't known Lee well before I knew him as a very sick man, but Terry was in my class at massage school. He looked great when we met and seemed well for months afterwards. He told me about the HIV, but when we met, he wasn't yet diagnosed with AIDS. It was wrenching when he dropped out of school and began a rapid decline. It was worse toward the end when his parents were caring for him. He spent his last days at Bailey-Boushay.

During that time I was in my forties and fifties. Death seemed a long way off (even though almost all of the people I knew who were living with AIDS were my age or younger). I had to come to terms with letting go of people I loved and still being here.

At the same time, having watched others decline and die makes my own aging and death seem more real. I notice the slow changes in my body and in my energy level (especially now). I am on the same path, just from years and not because of a virus.

I still feel connected to Michael and Jack and John and others. I hope the connection helps me as I age and contemplate my own death or that of good friends or family.

==========

In Truth

Michael said, "God is angry with me because I'm gay."

I said, "No, God just wants us to love someone."
He said, "Oh," and leaned into me
I held him gently to give him strength

==========

Lost Child
(For Albert S.)

> He waited in front of the black hulk high-rise, low-income housing
> Tall, thin, very thin, young in red sweat shirt and sweat pants
> Comfort clothes for those whose bodies are stiff and painful
> He got a ride to his doctor's appointment from me, a volunteer
>
> I offered a hug when we returned, opened a torrent
> None visit him in the hospital, a frequent event
>
> A call came from him on Thanksgiving Day
> Panic, blood filled his toilet bowl
> We went to the emergency room for IV hydration
> Tests confirmed CMV infection in his intestinal system
>
> It was almost a relief to have an answer
> Now he hooked himself up for daily gancyclovir
>
> For eight months, he waxed and waned
> Seemed close to death
> And then went out dancing with his cousin
> The last day came. An obituary. A funeral

==========

Alone
(For Jason S.)

> My assignment: drive him to treatment for PCP pneumonia
> At the hospital where I'd taken him once before
>
> At first no answer to the bell, then a voice over the intercom
> "Could you come up here to help?" weak and hesitant
> He sat on the bed, the door was unlocked, and he needed
> help with his coat and a shoulder to lean on getting to the elevator

As we drove, he told me about his former lover who sold everything
during the last bout in order to buy drugs for himself

There was a helpful volunteer with a wheelchair at the hospital
Took Jason to his appointment and back while I waited in the car

Back at his apartment, I hesitated as he coughed endlessly
Helped him into the bathroom to lean over the toilet and vomit
He was exhausted, lying on his bed. "Will you be okay?"
"Yes, my chore worker will be here soon. Leave the door unlocked."
His apartment was bare, clothing piled on shelves in the closet
A table and chair, some food and a few dishes, no pictures
It looked unloved and unnurtured as he did, and I wondered
if anyone really was going to come and help him and for how long

His death announcement was in the paper a few months later
Not an obituary, just name, age, place, and date

==========

The Volunteer Appears

      just a name and address on a list
      needs a ride from his home
      to the clinic and back again
      a little house north of the city
      roommates and dogs
      wander through the house

      he's just a skinny little guy
      sitting on a threadbare couch
      furniture looks like Goodwill
      no one speaks or notices
      as he leans on his cane
      down the walkway to my car

==========

No Words Needed

silent he slid into the car
silent he sat beside me

I knew where to take him
knew that I was to wait
take him home from the doctor

silently I sat on a bench
silently we walked to the car

I returned him to his house
two or three trips in all
later heard that he had died

==========

Step forward . . . Or Back
(Michael)

Can we choose to love when soon he will be gone
in a matter of months; knowing from the first day
that time is short. Stopping to consider
before joining in a hug. Nothing will change
the end of the story. How lucky to have the chance
to know, to talk, to sit together, a blessing.

==========

No Regret
(Michael)

That first time we met, I was assigned
to give him a ride to the doctor
to wait to the end of the appointment
seated on the hard chair with my book
to take him back to the tiny hospice

to walk him into the hallway
to say goodbye

That first time, he held out his arms for a hug
    as I hesitated for a moment
    to step into the possibility
        of love
    knowing his days were numbered
        in weeks, at most months

Living with the Virus

Bad as AIDS is, the HIV virus doesn't affect everyone the same way, and it isn't as contagious as other viruses, such as hepatitis.

I know two people who were exposed to HIV and never even got infected. One of them is a man. His partner died of AIDS. They had shared hepatitis B between them, but the man I knew never tested positive for HIV. (Hepatitis B is much more contagious anyway.) The other is a woman who was married to a man who died of AIDS (very young, in his early thirties, more than twenty-five years ago). They were married before he got sick and was tested eventually for HIV.

I also know several people who were infected with HIV (tested positive) but never developed AIDS. As far as I know, they didn't take medications either. My longtime doctor (Greg Allen) worked with a number of such people (so it wasn't that rare). I knew one man who had a longtime partner who died of AIDS in the early '90s. Another didn't have a partner, and I don't know how he was exposed to HIV. That man worked to retirement age without any problems. I knew another (Joel) whose partner (Clark) was very sick with AIDS while Joel had a normal T-cell count. Another person who was infected but didn't end up with AIDS was my friend Kelly.

Part of my volunteering for Chicken Soup Brigade (1990) involved preparing and packaging meals to be delivered to people living with AIDS. This was done under the auspices of FareStart, the creation of Chef David Lee. He was generally there in the kitchen of a building called the Josephinum on Second Avenue on the corner of Second Avenue and Stewart Street. It was once the New Washington, one of Seattle's premier hotels. In 1963, Seattle's Catholic archdiocese bought it, renamed it, and made it a residence for low-income senior citizens. It sounds like the building is now in disrepair although the archdiocese is trying to revive the old hotel dining room plus the former chapel as a church (2017, Christ Our Hope). The upper stories still have low-income residents.

It was hard to believe anyone lived above the kitchen where we worked. The lobby was always empty when we walked through it. We never heard any noise above us. The kitchen had long counters. The pots and pans were enormous. David usually had most of the food prepared when we arrived. (I think he did all the preparation although there may have been other volunteers.) We added some finishing touches and then divided them among containers (a hundred or more). All this usually took two to three hours. Other volunteers were responsible for delivering the packaged food.

I worked with two other volunteers. One of them was an elderly gay man (late seventies to my midforties). He was often gone on cruise ships, where he got lodging and board in return for being a willing dance partner to single women. The other was Kelly. He was about my age. He talked and laughed and cried a lot, sometimes at the same time, as we were packaging meals. He announced his HIV status the first time we met. He wanted to help others while he still could.

One time, we got there and the kitchen door was locked. We decided to wait for David Lee to arrive. During the next twenty minutes, Kelly sat down at the piano in the reception area. He played ragtime music and sang in his wonderful bass voice.

At that time, Kelly lived on ML King in a house with several other gay men. Two of them were a couple. The whole combination of people was dysfunctional according to Kelly's stories. He asked me for occasional rides, for instance to Safeway. One of those times was the day of the big Seattle snow (December 1990). I was driving home from Harborview about 2:00 p.m. and planned to pick him up on the way to take him grocery shopping. By the time I got there, it was too slippery and scary. No cell phone, so I called from home to cancel the shopping trip.

While we were packaging food, Kelly talked about his family. He grew up north of Seattle in Bellingham. One of the biggest traumas of his life happened when he (a young teenager) found his mother (an alcoholic) bleeding out in their living room. His grandmother raised him after his mother's death. He was close to his grandmother and often mentioned how much he missed spending time with her. However, Bellingham wasn't where he wanted to live.

By the time I was no longer volunteering for Chicken Soup Brigade (when I was in massage school in the spring of 1991), Kelly moved on to a different volunteer job. He worked in the thrift store in a small house on Harvard and

John. Mostly he sorted donations. He talked (complained) at length about the worthless and dirty items that some people donated.

Later, Kelly needed to move at the same time as my husband had an empty apartment on Greenwood. The downstairs of the building housed a secondhand furniture store. The upstairs of the building had four small apartments. Two of them had full bathrooms. The other two shared a toilet and a shower (two separate rooms) down the hall. Kelly took on cleaning the shared shower and toilet rooms. He was irritated by the disgusting way others left the two rooms.

He invited me for lunch one day. He cooked soup and sandwiches, and it was good. He knew what he was doing in a kitchen, even the limited one in the apartment.

Kelly earned a living by cleaning houses. He had a number of clients in various parts of the city. He had a car by the time he lived on Greenwood, making it easier for him to get his cleaning supplies to various places. He occasionally got rides from me when his license was suspended or he was having difficulty getting around. I drove him to a house in Magnolia (up and down curving roads on hills), to another in Wallingford (more than once), and to one in my neighborhood.

One time Kelly asked me to go to court with him. He had gotten a DUI and lost his license for a period of time. That court seemed to run like an assembly line with many cases in a couple of hours.

Sometime in those years, Kelly decided to get rid of his car. He couldn't trust himself to refrain from drinking and driving (after several DUIs). He was still cleaning houses and mostly taking the bus to his work. I respected his choice to give up the car.

By the time I lived in my current house (1993), Kelly offered to clean at my house in exchange for massage. I picked him up and brought him to my house on those days as well as driving him home. This was in the early years of my massage practice before I got frantically busy. He used to undress and get into the shower to clean it. I could hear him singing in his deep voice as he worked. He and Charlotte, my calico cat, teased each other and got along well. Charlotte seemed to understand his warm heart as well as his silly behavior (not unlike her own).

I tried to be cupid—Kelly and Rick (who had gotten some rides from me under the auspices of Chicken Soup Brigade) heard about each other and wanted to meet, so I gave them each other's contact numbers. They invited me once to visit with them at Rick's apartment. The romance was sweet but didn't last long. I think this was in about 1992. Later, Rick was a patient at Rosehedge, but by then, he and Kelly weren't together.

Kelly called me a few times when he was drunk and making no sense at all, talking about how much he loved me and couldn't manage without me.

On several occasions, I agreed to give Kelly a ride to my house or somewhere else, but he didn't come out when I drove up and honked under his window. This was before the days of cell phones. I went across the street to a phone booth and tried to call. The first time, he answered and said he was sick. He didn't answer the other times but later said he was sick. We drifted apart. I wasn't willing to go along with his flaking out on me and wasting my time.

Some time later, I found out that he had moved to low-income housing. He had gotten far behind on rent, and my husband told him he had to leave after a long period of giving him the benefit of the doubt.

I never saw the new apartment. Kelly was evasive, and I didn't push it.

I wasn't surprised when I got a phone call that Kelly was very sick and in the hospital. The hospital didn't have contact information for his relatives. All they had was my name and number. I had a name and phone number of his grandmother, which I gave to the hospital personnel. I think this was in the summer of 1999. Kelly never got AIDS. He was bleeding out, the result of alcoholism, just like his mother.

My husband went with me to see Kelly in the hospital. Kelly was lying unresponsive in a bed. They were giving him blood as fast as he was losing it. I think they kept him alive just so that his family had time to come to say goodbye. He was taken off the life support the next day, and that was the end.

Joel also worked and survived quite well with HIV. However, he had a recurrent brain tumor (not malignant). It may have been genetic. Someone else in his family (his mother?) had the same thing. He had several surgeries. Once he was in the hospital with suspected TB (which he didn't have). His partner Clark was HIV positive as well and had AIDS. Clark died from a side effect of AIDS medications. I don't recall if it was his heart or cancer. I don't know how Joel died. It may have been from the brain tumor. It may have been from a broken heart. We had lost touch before I heard he had died. By then, my massage practice was busy, and I didn't take the time to keep in touch. I regret my neglect.

Partial or full immunity to HIV is interesting. The most convincing explanation I've heard is that it's genetic and that the people who are resistant are descended from people who survived the Black Plague. This seems possible to me. I've heard that some sort of resistance to HIV is present in about 1 percent of the population and may be related to an inherited mutation.

==========

Refuge for a Night
(Kelly)

Late one night as I sat alone reading
My children and husband sleeping
A phone call filled with desperation

Drunk, slurring his words
Terrified of his neighbors
Needs transportation
Wants a place to stay
No way to bring him here

A call to another friend who accepts him
A silent drive across the city
Two lonely men living in desperation

==========

Love, Kelly

Blue ink across the page as taught in grade school,
Carefully rounded remnants kept within the lines.

(He was a Virgo through and through.)

A stamp, a red smiling sun atop of the page and at the end.
His words meander from today to years past and back again,
mourning the losses and clutching small joys.
Despite depression and booze and AIDS, he still wants love.

His words still send warmth to me.
I remember his voice, his laugh, his pain, all that I knew of him.

==========

Note from Kelly: Number 1

"the cat (calico) was indefatigable—
made love in a plethora of places and positions.

"Much following me,
jumping and caressing of tables, counters, etc.

"She also attempted,
a couple of times, to bite me.

"Hungry or horny?

"Guess they're both the same."

==========

Note from Kelly: Number 2

"I read your Advocate & SGN.
Hope you don't mind.

"Picture of dead friend in SGN.
"Chico" Mack Mead.

"Shit.

"Saw him not too long ago.

"Anyhow . . ."

==========

Sudsy Ammonia
(Kelly)

A slow leak at the base of the faucet—
my boy will replace it tomorrow.
In the meantime, my job: to clear out
bottles, cans, boxes, packages

crowded under the sink.
To pull out and inspect each,
to reorganize, to plan,
to dispose of useless items.

I pause, reluctant to move this bottle,
untouched for more than twelve years,
left by my friend who cleaned here.
I remember the pungent smell
as he scrubbed the shower.
I remember the cloth he put over his head,
the mask over his nose and mouth.
I remember the day he died.

==========

Kelly

He took a stack of books with him.
He wanted the Jewish story despite his Irish ancestry.
He was a gay man and wanted the lesbian stories.
He insisted that really he was a Jewish lesbian.
Then one day he returned them all,
some read and some unread.
He was moving.
He said nothing at all beyond that.
One day I heard he was dying.

==========

Kelly

something about the way his beard flowed from his bald head
covered often by a kerchief or cap
and the gloves he wore on the coldest days
carrying his scrubbing tools on the bus
I see a glimpse from a distance of him
hurrying to catch the ride
if I get close, it won't be true that he died years ago

Rosehedge

Mostly I remember the first Rosehedge. It was in a house near Temple de Hirsch, right in the center of gay Seattle. It was close to agencies, bars, and people. The location was convenient for friends to visit. Residents had opportunities to get out into the neighborhood as long as they were able to. I once walked over to 7-Eleven with a resident (Larry). He was a handsome man and looked totally healthy. Larry was cheerful and chatty at that time but became angry and reclusive when his health worsened. Rosehedge was also near a couple of restaurants owned by gay men, a comfortable place for them to go out to eat. I liked that it was convenient for me to get to as well.

The first floor of the house had three bedrooms, a large bathroom with a tub that allowed staff to bathe residents who could no longer walk, and a room for staff. The back yard had grass and a few flowers. I never saw anyone but the resident cat (known as Mama) in the backyard. A path led from the alley (where parking was generally available) to the back door. Most people used the back door to go in and out. The front door had a porch with heat lamps so people could smoke out there. The upstairs had three small bedrooms and a common area next to a full kitchen.

The staircase from the first to the second floor had a lift attached to it. Even when he was able to walk, Michael needed the lift to get back up to his bedroom. Unfortunately, the lift didn't always work properly. Sometimes patients had to be carried up the stairs by a staff person.

There was a television set up in the common area on the second floor. It didn't seem to be on often. The house had tape players and music tapes for patients to use. Many people brought their own players and tapes with them to use in their own rooms. Some got left behind after the person died. After Michael died, his sister asked me to take any tapes I wanted. I took one or two.

I guess she may have left the rest. Even though I'd never heard them when I was visiting Michael, the tapes made me feel closer to him.

These were the days before most people had personal computers or cell phones. There was one phone for the whole of Rosehedge house (with extensions on both floors). When I went to DC with Rebecca, while she looked at colleges, I missed Michael and worried about him. I called from the student union building at Georgetown while Rebecca was on a tour. (Trying to remember the process, I realize that I no longer know how to make a long distance call from a pay phone.) A staff person brought Michael to the phone. He was weak by then and close to death, so this took several minutes. I felt my heart lift when Michael began talking. Love flowed across the country.

Michael lived in one of the tiny upstairs bedrooms but preferred to spend his time in the common area. He was always interested in the others who lived in Rosehedge with him. He observed them when they came into the common area (but I don't recall him talking to them). When he couldn't be around the others or they stayed in their rooms, he solicited information from me or staff people. He was glad to hear when anyone had visitors. He was sad but wanted to know when someone died.

Michael moved into the large downstairs bedroom for the last couple of weeks of his life. Fans were set up on either side of him since he was having difficulty getting a full breath.

Michael never met the other resident Michael, MBH, but was happy when I told him that MBH's parents had visited from across the country. After that day, he expected me to stop and chat with the other Michael before coming upstairs to see him. I told him what I learned about the other man's life, including the fact that he had worked with precious gems. He heard about the details of MBH's death. I told him that the parents called when MBH was in a coma and gave him permission to die.

One day, Michael was having a bath when I came in to visit. A staff person checked with him, and I was asked to come in to keep him company (along with a staff person) as he completed his bath. I remembered then my complete lack of modesty when I was giving birth to my children. At a certain point, the needs of your body take over, and you don't worry who sees you. At least that seemed to me to explain Michael's comfort with my presence.

During his last months, Michael received blood transfusions about once a week. The medications he was on were hard on the blood and depleted his energy. (I see online that AZT, the most used medication at the time, can cause anemia.) The transfusions made a huge difference to his energy level.

However, that is an expensive way to add quality of life for someone who is dying, and eventually they didn't help. I was there once when he was done with a transfusion, and I was asked to help by pressing a bandage against the opening on his arm. Since I didn't have any open sores, I wasn't too worried about being near his blood. In retrospect, I was a little surprised at the casual attitude of the staff person.

Jack was in the same small bedroom as Michael, eight months after Michael died. By that time, Rosehedge had built a new facility in north Seattle. (I don't know if they lost their lease on the original house.) When Jack decided he couldn't stay in his apartment any longer, he asked me to take him to see both versions of Rosehedge. He had a choice about which one to go to. He needed help to walk at that point. We used a wheelchair, and he walked leaning on me. He decided for the original Rosehedge since it was so much more convenient for visits from his caregivers. Jack was sure he would die soon. He wanted to die at that point since there was so little quality of life. He was only in Rosehedge about a week.

I remember one resident mainly because smoking was so difficult and important to him. His hands were contorted, so that he couldn't use them normally. Some staff person put together a device that allowed him to hold the cigarette and smoke independently once the cigarette was placed in the holder and lit. The man (whose name I don't recall) had a face that showed the ravages of the disease and his suffering. Yet in those moments on the porch with other smokers, he was happy.

The lower hallway of Rosehedge was lined with many photos of people who had lived and died in the place. Even though it had only been open less than three years when I was visiting Michael (late 1990), hundreds of men had already died there. Michael was unusual in that he lived at Rosehedge for more than four months. Many were only there for a few weeks if that. I suppose, like Jack, they didn't want to move there until they knew they were dying. Albert refused to even consider moving there. He didn't want anyone to know he had AIDS.

I went to a twentieth anniversary of Rosehedge in 2008 and saw photos of Michael and others. Jayme, an RN, was still working there all those years later. She talked about all the men (hundreds) she had seen die and said that she had loved every one. I believed her. She used to sit with them and talk or play checkers with those who enjoyed the game. She was a nurse and a friend of the men with AIDS. I wish I could have taken a photo of the photo of Michael so I would have it for myself (but I didn't have a cell phone then or not one with a good camera). I do have images of him and others on a videotape of a show that was on television. There's probably some way to get stills from the show (if the tape is still in good shape, which it might not be), but it would be expensive.

The staff people were kind and loving. Some of them were HIV positive themselves. Peter, an aide when I was visiting Michael, died of AIDS a couple of years later. Most of the staff people were gay or lesbian, but not all. The staffing level was high enough that staff people had time to sit with patients, to chat with them, and sometimes to play checkers or chess.

One of the people I got to know during the months of visiting Michael was a man named David. Once he told me about thinking he was in the middle of Greenlake fishing. He interpreted that as being a visual memory coming back to him from years before when he really had been fishing on that lake. David was a small and bearded gentle fellow. Hanging out with him was always pleasant. He had a collection of beer steins on a shelf in his room.

David moved to the new Rosehedge when it opened. By then, I felt a connection with him, so I visited him there. He was one of the smokers, so I saw the smoking area in that new house. It was kind of a sunroom built as part of the house. David's hallucinations got scary. He thought people were conspiring against him. He told me that he took a medication called Halcion to help him to sleep. I had heard Halcion was implicated in paranoid ideation, so I mentioned that to a staff person. I think they stopped giving him Halcion not long after. I often chatted with another of David's visitors, a longtime friend of his, when I visited him there.

The new Rosehedge was almost to the northern city limits of Seattle. It was in a wooded suburban sort of area, not near any stores of restaurants. They had a large piece of land, and the building was quite beautiful. It also looked like a medical facility, not like a house. It was one story, making easy access for wheelchairs around the building. The nurses' station was in the center surrounded by six patient rooms. As was normal at the time, each door had the name of the patient who lived in the room. I noticed that Rick, whom I hadn't seen recently, was one of the people who moved in there. When I asked at the desk, they checked with him. He didn't want any visitors, so I never saw him again.

I didn't know anyone else who went into Rosehedge after that time. I guess that the opening of Bailey-Boushay (just about a year after Rosehedge moved north) changed things. The bigger and well-appointed facility probably attracted many more people. In addition, Bailey-Boushay is located close to the Capitol Hill neighborhood, much more convenient than the new Rosehedge.

After protease inhibitors came into common use (mid '90s) fewer people died of AIDS. However, many continued to live with the disease and needed help. Rosehedge transitioned to a different kind of facility. Rosehedge included several other houses, which offered support to people who were living with the disease but not dying. However, that wasn't sustainable long term. (And Bailey-Boushay also offered a day treatment program for the same population.) Rosehedge (and Multi-Faith works, which had joined Rosehedge a few years earlier) closed at the end of 2013.

==========

Still Himself
(For Shane D.)

They all remember him
All the men who went to gay bars in the '70s and '80s
Shane was tall, handsome, and muscular
The devastating bartender they all yearned for

He lived in a small apartment behind the QFC
Attended only by his care-giving cat

Even when he had spinal cancer
He wouldn't acknowledge that he had AIDS
He planned to go back to his restaurant
Expected to be standing erect again, without the wheelchair

He charmed all the people at the hospital
Smiled his way through radiation therapy

He moved from the hospital
To the AIDS hospice, Rosehedge, as he died
The family wasn't allowed to tell people he was there
Forestalled a deluge of calls and visitors

==========

Lonely Death
(For Brian G.)

We exchanged a few words
when I visited others at Rosehedge
Once he greatly enjoyed a treat
brought for the house
apricots drenched in deep dark chocolate

Then he was dying and no one with him
I sat for a while, perhaps a slow hour
Seemed like someone should care
At least a little, be with him
Wondering if this gasping breath would be the last
or perhaps the next one

Still Brian was there day after day
Each one seemed like forever
And then the bed was empty

==========

Let Go
(For Michael P.)

We looked deep into each other's eyes
Long and longer . . . He couldn't bear it
Begged me to move back
To break the intimacy
I offered him some water to drink
Our eyes locked as we held the glass up
Trembling hands tipped it . . . spilling
Ice water down his front
He laughed and laughed, freed from intensity

==========

Dregs
(For Tim S.)

> He outlived his partner
> By a few years
> Had nothing left of their life together
>
> They shared an apartment
> Before his partner's death
>
> His lover's family swooped in
> Took everything
> Even pots and pans
>
> After all he had AIDS
> Wasn't going to need all that stuff

==========

Many Years Gone
(David)

> Beer steins lined a shelf above the bed,
> his stash of cigarettes in a drawer,
> the coffeemaker always busy.
> His story leaked out in bits and pieces.
>
> I mused about meaning but sat quietly,
> waiting for him to tell, not asking,
> wondering about the unsaid.
> Too late, he may have wanted more.

==========

Turn About

> Sometimes it seemed I'd walked into the middle of a conversation.
> I did not know who they spoke of John, gone from Michael's life,

such a good friend until death loomed.
John never came to sit with Michael,
never watched Michael grow thin and weak.

But years later, when I finally met John,
I learned he was the one defended by Michael,
condemned by the loyal friends who sat at the hospice.
John spoke of Michael now that he was dying
and sighed about the friends who had disappeared from his life.

==========

A Vignette
(For Jayme)

Michael was dying. It seemed a matter of days.
Jayme stopped to say good night.
She was off for the next two weeks.

How could she stay away when he that she loved might die?

Now it's nine years later.
Many more have died. Many more that she loved.
She still works there and loves them.

Fully present when she's there. To her own life when she's not.

Michael: His Memory Is a Blessing to Me

I have no photos of Michael P., but I do have a taped piece when he was on television in a story about people living with AIDS at Rosehedge. I haven't looked at that tape in a few years. I hope it is holding up. I probably should have it transferred to something more durable. Now I want to watch it again.

After I had a fall and left my car near their house, Rebecca needed to bring my car back and retrieve her car that was parked at my house. She advised me to ask my parking angel to arrange the parking place. Rebecca showed up at 6:00 p.m. and found a parking place for my car almost in front of the house.

I told her a little bit about my parking angel, Michael. His years working as a Metro bus driver are one reason I call on him when I want to find parking. He liked the job and was grateful that eighteen years' seniority gave him a good retirement income. He owned his condo over on FirstHhill. He said I was a good driver—maybe because he wanted me to keep driving him. That also made him my parking angel.

Michael died of AIDS in December 1990. We met just a few months earlier. He was the first person with AIDS in my life. He lived in the hospice Rosehedge over by Temple De Hirsch. This small house had six bedrooms, a kitchen, and a common area. It also had an office for the staff (nurses and aides) and a large bathroom. They had the kind of elevator that traveled up the stairs when it was working. The front porch was partially enclosed so smokers could sit out there no matter the weather. Parking was available in the alley behind the house. There was a black cat who lived in the house and interacted with residents. The six bedrooms were always occupied. Most people died in a month or two, and then a new person came (from a waiting list) to live in the house.

On Thanksgiving of 1990, the family of one resident came in to cook a beautiful meal for all who lived there. They were grateful for Rosehedge and the loving care.

Michael had a bedroom on the second floor and spent most of the day in the common area. He didn't really interact with the other residents but did like to know what was going on with them. Even when he was bedbound at the end of his life, he asked me to let him know if anyone died.

He and his sister had an unhappy childhood with abusive parents. His sister depended on him to help and protect her. One time, she and her boyfriend decided to take Michael to Mexico for some kind of miracle cure. With the support of staff, Michael refused to go. The staff almost got to the point of calling the police, but Michael's sister relented finally and never brought up that idea again. She continued visiting him until the end of his life.

Michael had a large circle of friends. Many knew him from the old days when he was a drag performer in his free time. He was tall and strong. He loved to ride his bike around Greenlake. The friends from those days often visited him at Rosehedge. Most of them were also HIV positive. Another friend was a woman, Jackie, who supported several people with AIDS over the years. She even moved one man into her house with her and her husband and son. She took Michael to church. He worried a little because it was a Catholic church and not the church he had grown up in. We talked and decided prayer was prayer.

Michael wanted more connection with his faith. We talked about how I could help. Eventually Michael and I agreed on Psalms (suitable for both a Jew and a Christian). I read them to him during the last weeks of his life. The Twenty-Third Psalm suddenly made perfect sense to me: "Even though I walk through the valley of the shadow of death, I fear no evil, for thou are with me."

We were together, and that took away the fear of death. We were together, and that seemed to me to bring God into the room. Once he looked at me and said, "I never expected to fall in love with AIDS." I felt that too. We were together in a space of love, not in love in a romantic way.

(I recently learned about pantheism—according to Matthew Fox, God is in everything, and everything is in God. That is exactly the experience I had with Michael, where God was equal love and connection. For me, God was our connection and eternal.)

Before he became bedbound, when Michael was still hanging out in the common area, he liked to collaborate on doing the crossword puzzle. I brought the Seattle PI with me when I came to visit. I read the paper if Michael was dozing. We did the crossword together if he was awake. One way or another, I spent an hour there just about every day for several months. Sometimes we talked. He told me about a friend who disappointed him by refusing to come to visit him at Rosehedge. He thought the friend was afraid to come into the building. Much later, I met the friend (John) and became close to him. This was more than a year after Michael died. John told me pretty much the same story, but I didn't tell him that I knew Michael. I don't know why I kept that to myself.

Watching Michael change was like observing aging at super speed as his hair thinned, his muscles atrophied, and his bones began to show through his flesh. He was able to walk when we met but not a few weeks later (except for a brief improvement shortly before he died). At the same time, he looked very young and innocent and open to the world as if he was also reverting to infancy. He was forty-seven years old. He looked ninety-seven years old, and he also looked seven years old.

It seemed to me over the years of meeting people with AIDS that close friendship came about very quickly. When you know someone has that disease and you still want to spend time with them, you have shown yourself to be a trustworthy person. This allows for honest sharing. In those days, people died very quickly of AIDS. Knowing that death was close also helped honest and open communication. A few months felt like years of regular life.

I took Michael to a medical appointment the first time we met in September 1990, I think. He was the first person I met who had AIDS. I was afraid to be that close to someone with AIDS and yet reassured by what I'd learned in training. I knew in my head that I wasn't at risk, but anxiety isn't always logical. When we got back to Rosehedge, Michael seemed reluctant to say goodbye. And I thought he expected a hug. Despite fear, I stepped forward into the hug, and it was fine.

The next time I drove him to an appointment, he didn't want to go straight back to Rosehedge. He asked if we could drive around and look at the fall leaves. Either that day or another day, he had me drive him to the bank where he wanted to discuss some problem with his account. The teller looked at him (very thin with Kaposi's sarcoma on his face) and directed the conversation at me. This surprised and appalled me. I directed her back to him. We also stopped at my house. Pokey, the cat who was usually afraid of men, decided he was pretty nice and came out to say hello. After another medical appointment, Michael wanted to stop at his condo. I think he just wanted to check it out and wanted me to see it.

That December (1990), we had one of the worst snowstorms ever for Seattle. It was followed by a deep freeze. Many people abandoned their cars for days on the 520 Bridge and along major roads, including Madison. The cars remained for days. Mike took my four-wheel-drive car to work, and I walked (about two miles with a long hill) over to see Michael. When I got there the first day after the storm, they were dealing with frozen pipes. Staff people had spent the night, and they were coping somehow.

During the storm and the aftermath, Michael looked like he was fading fast. He became energized after the snow and ice were gone. Christmas was coming. He wanted to buy gifts for people. He wanted to send cards. He knew he was close to death. He wanted to thank all those who had made life better as he struggled with AIDS. He wanted to tell them he would miss them when he died. He wanted to say goodbye. I helped him address the cards. Others helped him with shopping. When that was done, he seemed to relax into his final days.

Rosehedge was staffed with loving and experienced people. There was always a nurse present and others who were hands-on caregivers. They saw so many people die and still gave their hearts to everyone. Their experience helped them to guide patients, friends, and family.

At one point, Michael requested more morphine. The nurse gently explained that increasing the morphine might mean he would no longer be able to interact with people. He also said morphine may repress breathing, so he would die faster. Michael chose to go ahead with the increase.

Michael was in a coma the last day. A nurse talked to me. He said people in comas still are aware and can hear what is going on around them. He anticipated Michael's sister would come in and would be greatly upset by the coma. The staff person urged me to talk to the sister if she came in while I was there. He said to tell her that Michael needed her to say she would be okay without him and that he could die.

The sister did come in, and I followed directions, speaking to her before she went into the room. Michael seemed agitated when she entered the room. I waited long enough to be sure the sister was reassuring him and then stepped out of the room. She came out in a couple of minutes and said he had died. I went back in. He was dead and at peace. I sat down with him and waited for his friends to arrive. I thought he had just a little bit of life energy left during the last couple of days, enough to keep him breathing in his coma. When his sister came and spoke, his response used up all of life that remained.

Between Michael's friends and his family, there were competing funerals.

One funeral was at an Episcopal church and was very formal. Someone had ordered food platters (maybe from Costco). I don't remember for sure, but maybe Mike came with me to that one. In any case, I didn't stay long. There wasn't much to say.

The second one was at the home of some of his gay friends. They had photos up from Michael's days of dressing in drag. The food was much better than the church event. His friends embarrassed me by calling me an angel for spending so much time with him. I didn't have a good answer. Nowadays I would stress how much I enjoyed his company and how much I learned from hanging out with him. I found that sitting with a person who was dying (and after he died) was a kind of meditation.

He seems so close even after so many years since he died.

I headed over to City People's Garden Store on a day last summer. I knew that a sunny Saturday might not be a good day to go. Parking might be awful and the place crowded. When I drove up, I saw not one but two parking places in their lot, close to the front. And as it turned out, I did well again when I came home, retaking the parking space I left when I headed to City People's. Thanks, Michael.

==========

Barely a Breath
(Michael)

> he was in his bed not far from death
> we read psalms together
> laughed a little
> learned to love one another
>
> looking into each other's eyes
> breathing together until he asked me
> to move back a little
>
> life force barely a thread
> easily overwhelmed

six inches was too close
twenty-four, perfect companionship

==========

At the AIDS Hospice
(Michael)

I was there to visit the dying man
We knew it would be soon
In a few weeks or months at most
For now he could still walk

His thin frame moving slowly,
painfully into the kitchen
I wanted to jump up to do for him
yet let him be the kind host

Two cups each with a tea bag
Mint, of course, to honor his guest
Hot water from the faucet
One step at a time back to me

==========

Goodbye
(Michael)

we walk through, walk through the valley together
hand in hand we walk
we walk together
under the forever care, sheltered by love

we walk together looking ahead to the end
we walk without fear, the shadow falling on us,
as we walk, led to the peace, led by peace and love

our hands part

we are still wrapped in comfort
we will walk together again one day
again we will be beyond the valley together

==========

**Beyond Time
(Michael)**

all the minutes ran together seemed endless:

laughing as we worked crossword puzzles
sleepy hours, sitting by his side as he dozed
walking slowly, as he leaned, into the kitchen
phone calls, good night at the end of each day

less than four months
it seemed a lifetime

==========

**Back with Them
(Michael)**

holding a special place on my shelf
a silver and black box
keeping memories
of quiet moments
tea in his new home
the last place he wanted to be
the last place he would be
a place for last goodbyes
the steam rising, the licorice smell

==========

Our Prayer
(Michael)

the Lord is our shepherd; we trust
comfort will be granted
we shall not want
all good will come in the end
we are led
on the path to green pastures
a table set before us
we will be nurtured
though we walk through
we walk hand in hand through
the valley of the shadow
of death
we fear no evil
one will be gone
still we will be together
hearts and souls
goodness and mercy always with us

==========

Michael and Pokey, c. 1990

tall and thin, every step painful
he walked into my house
a way to delay
a side trip before
returning to the hospice
better by far, he says
hello to the small tabby
usually runs from strangers
today she stops
waits to be patted
I tell him she sees how nice
he is, not dangerous to anyone

Wearing on Body and Spirit

I saw my friends with AIDS as their bodies wore out over time (and never realized that I might see some of the same changes in myself with aging). I saw the way being a caregiver can wear away at the spirit of a person and learned to take a little more care of myself.

Not long ago, maybe a couple of years back, a friend and I walked three mornings a week. This meant I got up early, before 7:00 a.m. if I wanted to do yoga first. Aging and time change everything.

Walking became challenging. Both of us got short of breath if we walked fast. Both of us had aches and pains. Mine were not as bad. I could walk even if I wasn't enjoying it. His were worse. We had to turn back after a couple of blocks several times. I told him that I'd rather just not walk. I thought I might get back to walking. Now I don't think I will.

Now I get up some time after 7:00 a.m. I often play online or with the cat before doing anything else. Sometimes I sleep until 8:00 a.m. and still have a leisurely start. This seems like a gift, a gift I've given myself. I'm glad that I was able to make the choice, and I won't go back.

Part of me thinks I should have just kept on forcing myself to get up no matter how much I wanted to sleep more. I wonder if I would feel better and stay younger longer if I did that. Part of me thinks I'm getting older and need to relax. I remember the frustration John had when he was no longer able to walk down to Broadway. He settled for getting a ride down and up the hill. Maybe I'm getting there.

Over the years, I've often reflected on the way stress can come out in accidents and injuries as if some of us need an excuse to give ourselves a break. I'm glad that I didn't fall or get injured during the many walks when I didn't want to be walking.

I remember when I broke my ankle in 1992 while walking with John. We were down by Madison Park. He walked with a cane and slowly, so he asked me to take the dog (Mo) down to do his business in a wooded area. The dog and I started down the wooden steps that were pushed into the hillside. They weren't in great repair, but I don't actually know why I fell, landing with my weight on one ankle. When I tried to stand, the foot just flopped. No pain, but I wasn't going to be able to stand and walk.

Someone who had seen me fall called for an ambulance. I told the EMT that I needed to go to Group Health. I was quickly taken up the hill and into the ER, so they could X-ray me and decide what treatment I needed. They did surgery and I stayed in the hospital for a couple of days.

After the ambulance took me up to the hospital and I was safely ensconced, I realized what a relief it was that no one could expect me to do anything that day or that week, not my family and not friends like John and Shawn who were living with AIDS. I noticed that John, who got a ride up the hill in the ambulance, was mostly concerned about himself and not about my injury. I decided that I needed to change my life. I had to stop offering too much and accepting too many demands.

The weeks after the injury were interesting. I couldn't drive Jacob places. Rebecca was away at college. I couldn't cook or clean the house. I couldn't do massage. I couldn't help people who were living with AIDS. Being forced to rest and read was wonderful. I did go back to my usual things after I got a walking cast, but I was more aware of limiting how much I did. And I learned everyone survived when I couldn't jump in and rescue them.

I was more aware but not perfect. Over the years, I worked at massage many, many hours and eventually developed arthritis in my hands. I did my best to treat the pain with ice and heat at the end of the day but didn't cut back on my hours. I especially didn't want to stop doing massage at the AIDS clinic. Then the day came when my hands hurt just as much in the morning as they had at night. An X-ray confirmed that the joint was worn away, and I simply needed to rest my hands. I decided then that I had to stop doing massage. I've often wondered if I could have continued doing massage for a few more years if I had worked less and used tools rather than my thumbs.

Some lessons come with observations of others and not personal experience.

Jackie and I met through our mutual friend Michael. She was devoted to him, visiting and taking him to church with her. He was grateful to her for the church services, albeit sometimes puzzled since it wasn't the version of Christianity he grew up with. She was Roman Catholic, and he was Episcopalian. She gave him a rosary, and he wondered what to do with it.

After Michael died, Jackie and I hung out a few times. We talked about Michael and about other experiences with the AIDS community.

For many years before we met, Jackie spent time with other friends who had AIDS. She invited one of the men to move in with her (and her husband and son) at the end of his life. It was the most difficult experience of her life. It almost destroyed her marriage. She decided that she would never again invite someone who had AIDS to move in until he died. She didn't want to be a caregiver anymore. In the end, her parents moved in when they both had serious health problems. This was extremely difficult for her as well, but she didn't think she had a choice.

Jackie was careful to limit her commitment to Michael during the time that he lived at Rosehedge. She simply took him to church with her once a week. This was enough for her.

Albert was the recipient of the same sort of offer from a friend of his. The woman had been a family friend as long as he could remember. When he was having difficulty managing on his own, she asked him to move in with her family. (He absolutely rejected my suggestion that he move to Rosehedge. He didn't want anyone to know that he had AIDS. He was sure his family would abandon him.)

I went to visit Albert at his friend's place. He was ensconced on the couch in the main room while the family (husband, wife, and two kids) went about their life. I believe it was a two-bedroom apartment. The couch was his place in the apartment. Albert complained about pain in his feet (neuropathy), so I did massage on his feet. He said it helped.

I think the friend took care of Albert for a month or so before she told him she couldn't do it anymore. It was just too difficult. He moved back to his apartment. They never spoke again. Caring for him wore her out. I guess she was ashamed that she kicked him out when it got to be too much. She must have thought he was dying when she invited him to move in with her family. However, Albert seemed to get a new lease on life once he was living with her. He demanded time and attention and interfered with their family life. He died two to three months after he moved back to his apartment. No one could have predicted when he would die. It could have been many months or even years.

I thought about my experience as well as about that of Jackie and of Albert's friend. I came to see those stories as lessons about burning out when too much is taken on. Albert's friend probably thought her caregiving would be just for a short time. I suppose Jackie may have thought the same thing when she took in her friend with AIDS. Time seems to change when someone is dying. Every minute of every hour of every day becomes larger than it ever was. A few months turns into a long, long time.

When Shawn was evicted a few years later, I thought about what I would do if he were dying and lost his home again. I decided then that I would never offer to take him in. I was certain we would drive each other crazy. And it would have been even worse if his friends had showed up to hang out at my house. The subject never came up, so I was spared the necessity to say anything. Now I think he probably wouldn't have accepted if I had offered.

For a year or two, I thought I was essential to Shawn. But I worried because he was so sick some of the time. I asked him to give me a key to his apartment so I could check on his welfare if he wasn't answering the door or the phone. He refused and stopped speaking to me for a long time after that (a couple of years, I think). When he resurfaced, he had managed without me.

John tried to persuade his sister Mary and me to take on 24/7 care of him (summer of 1993). He wasn't able to walk anymore and needed people with him in his apartment. He thought we were the logical people to provide the steady care while others could just visit as they liked. John was always willing to ask for what he wanted, and he often got it.

However, we both refused to take on the task of being with him. He had to move to Bailey-Boushay in October of that year. Mary agreed to keep his apartment as it was, with the idea that he could move back when he got better (though we were sure he wouldn't). He took his favorite possessions with him, making his room at Bailey-Boushay into a small replica of his apartment. Mary and I visited him often. One or both of us was there every day, along with many other people. Being able to come and go while knowing that John had full care was a great relief to us.

John lived at Bailey-Boushay from October 1993 into early February 1994. This seems like a very short time now, but it seemed like a lifetime then. Even with so many friends and so many caregivers, every day demanded time and care. We were glad he was there.

Sometimes it seems like I can stay strong and healthy no matter how old I am if I just keep on doing yoga, walking, doing Sudoku, writing, and so forth.

But I know that's not true. I watched John as he struggled to keep on. He insisted on walking again with the help of staff once he was at Bailey-Boushay. He seemed to be getting better for the first week, but then they all gave up. He still didn't want to talk about dying, but he didn't talk much about getting better either. AIDS was relentless, just as some other disease may be for me. In any case, time is relentless.

Since then I've reflected that doing everything can make me feel like a hero and a good person. I can imagine I'm not really old and won't get old. I was embarrassed when Michael's friends called me an angel, but part of me would have liked to believe it was true. But I knew I hadn't done that much. I also knew I enjoyed spending time with him and was rewarded in the moment by our relationship.

Wanting to rescue others isn't limited to those who are obviously in caregiver roles. Michael felt responsible for his sister. He thought she might not survive without him. He was able to die when he finally accepted that she could make it without him. Shawn used to take homeless people into his apartment until he realized they were stealing from him.

==========

On East Republican
(John)

Then, he seemed almost healthy except for pain that dug into his bones,
went off for hours by himself, down the hill and up again.
He knew which streets had harder slopes, could do them all on a good day.

Each time I plod up that hill, I think of him walking with his little dog.
I wonder when it was that the climb became too much.

==========

Years since We Saw Each Other
(For JW)

We sat by our dear friend's side
comforted him until he died

Learned love, respect for each other
We planned to be friends forever

Family Forever

Rick had two secrets. He was gay, and he had AIDS. He shrank from telling his parents he was gay. He didn't tell them until he also had to tell them he had AIDS. The gay part was more difficult.

Many men with AIDS had the same dilemma. Some had told parents they were gay and then been mostly rejected (kept at a distance). Others lived far away, so they didn't have to tell. A few were openly gay and were still considered to be part of the family. For the most part, being gay was shameful and hidden even in the big cities on either coast of the United States.

Back in 1990, almost everyone who got AIDS died within a couple of years. This was expected as far as we knew. The public was frightened. We didn't really know how contagious the virus was. However, people who worked in health care were confident that the virus was only transmitted through blood-to-blood contact (or possibly other body fluids, but rarely).

I volunteered to drive people with AIDS to medical appointments. One of the first people I met this way was Albert. He was very young, twenty-five years old, and African-American (his age and race were rare in those days when AIDS in Seattle mostly affected gay white men in their thirties and forties).

Albert lived in low-income housing. His apartment was in a building called Jefferson Terrace, across the street from Harborview Hospital.

When I drove Albert to a medical appointment, he explained that he got his medical care at Providence Medical Center. He had relatives who worked at Harborview, so he wouldn't go there. He was worried that they would access his medical records and tell family members that he had AIDS. He told his family he had cancer. He was also worried that somehow the people who worked at Harborview would somehow get access to his records at Providence.

Albert told me he was the youngest of fourteen children. He grew up in the Seattle area. When he was a child, his mother (a single parent) was often working. He said that the older sisters and brothers raised him and were hard on him. By the time we met, most of his older brothers and sisters had children of their own. He loved spending time with nephews and nieces.

Being gay didn't seem to be an issue in his family. Albert described being out in high school. He spent all his time hanging out with girl friends. When other boys mocked him for being gay, he pointed out that he was the one who got be with the girls.

He may also have been transgender. In fact, he said he should have been born a girl. He had no interest in surgery but did enjoy dressing as a beautiful girl. Once, he said, he dressed up and went out the back door of the family home. When he came around to the front and rang the doorbell, his mother didn't recognize him.

Albert told me about his boyfriend. They met when Albert was wearing drag. The boyfriend, according to Albert, thought of Albert as a woman. They kept in touch by mail since the boyfriend was in prison. Albert dreamed of the day when the boyfriend would get out, and they could be together. (I suspected that this was mostly a fantasy but never tried to find out for sure.)

Even though being gay was okay, Albert was sure AIDS would be a huge problem to his family. Since he admitted to being sick (cancer), he didn't worry what people would think when he was getting IV medications. He had the machine at his house and was proficient at resetting it when it went nuts. He worried someone who knew would take a look at his row of pill bottles on the windowsill in his bedroom and read the names. Then they would know he was being treated for AIDS. He was convinced that he would never see his family again if they knew because they would be so worried about getting the disease from him. I guess he kept most people out of his bedroom area.

I first met Albert a couple of weeks before Thanksgiving when I gave him a ride to a medical appointment. Then he called me on Thanksgiving Day. He was in the hospital (Providence). He was frightened and feeling very alone. I don't recall if he thought no one in his family would visit or if he didn't want to tell them in case they found out about his disease. He asked me to come visit. I agreed.

In those days before HIPAA, it was easy to call the front desk of a ward and ask about a patient. I did and found out what room he was in. Then I went up and found him in a simple cell, adorned with a huge crucifix at one end of the room. Albert grumbled about the room and the hospital staff. They wouldn't allow him to smoke in his room. He asked me to help him push his

IV pole down the hall and out onto the fire escape where he could smoke in peace (not approved but allowed).

I can't remember if I ever bought cigarettes for him. I might have even though I knew it was bad for him. It didn't seem to matter much. He was unlikely to live long enough to get lung cancer.

Albert thought he would die in the next year or two. He hoped to live long enough to see his boyfriend again when the boyfriend got out of prison. Other than that, he said he had no regrets. He had enjoyed his life and done what he wanted. He had found love. I don't know what kind of work he ever did or how he supported himself. He said he had asked his family to help him by buying household necessities, including forks, knives, and spoons, but no one wanted to. He only had a few of each in his kitchen drawer. So I bought an inexpensive set for him (from Costco). He was elaborately grateful, telling me that I was more of a mother to him than his own mother. I'm certain he told his family about me, probably exaggerating our friendship.

When he expressed unhappiness about Christmas, saying he wouldn't have a tree or any celebration, I bought him a little tree to put on his deck. I noticed over time that the tree had died. He probably never watered it. I hated seeing that and didn't say anything.

He also got me to help him with food. When I brought groceries, I had the challenge of getting into the building and up to his apartment. I learned that someone would always let me in the door, front or back. Albert laughed and said they all know the worst people already lived inside his building. He preferred going in the back door because of the old women who sat in the first-floor lobby in front. He said they were there all the time and had nothing else to do but gossip about their neighbors. Albert gave me a key to his apartment door but wasn't allowed to have extras of the security key to the building.

Most often, Albert was watching television when I came over, always cartoons. His apartment was a large studio with no walls between living room, bedroom, and kitchen. He had a couch and a large television in the living room area. His bed took up most of the bedroom area. One time, he had all the contents of the kitchen cupboards in the center of the room under a blanket. The building had let tenants know they were spraying for cockroaches, and all food had to be protected this way. He ranted about new neighbors who brought cockroaches into the building.

Later, when Albert wasn't able to walk, the roaches enjoyed free rein in his apartment. They shamelessly ran up and down the wall behind his bed. Albert squished them when he could using his slipper.

Somewhere in there, a longtime family friend invited Albert to come and live with her and her family. They lived in a low-income apartment. I'm not sure how many people. I think it was parents and three children in a two-bedroom place. Albert was installed on the couch in the living room.

I came to visit Albert in the new place. The people were kind, and the place was chaotic. He complained about his feet hurting and liked when I massaged them. By then, I was in massage school but just at the beginning and only knew a little about massaging feet. He figured out how to get an electric wheelchair from DSHS, but they didn't have any way to get it up to the apartment. He rode it around the block a few times, and then I don't know what happened to it.

I think he lived with the friend's family for about a month. Then the friend moved him back to his apartment. As far as I know, he never saw her or her family again.

As he got weaker, I suggested to Albert that he move to Rosehedge. He was absolutely against that. Everyone would then know that he had AIDS. But I said, if he didn't move, he could die alone in his apartment. He said dying alone would be okay. He got to where he couldn't really get out of bed. One time when I visited, he complained his niece had come into his apartment and stolen his big television. He still had a small one. She claimed he didn't need the big one.

One day Albert had managed to call 911. When they got to him, he was close to death and alone. He died on the way to the hospital. His mother told me about the funeral. She also told me about the viewing the day before. I went, and it was an odd experience to see him so changed by makeup. I also went to the funeral. When I got there, his mother and others were warm and lovely to me. They invited me to ride with them to the cemetery (I did) and to join them for a meal afterwards (I didn't).

Despite all his fears, Albert's family and friends who are like family tried to be supportive of him. I guess they may have figured out that he had AIDS but chose not to talk about it. I think it was the same with Rick's family (supportive) although they stayed at some distance.

I met another man, Joseph, who had the same fears about telling his family about his AIDS diagnosis. His family lived in Arizona. Since he lived at such a distance, the secret was easy to keep. However, he had no support group. He wasn't able to manage. His apartment had glasses all over with remnants of instant-breakfast drinks. This was all he could prepare for himself. We talked. He decided to risk calling his family to let them know his situation. His father subsequently drove up here and took Joseph back to the family home. I called once and was told he was doing okay, so I don't know what happened next.

Peter worked at Rosehedge. He was an energetic redhead, always loving and smiling. And he was HIV positive. He grew up in the Midwest. When he was thirteen, he came out to his family. They told him to leave, to go to San Francisco to be with his own kind. He had a hard life there. Somehow he was strong and connected with other people. He found family and joy at Rosehedge among the patients and with his coworkers. Peter died of AIDS a few years later. He hadn't talked about being HIV positive when I knew him. I guess there may have been others on the staff who lived with the virus as well.

==========

Jefferson Terrace

My friend Albert lived on the sixteenth floor of
The hulking building on the edge of downtown
With a view of the bay
Had a small terrace
Where the little Christmas tree I gave him died

He railed against the old women who had nothing
Better to do than to sit in the lobby
Watch their neighbors
Gossip about them
Tell stories to anyone who was interested

I usually came in from the back parking lot
Always someone would let me in
Security meant nothing
Didn't really matter
As Albert said, the really scary people lived there

Everything Takes Longer

I notice as I age that things (such as getting ready for bed) take longer than I thought they would and longer than they used to take.

Back in the days when I drove John to appointments, I learned to allocate twice as much time as I thought I would need. If his appointment at 3:00 p.m. was twenty minutes away, I showed up to drive him at 2:00 p.m. This way, we were generally about ten minutes early for the appointment. Sometimes I had to help him get dressed. Usually we had to gather his possessions together for the trip. Getting him into the car and then out at the other end was often difficult.

Once I drove John to an appointment in Magnolia in the days before GPS. He said he knew the way, and between us, we were able to get to the right neighborhood in a reasonable amount of time. We drove up and down various streets until we found the address. With his slow walking, the trek between car and front door took five minutes. He was getting some sort of energy treatment, meant to take an hour. I stayed in the car with a book. The front door finally opened ninety minutes after he went in. We began the drive home. When we got close to his apartment, he asked me to drive slowly through Volunteer Park. We stopped for a few minutes to watch people and dogs. In the end, one appointment ate up the entire afternoon.

Doug was another who could stretch an appointment into hours of time together. Once he asked me to stop at QFC before driving him home so he could grocery-shop. I trailed him through the store as he compared prices, sizes, and brands. That wasn't too bad. Then we got to the check stand. He watched the bagger all the way through the bagging process.

When the groceries were all bagged, Doug got upset. He said the groceries were bagged incorrectly. He insisted that various items were going to be squashed and ruined. He made the bagger take all the groceries out of the bag. Then he determined which item should be put in first and next until we were finally ready to leave the store.

Doug was in his fifties, very thin with a leathery face. The skin on his face seemed loose. Doug was short, maybe five feet seven inches. He always looked disgruntled, and anger wasn't far below the surface. He had grown up in the Midwest and had an obvious accent in his speech. He sounded like a country boy to me.

Whenever I took Doug to an appointment, he made me wait. I parked in the load zone in front of his apartment. After I parked, I walked over to the door and buzzed him to let him know I was there. He always took ten to fifteen minutes to come out.

Doug managed to use up a lot of my time even when we weren't together. He put his favorite music on his answering machine. No one could leave a message without listening through several minutes of music (like one movement of a symphony). It was kind of cute the first time but got old very quickly. There was no way to skip through it. Eventually I ended up hanging up and calling later, hoping to get him in person. Then I learned he was angry with anyone who wouldn't listen through the music. He said hanging up was rude. He was there all the time but wouldn't pick up until I began to leave a message. Even though I called often, he was offended I didn't want to listen to the music over and over. Possibly he didn't want to answer until he knew who was calling.

One time, after a medical appointment, Doug asked me to take him to the Crypt. The store had leather, fetish, and fashion wear, plus many magazines and sex toys. It seems to have closed in 2015. He wanted supplies for his next trip to the gay bathhouse (seemed to be his only social outlet). I had never before been in the store, which I admitted to him. When we went in, Doug made sure I didn't miss anything. He kept pointing to various sex toys. I did my best to keep my face blank since I suspected he was trying to embarrass me.

Doug talked several times about his experiences at the gay bathhouse. He hooked up with people there. He gave out his phone number and waited for the phone call that almost never came. He was bitter about this unkindness. Finally, one man called him. They got together once, and then the man disappeared. Doug raged about the man, saying he used him and then abandoned him.

He also talked about experiences at truck stops when he was young. He went over at night and went from truck to truck looking for someone who was interested in sex with him. He said that many truckers were willing to hook up with gay men. He always found someone. Doug didn't seem to have ever had a long relationship. Once he was grown, he moved away from his birthplace, initially to San Francisco and later to Seattle. He indicated that his parents didn't want anything to do with their gay son.

He lived in low-income housing in Bell Tower. That building is in downtown Seattle on First Avenue, overlooking the waterfront. It is close to grocery stores, pharmacies, and other shops. It is also located near Downtown Public Health and Neighborhood Service Centers and is a short bus ride from Seattle Public Library's Central branch. His studio apartment was on one of the higher floors of the seventeen-story building looking out over the waterfront.

It occurs to me that Doug moved after the first time I gave him a ride. He was living in a building in Greenwood that first time. I don't know why he moved.

His apartment was not big, but he had a grandfather clock that had belonged to his parents, a beautiful couch, a plush rug, and a few other nice pieces of furniture. Everything looked beautiful and untouched. It was like a display rather than a home. He had inherited all these pieces from his parents. His parents were older when he was born, and he was an only child. When I was there the first time, I commented on the fantastic view and about how beautiful his apartment was. He responded that the view didn't look good if you looked straight down at the drug deals on the street below him as well as the homeless people urinating on the sidewalk.

One time, Doug suggested that we go to Volunteer Park and climb the water tower. I hadn't ever been up there. He told me the view was wonderful. As we began to climb the stairs, Doug directed my attention to the walls and all the graffiti. Both the pictures and the words were pornographic and directed at gay men. He stopped at every step to get me to look.

After a few of the decorations, I got bored with the topic and went ahead of him. We got to the top finally, and I walked around looking out at the view. He kept telling me to look at the decorations even up there. According to Doug, gay men had some wild times there at night.

Once, Doug called me when he had an emergency stemming from a sex toy that had been inserted too far into his anus, so that he couldn't remove it. He was in enormous pain and bleeding. We arranged for him to go to the hospital, and I drove him. When we got there, he was examined in the emergency room. They decided to admit him since he had CMV in his colon.

After they admitted him, Doug handed me his keys and asked me to go back for items he would need during his stay. He had no one else to ask.

When I got over to the apartment, I noticed blood on the carpet by his bathroom. I didn't want him to come home to a mess, so I pulled out cleaning supplies and scrubbed at the blood. I couldn't get the stain out completely, but I thought it was better.

When Doug got home from the hospital and saw the carpet, he was furious with me. He said I shouldn't have tried to do anything when I didn't know what I was doing. (I can't argue with that.)

Even though Doug was cold and angry with me, he continued to depend on me for rides to appointments. One time, I fell asleep in the afternoon and woke up when I was supposed to be picking him up. He called. I went. He did not accept my apology.

After that, Doug would not accept my phone calls and wouldn't accept rides from me. My friend Bob, who worked for the volunteer agency, ended up offering to drive him. He reported that Doug talked about his anger with everyone, especially me. Bob was with Doug when he died.

All this must have happened over several months and no more. Doug and I were together no more than a dozen times. He never asked me about my life.

When Doug stopped talking to me, I was sorry that he didn't want my support anymore. He thought I was a bad person, and I don't want anyone to think that. I thought that I had failed. At the same time, I was glad to not have to deal with him anymore. He was always cranky and demanding. I had to watch what I said and did. I was embarrassed to admit that I was happy to be free of him.

John was often cranky and demanding, but it was different. He often expressed appreciation and love for the people around him. He enjoyed many parts of his life, especially if they distracted him from AIDS

John and I had some bumps in the road but continued to be friends for more than two years until he died. John met several members of my family, including Mom and Gigi. He also knew Steve (husband of Carol from Mike's work). Steve and Carol invited John and me to Thanksgiving at their house one year. Our family Thanksgiving had fallen apart that year. So John knew some of my people and was interested in any juicy gossip.

John took up a huge amount of space in my life. Over time, we got to where we talked every day and saw each other most days as well. I used him as a subject for a project when I was in massage school. We were supposed to do weekly massage on the same person for ten weeks and turn in notes on how it went, showing any changes. John was delighted to have the opportunity to get even more massage than usual. He was always happy to have me try out new techniques on him (which helped me a lot). Massages were supposed to last for an hour. They went on much longer because he kept thinking of new painful spots and asking for fixes.

==========

"Z"

His club: for a night to forget pain and rejection,
the virus dragging him along to the end of his life.

His time: to pretend in the dark.
Among strangers, life is good after all.

His bag: all he needs, his hope
a jar of Crisco, his toys, pills to enhance the fun.

Chicken Soup Brigade

My work with Mike's company had dwindled by 1990 (because computers took over inventory and I wanted something different). I decided to volunteer while I was thinking about what to do next.

When I was a teacher, I thought that I was helping people. Working in a business seemed to be the opposite. I wanted to find another way of helping, especially since my children were teens and needed a lot less from me. I felt drawn to the gay community and wanted to learn more about it. AIDS was a huge part of knowing about the gay community at the time. I looked into volunteer opportunities and discovered an organization called Chicken Soup Brigade (CSB).

Chicken Soup Brigade was separate from the Northwest AIDS Foundation (NWAF) at that time. Years later, NWAF became Lifelong AIDS Alliance (still in existence), and Chicken Soup Brigade became part of Lifelong. CSB began from the realization that many people living with AIDS were poor and couldn't afford food. They also might not have the energy to shop and cook for themselves. The organizers found a kitchen (in the Josephinum) and a chef to run the program. Volunteers cooked, packaged, and delivered food to clients. These jobs were done by three different groups of volunteers. The organization also found volunteers to provide rides (to medical appointments and the like) for people with AIDS. NWAF focused more on housing, counseling, practical help, and a thrift store.

I went to the CSB office in a tiny storefront on Pike and found out about the training program (one day in a rented space). This was scheduled for July 21. At the training, we received a lot of information and were given the opportunity to sign up for volunteer tasks that interested us the most. The presenters emphasized that the warmth and kindness was a huge benefit to people with AIDs who had often experienced a lot of rejection from friends, family, medical personnel, and workplaces. Hugs were encouraged. However, those who weren't comfortable with one-to-one contact were encouraged to sign up to cook or package meals, another good way of helping.

I looked around at the other potential volunteers as well as the people presenting the program. It seemed that perhaps half were young gay men or lesbian women. Many others were older straight men and women. I guessed that most of the people running the organization were gay or lesbian. Ironically, the failure of the U.S. government (Reagan) to recognize the crisis may have energized others. I heard over time that gay men and lesbians were drawn together by the crisis. Lesbians gave love and care while gay men learned to love them back. The two groups had been quite separate previously.

I had a lot of free time since I only worked at Mike's business for a few hours in the morning and had few demands from my children, so I signed up to package meals and to give rides to people with AIDS.

That day, after the training, I was scheduled to go over to Husky Stadium to meet up with Mike and some friends for the first day of the Goodwill Games. I walked down the hill and across the Montlake Bridge. Mike and the others (Mike's banker and his wife) were already there. The wife, Linda, was interested in my volunteering. The men weren't although Mike expressed approval when Linda commented on what a great thing it was.

When we pulled up to our house, Rebecca (aged sixteen) came running out of the house in tears. She sobbed out the information that my father (Grampa to her) had died. I got into my car and cried the whole way over to Mom and Dad's house. I think Rebecca came with me, but I'm not sure. Mike probably came in his own car. He calmed Mom and offered to help her with all the required details, from having Dad's body taken to a funeral home to persuading the *Seattle Times* to print a news obituary.

Not long after that emotional day, I began my volunteer activities. I went over to the Josephinum, on the bus I think, one day each week and packaged food. The food had been cooked earlier in the day by a different group of volunteers. Another volunteer, Kelly, and I (sometimes others) followed instructions on how much to put into each package. The packages were then ready for the volunteer drivers to pick up and deliver to people living with AIDS.

Over time, I knew a number of people who received the food. They generally appreciated the thought but sometimes thought the food wasn't very good. Of course, people who are sick often can't eat as much, and food may taste wrong. Shawn used to get the food delivered, but he rarely ate it. He froze them when they were delivered. He was an excellent cook and preferred to cook for himself. However, he knew a large number of homeless or very low-income people who didn't have food. He gave the frozen packaged meals to them. Many others who received the meals wasted part or most of the food.

The volunteers who provided rides needed to go into the office and look through the list of ride requests. People were listed by name and the destinations in a large notebook, along with the date and time. (This was in 1990, before HIPAA mandated more privacy than the notebook provided. It was also before computers made such scheduling easier. I suppose this might be done on the computer nowadays.) Some requested a driver who would take them both ways. Others were fine with two different drivers or finding their own way one direction. The volunteer signed up in the notebook and then wrote a reminder for him or herself.

In some ways, the organization seemed very casual. Employees were crowded into a small space. They were often willing to describe the people looking for rides, not always in flattering terms. I don't mean that they gossiped about the clients. They gave information useful to volunteers such as if the person was always late or always angry. All of the people working at CSB were grateful for volunteers and treated us as honored coworkers.

Everyone on the CSB staff was friendly. Bob was especially easy to get along with. He and I became friends and over the years often spent time together. We met for coffee and talked about our lives. I practiced (during massage school) on him a few times. Bob took me to a fundraiser for politician Cal Anderson (that famous occasion when the backyard deck collapsed under the weight of people attending the event. It only dropped a few feet. No one was hurt, just startled.) Even though Bob wasn't feeling well, he came to my graduation from massage school (spring 1992).

One of my memories of Bob was from a day when I was meeting him at his apartment. This was after I lived in my current house (probably early 1994), so I walked down, about six blocks. I rang the bell, and nothing happened. I rang again. Still nothing. I gave up and went home after fifteen minutes. When we talked later, it turned out that he had forgotten. After that, I made sure to check before meeting up with him. That was the only time he let me down. We didn't see each other often. When we did, we talked about our lives in an open way and supported each other.

Bob was a gay man in his thirties. I don't recall what sort of jobs he had before coming to Chicken Soup Brigade. He was frustrated by not finding a relationship. Bob talked a little about the worst trauma of his life when his mother committed suicide. He was just a boy, and he found her body, I think, in the bathtub. (Bob was not HIV positive.)

Bob had a long friendship with a man he met through the AIDS community. Bob drove him around, brought him meals, and spent nights with him. The family was at a distance. Then the end came when the man was close to death. Suddenly the family swooped in and shut Bob out. This was devastating to him. He didn't want to blame his friend, but he didn't know how the family couldn't have done that without his agreement. He struggled with blaming the man with AIDS for allowing that to happen.

Other than the man with AIDS, Bob didn't have a long-term relationship, and I don't know if he ever did. Once he told me about going to meet men in the park for anonymous sex. He met someone and then asked for his name. The other man was annoyed and said names destroyed the whole meaning of anonymous sex. Bob also had a fairly long (months at least) relationship with a man who was already in a committed (but open) relationship with another man. I don't remember how that ended.

The communication went both ways. I told Bob about the friendships I developed with several of the people who got rides from me. He knew that I looked for people I knew when I signed up to give rides. That was acceptable. Creating a private relationship where people directly asked me for rides seemed to be okay as well. Bob knew I gave my phone number to people I liked and was open to friendship with them. He was always supportive.

Over time, Bob decided to move on from his job at Chicken Soup Brigade. He wanted something more challenging. He learned that a physician who ran a clinic that served people with AIDS needed a personal assistant. He was excited about applying for the job. He felt that he would finally feel validated as a person if he got the demanding job.

He was happy when he got the job. He often found that it was more challenging than he expected. This was difficult for him. He was doing good work, and there were more challenges every day. He said his boss thought work should get done when he walked by her desk. He had heard ahead of time that she was a demanding boss and had gone through several assistants in a year.

I didn't listen carefully enough to Bob. Though he told me a lot about his life, I didn't realize that he struggled with lifelong depression. I was surprised when I learned he had committed suicide. Many other people knew he had thought about it for years. They thought it was associated with his mother's suicide, both from his grief and knowing it was one way to end pain. Perhaps there was some kind of survivor's guilt too after all his years of working with and knowing people with AIDS.

Bob died by swimming out into the ocean by Neah Bay. He didn't want to take a chance that anyone would find his body. As far as I know, his body never turned up. (He was born in 1959 and died in 1995.)

Before Bob swam out into the ocean, he left messages for many people, including his psychiatrist. He wanted everyone to know that there was nothing they could have done or said to change his mind. He wanted them all to know that he loved them and thanked them for their caring. I heard about the messages from others but didn't have one myself. The people who worked with him were stunned, angry, and sad for months afterwards.

Helpers and those helped—sounds like a neat division. But often those who are helping are suffering or helping themselves in the process. Often the people being helped have something to offer to the helpers. Many of the volunteers for Chicken Soup Brigade were people who were living with AIDS and wanted to give something back. Bob was suffering in a different way and giving back.

==========

No Freedom
(For John N. and Bob M.)

> He worked for an AIDS organization
> Spent time with his friend who had AIDS
> Once in a while
>> He'd go to a movie
>>> Hike in the country
>>>> Ride a roller coaster
> He liked having an AIDS-free day
> Claimed it for himself
>
> We talked it over
> John wished that he could do the same
>>> When you have AIDS
>> Every day it's there
> In the bones and blood
> In every thought
> Whether you're at a movie or on a hike
> Life is about living with the disease

==========

Community Project
(For Bob M.)

Walking to honor the NW AIDS Foundation
We shared the tradition
Never solicited donations
That part didn't interest us

The group gathered for breakfast
Drove close to the Seattle Center
Complained about boring speakers
Laughed and talked as we walked

Celebrated at the end with a ride
(The roller coaster was mandatory)
Greeted others from the AIDS community
We had our traditions

==========

Bill's off Broadway

not every time but often, when I walk along this street
I look over at the small pizza place
look over, remember the one time I ate there
the one time I was there with my friend Bob
my friend Bob liked the place, the name or the food
the food was pretty good but not great
the greater blessing, time with my good friend
my friend, gone now for more than ten years
years ago, lost his fight against demon depression
depression pulled him, away from us
pulled away, and I remember his kindness
wonder if I listened to him
or listened without hearing his pain

Some Family Nurtured

I met many people with AIDS over a couple of years. Most had family or friends in their lives. Some seemed to be almost totally alone.

What does it take for a child to reject parents and the parents to reject the child? Does the child turn away in order to live the life s/he wants? Does the parent reject the child who goes against what the parent believes? Perhaps there is shame and guilt on both sides? I felt so sad for those who were totally alone and comforted by those who had family love around them.

Marty was short (about five feet four inches) and thin. He lived in a Seattle Housing Authority building above the freeway. The tall brick building looked good from the outside. When you went inside, it smelled of old food and cigarettes. I thought it had a feeling of despair.

Marty needed a ride to a medical appointment from his apartment over to Swedish Hospital. He had difficulty walking. When we got back to his place, I accompanied him from the car up into his place. I waited while he made it to his bed and got settled. As we walked, he said he needed new T-shirts and socks but wasn't able to go shopping and didn't have the money. There was no one to help him.

I told my husband about Marty. Mike told me to take some T-shirts and socks from the warehouse to give to Marty. I picked out three T-shirts, plus some socks that seemed to be suitable and then called Marty. He asked me to bring the clothes to him. I parked in the loading zone. I didn't intend to stay for a long visit. Marty was mildly grateful. I suppose the T-shirts weren't stylish and the socks weren't either.

Later, when I was visiting Michael at Rosehedge, Marty was a resident there. The door to his room was open. I recognized him sitting on the bed. By then, he couldn't walk by himself and was often unresponsive. I sat with him several times. Once he expressed sadness about his life. He said that he had never been in love and never had a relationship. He was in his thirties. Nurses told me that he had been quite a character before he became bedbound. He used to race to answer the phone (and say silly things) before staff could get to it.

Another time, when he was close to death, Marty talked about his family. They lived in Ohio. He had called them several times since he moved to Rosehedge. He begged them to come to see him. They refused. Everything else in their lives was more important than coming to see him. They never came. He hadn't seen them for many years.

One of Marty's friends invited me to an informal gathering, a memorial service after Marty died. This was in a house south of Seattle. I guess there were about ten people there. People talked about Marty. It sounded as if no one knew him well. Most of the people had met Marty through their positions as caregivers in the AIDS community.

Joseph was one of the rare people who were able to go home when he was very sick. When he finally agreed to call his parents to tell them he had AIDS, his father drove up from the southwest (maybe New Mexico or Arizona) to Joseph's apartment. Then he took Joseph home to stay. I talked to one of Joseph's family members after he had gone home. I suppose they took care of him until he died, but I never heard.

Another who was able to go home was my cousin David (1951–1987). He was gay and moved to San Francisco (from Vermont) as a young man. At the time, San Francisco was the place for gay men. His experiences with living and dying from AIDS were quite different from Marty's (as far as I know from what Mom said, based on what she learned from David's mother, my dad's sister). I see that San Francisco is where my aunt (David's mother) was born, which seems like an interesting coincidence.

At some point, David got so sick that he knew he was going to die soon. He wrote to his parents to let them know. His mother, my aunt Jean, told him to come home. Mom said David's father didn't approve, but Aunt Jean insisted on taking care of their son. She took care of him until he died. David is buried in a tiny graveyard at the farm where his brother John and wife, Carol, live.

I looked at the AIDS Memorial Quilt (http://www.aidsquilt.org/view-the-quilt/search-the-quilt) and asked for his name. There is a square with the correct name (David Reynolds), and I decided it was for him (block number 04060). It just has the name in sparkly letters. I guessed I could ask Cousin

John (or his wife, Carol) for more information. (David was at the wedding when John and Carol married in 1978, I think).

I sent a message to Carol on FB, "Hi, Carol, I've been writing about the people I knew who died from AIDS and got to thinking about David. I remember a little about him as a small boy (seven years younger than I) but know nothing about him as an adult. I wondered if you could fill me in a little. What were his interests? How did he earn a living? How long did he live in San Francisco? Mom said that Jean took care of him at the end of his life. Do you know how long he lived with her? Did you see him during that time?

"Also, one thing that especially interests me about this is that so many families totally abandoned their children who had AIDS, or visited but wouldn't care for them. David was lucky, I think."

Carol: "I can send you some information/ stories. Get me your mailing address.

"We made a panel for David. If you search for David Reynolds, it's in the upper right corner of the thirrd section, I think. It features a map of California and a map of Vermont along with a garden of lilies made of family hands" (http://www.aidsquilt.org/view-the-quilt/search-the-quilt).

Me: "Good thing you described it. There is more than one David Reynolds."

The square I found initially was not the right person. I looked back at the quilt and was able to find the square Carol described. It seems very appropriate for him.

I remember helping to make a square for someone (maybe John), but he isn't in the official quilt. I tried a couple more names. No one else I knew was on there among the more than 48,000 panels (http://www.aidsquilt.org/about/the-aids-memorial-quilt).

I barely remember David from when we were young. He was seven years younger than I am while his older brother Tommy was only three years younger. Tommy and I used to go out on the lake in rowboats and try to capsize each other when I was there for the summer. I was almost thirteen and Tommy was ten. David was too young to have that freedom. So he was just an annoying little kid.

When I visited Michael at Rosehedge, I got to know other people who were living there. Only six people lived there at a time. Doors to rooms were generally open. Staff and visitors interacted almost like family. Residents who were healthy enough spent time in a common area. Even though they hadn't known each other before, Michael cared about the welfare of others and wanted to hear even when one of the others died. He encouraged me to visit and chat with others and then report to him.

One of those others was also named Michael. The first time I met him, he had many visitors. His parents and other family members had come from another state to see him. They may have initially assumed I worked there as they included me in the conversation when I paused by the room. They were planning to go home the next day. They asked me to visit with their son when I was there. I agreed.

Since I was visiting my Michael every day, I spent time with the other Michael a number of times even though he was close to the end. He told me that he had worked in a jewelry store and had a collection of precious gems. Then he gestured to the other side of his room, wanting me to see his treasures. There were no gems and no display cases in the room.

After a few weeks, the other Michael was no longer able to talk. He was in a coma. Then there was the day when the bed was empty. A staff person told me his family had called him and, with guidance from Rosehedge staff, told him they loved him and that it was okay for him to die. He died within a few minutes of hearing those words.

Jack's family wouldn't let him come home, but his father helped to care for him and then stayed with him at Rosehedge during the last few days of his life.

My Michael had only one sister. Their parents were long gone. His sister and boyfriend got the idea that he could get cured from some sort of alternative treatment in Mexico. They tried to persuade Michael to leave Rosehedge with them. When he was reluctant, they got on either side of him and attempted to force him out the door. The Rosehedge staff eventually called the police to come and protect Michael. The sister agreed to let him stay there, and she never pushed anything like that again during the last weeks of his life. She continued to visit him most days.

Others at Rosehedge, like Marty, had no family who visited. One man, Larry, seemed to have no one at all. I stopped in and chatted with him occasionally. He liked to have someone to walk with him a couple of blocks over to the 7-Eleven. Larry wasn't able to walk at all by the next month. I stopped to say hello. He was angry and did not want to talk. After that day, he demanded that the door to his room be closed (which was unusual) and said he did not want any visitors. He didn't even want to talk to any of the people on the staff there. He died a few weeks later.

Bill always sat in the common area. He chatted with anyone who was willing to talk and even when they didn't want to talk. When he couldn't walk anymore, he had someone carry him into the common area. I went to his funeral in the chapel at a mortuary. There may have been eight people there. I don't think any were family, but some were probably friends.

There was another man (and I don't recall his name) who never had any visits that I saw. I sat with him during the last days of his life just because I didn't think anyone should be alone while dying. He was in a coma. Perhaps he didn't know that he was alone. Staff also spent time with him.

I wonder if the families who never saw the child again might regret it now?

My sister said, "I remember Aunt Jean talking about being the hostess at Middlebury College and how difficult it was for her when guests made derogatory remarks about gay people or people with AIDS at her dinner table. She believed it was impolite to embarrass a guest in your home. (A guest had a lot more freedom.) I will never forget her words, 'and my Davey dying of AIDS.'"

==========

Too Naughty
(For Marty J)

He lay helpless in the bed at Rosehedge
A seizure might be bringing him to an end
He asked me to call his Shanti volunteer
She knew where to get good chicken soup
She was surprised to hear after so long

Then he felt better but still at Rosehedge
Drove them crazy by answering the phone
In the office across from his bedroom
They thought he was very naughty at times
He delighted in being so

As the end approached, he begged his mom
At home in Connecticut to come
She made excuses, said it wouldn't work
She had to mow her lawn today or next week
She never saw him before he died

Demonstrating Solidarity

These days, protests often involve blocking traffic and annoying everyone else. Those protests seem quite different than ones I was in.

I guess pride parades count as public demonstration. Some people may have been irritated when roads were blocked, but the route was known well in advance and easy to avoid. Others were offended by some of the floats, including gay parents who worried about their kids seeing outrageous clothing (or rather lack of clothing). I went to a number of the parades and took John to one or two. I left him off on Broadway and then parked my car up the hill. One of those years, during the gathering in the park after the parade, John held court under the largest tree. I felt extraneous. Another year, Shawn came up to John and me. We were irritated with Shawn's behavior and were unfriendly to him.

If the pride parade was a demonstration, we even had counter-demonstrators. Usually four to five people with signs pronouncing that gay people were going to hell stood on one of the main corners. The marchers and the watchers of the parade ignored them as far as I could see. Actually I thought the protestors were brave to stand out there since they were outnumbered so completely. Either they were brave or they trusted that gay people wouldn't attack them.

The pride parade and the celebrations in parks (actually several parades) has continued, but I haven't been to them in years. I got bored when it seemed that they had been taken over by politicians and groups selling things. I think this is the sort of event that appeals more to younger people, who don't mind being in the middle of crowds. And they are helpful for those wanting to edge out of the closet. Even in June, Seattle weather often isn't friendly to parades and celebrations in the park. The happiness of the crowds seems to overcome any dismal weather.

The NW AIDS Foundation (now Lifelong AIDS Alliance) walk, and fundraiser is another sort of demonstration. I walked in it a couple of times but don't recall trying to raise money. We walked downtown and to the Seattle Center on a Sunday when there wasn't much traffic or many people to annoy. (The bit about getting people to donate reminds me of my first awareness of the homeless man, Robert Lee, who was gay but not HIV positive I think. He had a ragged donation sheet, supposedly for the walk. I don't think he raised much money. No one thought he was actually raising money for the NWAF.)

I wrote, thousands walk each year for the Northwest AIDS Foundation, a river of people, near the end of September, sometimes damp usually sunny. Volunteers along the route offered coffee, juice, Tootsie Pops. We waved to friends going the other way, some carrying names of those who died.

I see that the AIDS Walk continues (https://give.lifelong.org/seattle/events/2017-end-aids-walk/e127102): "After 30 years of walking, Lifelong has renamed the *Seattle AIDS Walk* to the *End AIDS Walk*. Funds raised will support HIV prevention and care services for people living with or affected by HIV and AIDS." I couldn't walk that far nowadays.

I guess I walked once in the AIDS Walk with a group from NW AIDS Foundation and another time with friends (talking and laughing the whole way). Most AIDS organizations had teams representing them. People with AIDS sometimes marched, as well as family and friends.

Shawn got me to go to an ACT UP (AIDS Coalition to Unleash Power) meeting, but for some reason, he didn't come to the meeting. Or maybe he just came the first time I went. I don't recall details now. I went and kept going for quite some time, including participating in a demonstration.

One thing I appreciated about ACT UP was how well organized it was. Every meeting was planned for two hours. At the beginning, the coordinator would ask for topics and list them on a board. The topics were put in order and allotted time for discussion and disposal. The coordinator kept everyone within the allotted time. One block of time, at the beginning of the meeting, was provided to check back on tasks assigned at the previous meeting.

The ACT UP group was planning a demonstration when I joined it. The issue was whether HIV-positive people could go to medical or dental school. Some people (not those in ACT UP) were convinced that HIV-positive doctors or dentists posed a great risk to patients. This was never true as far as I know, but the University of Washington was under pressure. We had signs and a chant we learned. About a dozen people showed up for the demonstration. We marched and chanted near the UW medical school. We didn't interfere with anyone, and we made our views known. I don't know if we had an effect, but the UW dropped the idea of keeping HIV-positive people out of the dental and medical schools.

Some time after that demonstration, I stopped going to ACT UP meetings. I think the group lost fervor in general and disappeared.

Wikipedia says, "ACT UP chapters continue to meet and protest, albeit with a smaller membership. ACT UP/NY and ACT UP/Philadelphia are particularly robust, with other chapters active elsewhere." This suggests to me that it's gone in Seattle.

Looking further online, I came across this article, http://www.bailey-boushay.org/body.cfm?id=114&action=detail&ref=58. I didn't realize that ACT UP helped to ensure that Bailey-Boushay House opened. Phil Bereano describes an action that was canceled when it was no longer needed. "ACT UP's activist strategy of 'challenging and publicly taunting the powers that be' changed history," Phil says. Most important: "This house would have been stuck in the legal process and delayed at least two years. The lives that were touched and affected in that time were real. I think it's something that all of us [in ACT UP] feel very good about.'"

The other vivid experience of public demonstration for me was the AIDS Memorial Vigil (http://archiveswest.orbiscascade.org/ark:/80444/xv00820). "The Vigil was begun by a man named Laughing Otter in the mid-1980s as a way for the gay community to come together in grieving and to memorialize their late friends. Responsibility for organizing the annual event on the lawn of Seattle Community College was assumed in 1988 by Dale Inman. His wife, Carol, continued it after his death until 1998." (She may have died then. Plus, fewer people were dying of AIDS.)

The vigil was sad and joyous at the same time. People set up makeshift altars, usually showing the creativity and other powerful aspects of the person who had died. The organizers were people who lived with AIDS, as well as family and friends.

"Album of photos, obituaries, tributes and objects related to a Vigil begun as a way for the gay community to come together in grieving and to memorialize their late friends."

The grassy area at the southeast corner of the SCC campus was the site for the vigil. Sometimes I look at it when I pass by and remember the tables set up between the grassy areas. Some people stayed in tents through the whole weekend.

I learned of the vigil in the *Seattle Gay News* (still published and free at various locations). Each year, before the vigil, the *SGN* posted a list of Seattle people who were known to have died from AIDS. The list covered several pages of the newspaper in columns of small print (http://www.sgn. org/sgnnews46_08/index.cfm). Nowadays, a public list like that probably wouldn't be allowed and would be seen as an invasion of privacy.

He didn't know me, but I remember Dale Inman. I saw him once in the Chicken Soup Brigade office. He was tall and rough looking, with many tattoos and piercings. He was handsome and looked healthy. He surprised me. Other gay men I'd met looked middle-class and mild compared to him. I wasn't sure if he was gay since he was married. Now I think he was gay, and the marriage had survived his truth. His wife was supportive of him and other gay men.

I saw the vigil as a place where people put names and faces to the deaths from AIDS. Some had artwork or other items that meant something about the people who had died. One of the rituals had us all in a circle. Holding my hand on one side was the governor of Washington, Mike Lowry.

I think this was before HIPAA, but Chicken Soup Brigade had taught us not to reveal the names of people we knew who were living with AIDS. Opinions varied about whether confidentiality extended to after the person died. I never put anything up at the AIDS Memorial. I saw some tables dedicated to people I had known, which made me cry even though I already knew they were dead. One of those was Lee. It looked like many people had contributed to his memorial.

When I was a volunteer for Chicken Soup Brigade, I got to know a gay man named Joe. He also helped to prepare meals. He was mostly closeted, especially from his family. He was one of three brothers. All of the brothers were severely diabetic. The other two had died because of diabetes. Joe wasn't HIV positive. He was shy and hadn't dared to approach any of the men he wanted to date. He was glad not to be infected and also felt like a failure as a gay man. We both remembered one charismatic man (Shane) who had been a bartender. Joe used to hover at the back of a crowd of admirers of this man. Shane died a number of years before we talked about him.

Joe had a difficult relationship with his mother. I can't really remember, but I think they shared two halves of a duplex, so he thought she was always keeping track of him. He wouldn't invite anyone over to see him at his house. He didn't want his mother to meet his friends. Joe told his friends that they could meet his mother, but then he would never speak to them again. He resented gifts his mother gave him since she always seemed to choose colors and styles he was sure to hate.

Joe and I talked about the AIDS Memorial Vigil and the pride parade. He had never been to either one. He decided he had the courage to go to them with me. He parked in front of my house, and we walked down the hill. The parade was on Broadway. We could get to it by walking straight down the hill and then went to the booths in Volunteer Park afterwards. We walked down to Broadway and Pine when we went to the AIDS Memorial Vigil.

I rarely saw anyone I knew from AIDS organizations or people who were living with AIDS at the memorial. But then I only went for a couple of hours of the memorial weekend. It felt like a funeral and not a place to socialize, so I never connected with anyone at the event.

As demonstrations go, these were all pretty sedate. ACT UP had much more confrontal demonstrations in other cities. Blood was scattered in a Catholic church in at least one demonstration, symbolic of the anger about the way the church continued to prohibit condoms, which could inhibit the spread of the virus. Also there was the sense that the Catholic church (like the Reagan administration) didn't care if gay men were dying. I remember something about men who died from AIDS directing people to spread their ashes in government offices to make the same point.

So maybe I was just involved in the polite protests . . .

==========

A Public Person
(AIDS Memorial Vigil, Dale)

>he seemed to be everywhere
>volunteering for AIDS groups
>tall and weathered
>pierced and tattooed
>a chain through vest and jeans
>answering the phone
>at the support group
>always a smile
>organizing, directing traffic
>gone too soon from life

==========

At Seattle Community College
(AIDS Memorial Vigil)

> often when I pass that grassy hill
> when I see students
> lounging in the sun
> when I survey the familiar walkways
> I remember
> all those years ago
> the first walk
> among memorial tables
> names, people I knew, people
> dead of the virus
> talked to others
> those others since then
> joined their brothers in the grave
> now all gone
> memory hidden in the past
> erased from the carefully tended grass

==========

A Vignette (for Joe)

> We worked
> Together
> Packing food, Chicken Soup Brigade,
> Chatted each time
> Shared our lives
> Became some kind of friends
>
> We three decided
> To have
> A picnic at the Triangle campground
> For gays and lesbians
> In the mountains
> Sharing sandwiches and veggies

We walked
Through
A woman stopped us, asked if we
Were Gay and lesbian,
They were, could stay
I said that I was bisexual, forced to leave

We all
Told the story
Now the campground is gone
We no longer pack food
Haven't talked
In years since we went our separate ways

Offering Massage

I was restless and ready to move on once again and to reinvent myself. I thought and said little to anyone else until I had a plan. This was in 1990–1991. Looking back, I'm not really sure how I ended up in massage school. I wanted flexible work. I wanted to do something that helped people.

I was always interested in medical matters and healing. Spending time with my friend Dick in the months before he died (1988) made me want to learn more about death and dying. I wanted to connect with the gay (and lesbian) community in Seattle. In 1990, I decided to volunteer in the AIDS community, preparing food for the Chicken Soup Brigade, giving rides to people with AIDS, and learning about the disease.

I went to training for Chicken Soup Brigade on July 21, 1990. One of the things we learned in the training was that people with AIDS often aren't touched at all. I wanted to change that, and massage seemed like a good way to offer healing touch. Finally, I had a plan.

I looked up massage schools. Picking Seattle Massage School was kind of random. It was located next to Greenlake, my old neighborhood. I went over to talk to them, found out about classes, and signed up, to begin in February 1991 for the one-year program. We had classes two days a week, every other Friday and a few weekends. Some of the classes were academic, learning the names and locations of bones and muscles, studying the various body systems and how massage can affect them, and learning contraindications (when massage can make things worse). Other classes were all hands-on. We practiced massage on each other and occasionally on advanced students or teachers who could give us more coherent feedback. We got evaluated for every massage.

At that time, my son Jacob was thirteen. My daughter Rebecca was away at college in DC. My husband traveled a lot for work. I was happy to dive into memorizing for the academic tests (and pleased to realize I could still learn). The hands-on part was more challenging. Developing the skill to feel the muscles and bones beneath the skin was the biggest challenge (seemed easier with my eyes closed). I drew (over and over) pictures of various muscles and how they connect to the bones. I bought a book that showed a model with muscles painted on the nude body. That model flexed in various ways to demonstrate how muscles change shape with motion. That seemed to help me to know what I was touching.

One of my close friends at massage school was a gay man, Terry, who confided (early on) that he had AIDS. He dropped out of school. I visited him and gave him massages a few times after he dropped out and attended his funeral. Another friend, Jack, whom I met when I gave him rides to appointments, needed support during that summer (help with grocery shopping, laundry, hanging out). I often spent afternoons with him. I practiced massage on him and studied while he watched television, usually with the sound turned off so he could invent dialogue. Jack died in August 1991.

Later in the fall of 1991, I met John (through Shawn and Susan). John absolutely loved every kind of bodywork. He had volunteer chiropractors, Reiki practitioners, massage therapists, and acupuncture practitioners. He had at least one person working on him every day. He hoped that this would enable him to get over AIDS. And he wanted pain relief. We had to do many practice massages as homework for massage school. And we were supposed to focus on one client in particular. For me, that was John. I took notes of weekly massages massage and then wrote up the whole experience.

One of the last classes in massage school covered the practical aspects of getting licensed. Hints about advertising and finding clients in general were part of this class. The class included warnings about people who would try to take advantage of massage therapists. I always thought that doing massage primarily in the AIDS community spared me that sort of worry.

At the end of the program, we had a long written test (not difficult) and on another day, a two-hour practical test. My friend Scott offered to be my "victim" for that second part. I barely made it through that test, but I did make it through. Now that I think about it, I had a bad cold that day, and there was no way to reschedule. I think that had something to do with some of my mistakes in that test, where we were asked questions as well as having to demonstrate massage strokes. My brain was fuzzy.

One way that I hoped to build a practice while getting lots of experience with massage and working with many eople, was by being a volunteer at two clinics of Harborview Hospital. (I originally signed up with Madison Clinic and expanded to the ACTU later.) For that, I bought a massage chair. I approached the nurse manager at Madison Clinic, Harborview's AIDS clinic. They were happy to have me as a volunteer, doing chair massage in the clinic.

I started with shorter hours and increased until I was at Madison Clinic for six hours (plus an hour off for lunch) on Tuesdays and at the AIDS Clinical Trials Unit (a UW clinic) for four hours on Wednesdays. I set up sign-up sheets with appointments every twenty minutes (so I could see twelve people on Wednesday and twenty on Tuesday). After they got used to me, my whole schedule was filled, often with a wait list at the bottom of the page. The receptionists in each clinic posted the schedule on Monday of each week.

When I proposed doing massage there, I envisioned working on people living with AIDS. I saw some of the patients from each clinic. However, staff people (social workers, nurses, doctors, and medical assistants) filled the majority of the massage slots. The staff gave a lot of themselves in a difficult situation (many deaths), and I was glad to offer respite to these wonderful people. I guessed patients were helped indirectly by having happier caregivers. I really liked the idea that the two groups mixed in my room and under my care.

Volunteering at the clinic was hard work and paid off as I had hoped. Many who came for chair massage at the clinic chose to pay for Swedish massage. At first, this meant that I went to the homes of clients (because my husband didn't want me to do massage at our house). When I moved out after initiating divorce proceedings in 1993, I looked for a place that had a room suitable for massage. I found the right one. This house had a tiny room close to the bathroom and the dining room. It was just the right size to be a massage room. I had space to walk around the massage table. The room was long enough that I could provide a chair for the client to sit on while changing clothes. I had space for music and candles as well. The driveway was also useful since it provided an option for clients who needed to park. I offered special low prices for people in the AIDS community whether patients, family, or staff.

I was so excited about working with people in the AIDS community that I offered free massage to many people with AIDS both during and after massage school. This was was okay while I was in school and needed practice but not after I was done with school. Free massage in clinics was fine, but with individuals, it often caused a weird tension. I couldn't help thinking they should like and appreciate me while they felt indebted. The imbalance made things uncomfortable. I decided not to do that anymore.

When we started massage school, we learned about necessary tools and supplies. All of us bought tables, and some bought chairs as well. We needed sheets for the tables and coverings for headrests. A bulletin board in the hall advertised used tables, chairs, sheets, and other items at low prices. We needed oil and/or lotion. Everyone acquired music and something to play the music.

Beyond the basics, I bought a heated mattress pad to warm up the massage table. I bought ice packs and heat packs and small towels to wrap around the ice packs. Mom cut up pillowcases into fourths and made small cases for heat packs. I bought a variety of essential oils to mix with oil and lotions. Most people seemed to prefer oil with lavender, juniper, and other essential oils added. Next most popular was plain lotion. A few preferred lotion with vanilla added, and a smaller group wanted grapeseed oil with nothing added. I bought small candles for a very low light in the room. At first, I used scented candles, but they left the room scented, which was often a problem to the next client, so I switched to unscented.

Zenith Supplies was where I bought oils, lotions, essential oils, and a few odds and ends. And that's where I bought my massage table and chair as well as the fitted covers for headrests. Sheets and mattress covers (which wore out over time) came from Penney's. Ice packs and heat packs came from another company. Over the years, I bought several tape players and then CD/tape players from Magnolia HiFi. I had hundreds of tapes and CDs from East West books, the University Book Store, and other places. I also bought many books over the years, trying to learn more about muscles and about techniques. I bought water glasses from a secondhand store since I always supplied a glass of water for each client.

Teachers in the massage school promoted New Age music and nature sounds. I bought a few of those recordings. I preferred other kinds of music such as that of Bill Frisell, Taj Mahal, Yo-Yo Ma, or others, where I could plug my brain into the interesting sounds and allow my hands to focus on what I was feeling. I asked clients to pick out music as they undressed. Many preferred to have me pick, and some didn't want music at all (especially the talkers).

During the years that I did massage, I always got massage myself, generally once a week. At first, I traded massage with a friend. We had increasing difficulties coordinating our schedules. After he missed a couple of times (forgot), I decided that I'd rather pay for massage and know that it would actually happen. Continuum was also helpful to me during those years (classes generally over a weekend). Getting massage myself was a way to demonstrate that I valued it. And I liked being on the receiving end so that I could better understand what clients felt.

When a new client came to me, I spent half an hour or so on a basic intake form based on one used by the student clinic at Seattle Massage School. We talked a little about what the person hoped to get from the massage and anything they didn't want. Some had particular painful spots to work on. Others simply wanted relaxation. Some knew that they liked deep pressure. Others wanted only a light tough. Some wanted lots of work on feet. A few were ticklish and didn't want any touch there.

I had worked out a basic routine during massage school (and had the cheat sheet, on a four-by-six card, to prove it). During the massage, I would check in frequently, especially about the amount of pressure.

After the first massage, I sent the client a card (stamped, addressed to me) on which they could evaluate the pluses and minuses of the massage. I encouraged them to keep it anonymous if they wished. I had a card for each client with his or her personal preferences. I wrote notes after each massage, occasionally adding to the client's card so that I would remember next time.

The best massage I ever gave (I think) was one in which I was almost hypnotized by the music and the touch. The client, normally chatty, gradually became very quiet, and I think she had the same experience. It was like a prayer, a God connection.

Over the years, I gradually increased the amount of time I spent doing massage. I was available for clients seven days/week, except for specific events such as birthdays and Jewish holidays. I was willing to make appointments as early as 8:30 a.m. and as late as 7:30 p.m., planning for an hour massage and half an hour in between to change sheets and write notes. Some days I did one or two massages. Other days I might do as many as four or five. This was a ridiculous schedule. I liked making deposits in the bank. And I didn't like to disappoint anyone who wanted a massage.

Many of the clients came from my volunteer work or people who knew people at Harborview. Some came from people I knew. Many referrals came from old friend and neighbor and from people who got referrals from her friends. (I made kind of a family tree, "lineage of clients.")

Over time, I had increasing pain in my hands in the joint between thumb and other fingers. Generally the pain would go away overnight, and I could start over. I wanted to keep doing massage for at least ten years (as I did with teaching and working for J-M.) But one day toward the end of 2000, the pain was still intense in the morning. An X-ray confirmed arthritis in both hands. And I knew I was done. I called Harborview to let them know I wouldn't be back. I called the clients who had appointments that week and sent a letter to the rest. All done.

Stopping massage was painful. I hated leaving the community at Harborview and losing my connection to all those people. I was sad that no one was there to take my place. Now I wonder if I should have gone over to the massage school and tried to recruit someone. However, I guess the clinic could have done that if they wanted the program to continue.

Jack Living with AIDS

Even after all the years, the moments with my friend Jack are bright and present to me. His illness, knowing he would be gone soon, shone a spotlight on times together.

For Throwback Thursday recently, I posted a photo of Jack on Facebook with this comment, "Twenty-ifve years ago, my friend Jack knew that he would die soon (AIDS). He had me take photos and he picked the one he liked most to share with family and friends. I made a bunch of copies of those. I kept one and he sent the others out by mail. And, yes, he died in August 1991. His photo stays on my refrigerator, and I love remembering him." After all these years, it felt good to name him and to remember he used to speak at various places, explaining what it was like to live with AIDS and to face death.

Several people said how sweet he looked. I added, "His friendship was a gift to me . . . Looking back, it's hard to believe that we met in January and he died less than eight months later. He said that he learned a lot from having AIDS. Living with the disease was a spiritual process for him. At the same time, he freely acknowledged that he would rather have not had AIDS and not learned all he did." I don't know if he was exactly sweet. He was open and vulnerable. Probably that was part of what he learned. On the other hand, part of what he was working through was anger at family members. He was angry about his childhood and angry that they wouldn't let him come home when he got sick. However, his father came across the country to stay with him for several weeks when he got out of the hospital.

I met Jack when I arrived at his door to drive him to an appointment. I was a volunteer for Chicken Soup Brigade. I think it was to acupuncture, but it might have been to a support group. (My memory is faulty after all these years.) We were immediately at ease with each other, talking the whole way back and forth as I drove. I gave him my phone number. He began calling me directly for rides. People at the organization knew we were connecting on our own, but not always when. I wonder if they were supposed to list all the hours donated by volunteers (often true for nonprofit organizations).

Jack moved to Seattle from San Francisco after his first round of pneumocystis pneumonia. He was horrified by the way he was treated in the hospital in San Francisco. Everyone who came into his room was swathed in gowns and masks and gloves. He hoped Seattle hospitals would be different. His brother David lived here in Seattle. David was also gay and also had AIDS. He told Jack that the medical care here was better. Jack thought David was happy to have his brother move here.

Before, when he was working, Jack was a headhunter. He had a wicked smile when he explained to me what the term meant. He seemed kind of proud that businesses didn't like him (because he might steal away their best workers).

During one conversation, Jack mentioned that he was bisexual. However, he liked the gay community, and so he always identified as gay.

Some of his mail went to a PO box. He knew that he was likely to die soon. Using the PO box was one way to keep some of the bills away from him. His income was so limited that he sometimes had to pick and choose which ones he would pay at any particular time.

Jack was angry with himself for getting AIDS. He knew how the virus was transmitted. He was in a relationship. After a fight, he got drunk and then went out and picked up some random man. They didn't use any protection. Jack was convinced that he was infected that night. He knew of no other risk factor, and he knew better before he did it. However, he was so angry with his partner that he didn't even care about the danger when he took the risk.

Part of Jack's path was educating others about AIDS. He volunteered to speak to nursing classes at community colleges. I have a videotape of him speaking (1990), and a small piece of paper with notes he wrote before one speaking engagement. He says that he went inward during the two years since his diagnosis and wanted to share with others. Jack stresses that this was his path and not for everyone with AIDS. Others might try experimental drugs as hard as that is for Jack to understand. He noticed his own judgments about the way other people live with AIDS. It turns out that public speaking is his joy even though it is scary for others. One of the most difficult parts of living with AIDS for him was giving up control and asking for help. He said, "Who's going to be there for me when I die? Will I be there for me when I die?"

When he got very sick the first time, his parents refused to take him in, and he'd had to learn to nurture himself as well as being realistic about what his mother and father are capable of doing.

When we met in January 1991, Jack was beginning to worry about shortness of breath and a cough. A couple of weeks later, he ended up in Swedish Hospital with his second round of pneumocystis pneumonia. Jack spent months in the hospital until late April. During much of that time, he had all sorts of tubes all over his body. One of his lungs collapsed. He needed hydration. He had a catheter for urine. He sometimes joked about his situation with tubes everywhere.

Jack wouldn't agree to have the hospital door left open. It was always closed, with a sign directing anyone who wanted to come in to knock and get permission. Jack also wouldn't allow guests to come and go as they wished. He never allowed more than one person to visit at a time. He asked people to call and set up a specific time to visit. Once, he couldn't get attention from the nurses after the call button had been on for over an hour. I think he needed a nail file. In the end, he called his doctor's office (across the street from the hospital) and asked someone from there to bring him the needed item.

Before he left the hospital, Jack talked to people who visited regularly and made up a schedule so that at least person would visit him at home each day. These were people who were willing to help with laundry, grocery shopping, and meals.

I was in massage school at this time. Jack agreed to have me practice massage on him, so I brought my table over to his apartment on my visiting day. I also sat and studied while he watched television. Over time, some others in the group of supportive friends had responsibilities that stopped them from sticking to the schedule. I ended up spending a few hours there most days.

While I studied, Jack often sat in front of the television. Sometimes I sat next to him with my books and notes. Other times, I sat on the floor. His favorite show was *In Living Color*. He often entertained himself (and me) by turning off the sound and making up dialogue.

In his talk to the nursing students, Jack described a period of time (before AIDS) when he drank too much. Then he stopped drinking and switched to pot. He tried cocaine a couple of times, but it was too expensive to use often. At the time of the talk, he was no longer drinking or taking drugs. As a side comment, he mentioned reading that we often become addicted to whatever is bad for us. Someone brought it to his attention that he might be addicted to sugar. This made sense to him even though he wasn't overweight. Once or twice, he asked me to buy Dreyer's ice cream bars. Then he tried to get other people to eat all but one so he wouldn't be tempted to overindulge.

Even though Jack loved massage, he couldn't endure much touch toward the end of his life. One day, he spoke of people who come up and hugged him so hard that it was painful. He was uncomfortable with people who stroked his arms or hands as well.

Besides hanging out with Jack in his apartment, I also drove him to various appointments (acupuncture, support group, primary care provider). When he got out of the hospital, he was able to walk around his apartment. Over time, he got stronger until he was able to walk two blocks to the QFC on the corner of Broadway and Republican. This was in June. After that, he began to reverse direction. Finally, toward the end of July, he was barely able to walk into his bathroom. He decided he was ready to die and ready to move from his apartment and into Rosehedge. He and I drove up to the new Rosehedge. He didn't like it much and chose to go into the old one, in the little house near Madison on Sixteenth.

At first, when I took Jack to see his primary care provider for routine appointments, Jack was very sure that I needed to stay out in the waiting room. By June, when he had some kind of crisis, he asked me to stay in the examining room with him when we were at the emergency room.

Luckily, others who lived in Jack's apartment building weren't generally home during the day. I was able to park in the lot in someone else's space. This worked until the last weeks of his living there. Then he couldn't make it up the steps to the parking lot. He needed me to stop on the street so he could come down those stairs. Once a police officer forced me to move no matter what I explained. Somehow Jack made it up to the lot, leaning on me.

At one point, Jack's parents came out from the East Coast. His mother went home after a few days, but his father stayed for a couple of weeks and took over the caregiving during that time. Jack never forgot his anger with his parents, but he was at peace with the past and able to relate to them in the present.

In the taped piece, Jack had everyone take off one shoe. He directed them to wiggle their toes. Someone told him that death is like taking off a tight shoe. He feels comforted by this idea. It allows him to see death potentially as a relief. He imagines being on his deathbed and someone holding his hand, saying, "You've done what you came here to do. You can go now." At the same time, he acknowledges he's afraid, very afraid of dying.

Jack said he used to think of suicide as kind of a back door, if things in life got too unpleasant. At the same time he'd always had an enormous curiosity. He never could have imagined all the people, the growth, and the opening of his heart that happened after his diagnosis.

When Jack talked about the wonderful people he'd met since he got sick, he meant his Shanti volunteer. He meant his friend from Multifaith AIDS Support. He meant people he knew from Northwest AIDS Foundation. He meant his doctors, the receptionist at his doctor's office, and others. He meant me. He appreciated all of these people and talked about how wonderful we all were. Once, he acknowledged that he probably would never have been interested in knowing any of us if he didn't have AIDS.

Jack's speech at the community college took place less than two years before I took the photo. He looks much older in the photo. His hair is thinner and has receded. He is gaunt. He had been through a lot and knew that he was close to death. At the same time, he looked young and innocent, not polished. And he actually was young. I think he wasn't even forty when he died. (I was forty-six.)

Some people with AIDS had the very visible stigmata of Kaposi's sarcoma (a cancer associated with weakened immune system). This looks like a purplish bruise or abrasion. Jack never had this. However, his doctor told him in June that he had KS in his lungs. That seemed to be worse and more dangerous than the external KS. He understood his doctor to be saying it would kill him.

At the end of Jack's life, his father and sister came back from the East Coast. Friends gathered at Rosehedge, the hospice. Jack was no longer able to talk. We honored his requests from the hospital months. Only one of us went into the room with him at a time. I think we all told him he had done what he came to do and could go now. His father was in the room with him when he died.

==========

No More Privacy
(For Jack S.)

> Jack in his wheelchair
> Filled the empty space
> In the examining room
> His dad and I sat

On the small plastic chairs
Waited with him

He had to pee
We requested a urinal
From a nurse
She handed it in to us
I averted my eyes
As best possible

Six months back
When we first met
He asked me to
To leave the hospital room
Even to shut the door
As he peed

Now it didn't matter
Too many procedures
Too much pain
Death looked him in the face
Modesty is nothing
As the body disintegrates

==========

Not Too Hard
(For Jack S.)

I reached out to hold him, my dear one
He stopped me and told me that sometimes
Hugs hurt, and sometimes
He feels like he can't breathe

His body so fragile coming to an end
Still he wanted to be touched,
Just the gentlest hand resting on his leg
Or heads leaning together

==========

Just Like on TV
(For Jack S.)

A walkie-talkie for the handicapped
Advertised on TV
Jack laughed a little
It was so dramatic

Until the day he called Bob on the phone

Asked him to come
From across the street
Now it was real
"Help, I've fallen and can't get up"

==========

Bisexual
(For Jack S.)

As death lurked
Clearly coming closer

We clung to each other and talked
About what was
And what could have been
His dad was sure that we were lovers

Jack said it might have been
Back when he was healthy

==========

Spring
(For Jack S.)

More than once Jack mentioned
That he wouldn't change
The three years
Of living with
AIDS
For anything

He reclaimed lost pieces of himself
In the midst of grief and loss
He saw himself
Like a flower
Unfolding
Petal by petal

==========

Presence
(For Jack S.)

A key question
One he thought of often
Talked about
To me and others

Imagined the day
Who would be there when he died
Jack wondered
Who would he want to have
By his side

Would he be there
For himself
Would pain and drugs
Take him off

==========

Raison D'être
(For Jack S.)

He had insurance
Barely enough income now that he was
Disabled and dying

When he had no speaking dates
He was sluggish
The TV was on more
He felt depressed
Then someone called
It was life giving
Suddenly he was making plans
He had a future
And a reason to live

And he had extra money
To pay for alternative treatments
Especially acupuncture

==========

Recognition
(For Jack S.)

Maybe nothing more is required
As you stand at the bedside of your dying friend
Than to gently touch his wrist

His greatest fear
And he had a lot of time
To consider this
To have a life not fulfilled
To know that it
Didn't serve its purpose

He imagined lying on his deathbed
A friend holding his hand says, "It's okay to go now
You've done what you came to do."

==========

His Way
(For Jack S.)

His life
Being an example
Standing up in front of people
Being vulnerable and open

He doesn't need our fears
He has enough of his own,
Thank you

He's busy scraping away
The barnacles around his heart
Finding a place of healing

Not much else matters in the end

==========

Spring 1991
(Jack)

We could sit and measure his losses,
count the people gone from his life,
his job only a memory,
his home miles away and years past.
He is surrounded by friends who love him.

We could count his limitations,
as he struggles to walk up hill,
his breath coming slow and shallow,

one more stair up to his doctor's office.
He sits with us, the room filled with laughter.

He stands before a class of nurses,
speaks of expecting death,
they say, like taking off a tight shoe.
His smile comforts us
as we hope that he will survive.

==========

AIDS Perks
(Jack)

One day, he sat with a sideways smile,
recounted it all
The food brought to his home
Free massage
A clinic for acupuncture

Oh, so much better than if he had cancer
More than for pneumonia
Or for heart disease
Anything else
All this he had, with love and smiles

==========

(Jack) I wrote this in a comment on an advice column, "A friend, who was living with AIDS (and died a couple of months later), was fully supportive and sympathetic to me. I wondered at the time of I could have been so generous and said so. He said I was entitled to have pain in the context of my life and it had nothing to do with what he was dealing with."

==========

Saying Goodbye to Jack

late summer, the sun still sleeping
harsh sound of the phone
a fumble and grab
alert immediately to the news

easy clothes: soft sweats, socks, shoes
no one else about on the street
two miles to the hospice

we gather, take our turns, sit by the bed
murmur him on his way
after the last breath
leaves emptiness, where he isn't now

Jack Aging Too Fast

So many diseases have treatments that are uncomfortable and difficult. When there is success, it seems worth it. What about the rest of the time?

I had pneumonia when I was three and a half years old and spent a long time in the hospital at the time when my mother was on bed rest because of her pregnancy. Then I had pneumonia again when I was thirty-two and pregnant with Jacob. Either that case was less harsh or treatments were better. Antibiotics had me feeling better within a few days. I would have died either of those times back in the sixteenth century. Any kind of treatment would have been doomed to fail. So here I am likely with some scarring on my lungs from the two rounds of pneumonia. I'm glad to have had treatment and to have survived to old age.

Then I think about Jack. When we met (January 1991), he seemed healthy and cheerful despite having had pneumocystis pneumonia before he moved to Seattle. He was part of a speakers' bureau and talked to various groups about what it was like to live with AIDS. At that time, he said, people with AIDS generally died less than two years after diagnosis. By then, fall 1990, he was two years past diagnosis and thus was a long-term survivor.

Jack lived independently in an apartment on Capitol Hill after he moved from San Francisco. He attended support groups at Seattle AIDS Support Group. He had a team of caregivers from various AIDS organizations. He walked to acupuncture (about half a mile in one direction) and to SASG (Seattle AIDS Support Group, less than a mile in the other direction). He walked to the Northwest AIDS Foundation (less than half a mile). He shopped in a QFC two blocks from his apartment, did laundry, cooked, all the regular life tasks. I guess he took a bus to his speaking engagements since he didn't have a car.

By the time we met, Jack was beginning to worry about shortness of breath. He was no longer able to walk to appointments. I took him to an acupuncture appointment the first time we met and to SASG the second time. He feared that he was in for another round of pneumonia. What he was feeling was very similar to the first time. He talked and worried about whether to do anything.

Eventually Jack had me take him to the emergency room. They examined him and admitted him (Swedish Hospital). When I asked if he wanted me to bring him anything from his house, he hesitated and then agreed. We hadn't known each other long (maybe a couple of weeks). He decided to trust me. In the end, he was in the hospital for months (January to April) with collapsed lungs and various other problems with pneumocystis pneumonia and AIDS.

Once, I came to visit, and he laughed about all the tubes attached all over his body. It wasn't just the lungs. He had a catheter for urine and diapers, so he didn't have to get up to sit on the toilet. As time went on, he felt better. He found it more and more difficult to be stuck in the hospital. Sometimes, just to get past boredom, he sat in a wheelchair while I wheeled him around the hospital. We enjoyed looking at the art on the walls and even ventured outside on a couple of mild days.

Jack had many visitors when he was in the hospital. He wouldn't allow more than one person at a time, so we didn't get to know each other except by what he had to say. I guess that Swedish Hospital may have encouraged him to have a plan for when he went home. At that time, he could barely walk around his apartment. He asked around among those who visited in the hospital. Several of us volunteered to help. Jack assigned days and times. He had people coming in to help him every day (preparing meals, doing laundry, washing dishes, and sitting with him) for an hour or two.

Soon after Jack got home, his father came for several weeks, which meant a lot of healing for their relationship. His father took on all the caregiving during that time. He shopped for groceries, cooked, and did laundry. They watched television together. Jack's mother came for a few days of that visit. Jack was relieved when she went back home (and she was too). Those of us who had agreed to help came for visits and met Jack's parents.

Then Jack's father went back home, and the care team took over helping. I came by on days when no one else was planning to come in. I was there for several hours, so I could shop, do laundry, and also practice massage on him since I was in massage school. I studied for tests while Jack watched television (often with the sound off so he could improvise dialogue).

Jack talked about his life. He said he was bisexual but liked the gay lifestyle, so he lived as a gay man all those years. He was in a monogamous relationship in San Francisco. They had a fight, broke up, and Jack went out and picked up someone to take revenge. He believes that was when he got HIV.

I talked about my life as well. My troubles seemed small in comparison with having AIDS. Jack said my pain was just as important in my life as his pain was in his life. I had the right to feel it. One time I began to cry because he was getting worse. Then I apologized for my tears. Jack said that knowing I would grieve when he died comforted him.

Sometimes I hugged Jack when he talked of his painful life experiences. He explained that he loved to be touched, and it had to be gentle touch. He couldn't take a hard hug or a strong touch on his hand. I learned to leave some space during a hug and to rest a hand on his arm rather than holding on. I'm glad he explained in a way that I was able to accept and to remember with others who were fragile.

Jack worked hard to regain his strength. He walked a little more each day. By June, he was able to walk to the QFC, three blocks from his apartment. He was optimistic about reclaiming his life. After that, his strength plateaued and began to go downhill.

He used to come down the stairs to meet my car when I took him to a medical appointment. Then he got to the point where the stairs were difficult. I parked in the lot behind his apartment, taking the chance of using someone else's spot so I could go to the apartment and help Jack to my car (this was a much shorter staircase).

Jack never was able to take back the life he had before getting sick again. He needed help to walk around his apartment by July. Some of us spent occasional nights with him, but it wasn't enough. Even with all the help, there were many hours when Jack was by himself. He would have been in trouble if he had an emergency in the night. He couldn't even reliably get to the bathroom by himself. (He joked, "I've fallen and can't get up.") It was time to look for another solution.

We went to look at Rosehedge, the original AIDS hospice. We looked at the old one (Capitol Hill) and also at the recently opened new one (north Seattle). I pushed him in a wheelchair in the new one. I guess he walked around the old (smaller and more compact) one. The old one, in a house, had the feel of a home. The new one, built to be a hospice, seemed very much like a medical center. He chose to move into the old one in August.

Once he was moved into the new place, Jack thought over his experiences and what he had learned. He considered all he had gone through between January and August, including the months in the hospital. He had such a short time of beginning to enjoy his life again. He said he wouldn't have gone through the treatment in the hospital if he'd known how it was going to turn out. He would have chosen to go without treatment and die sooner.

This was Jack's second round of pneumocystis pneumonia. He never regretted treatment for the first time. There was no way he could know ahead of time how the second would turn out.

When Jack and I met, he described grudges he had from his childhood. He was unhappy with both of his parents as well as other family members. He thought he and his brother were blamed for being gay even before they knew were gay. Some of the complaints related to food he didn't like. Others involved abuse on fishing trips. Because of all these, he indicated that both he and his brother chose to live a long way from family and have little interaction. Sounds like Jack interacted more than David but not much. Jack told these stories with humor laced with bitterness.

After we knew each other better, Jack added to this story. When he moved away, his parents told him he could come home if he needed to. Then the day came when Jack needed them a lot, the first time he had pneumocystis pneumonia (1990). He asked to move home (across the country). They said no. (Many people were terrified of being around AIDS.) He was devastated, frightened, and felt alone. He made it through time in the hospital and then moved from San Francisco to Seattle to be close to his brother.

Once when I was visiting Jack at Rosehedge, he asked the nurse if he would benefit from IV hydration since he wasn't even able to drink much anymore. The nurse said that hydration would prolong the dying process, but he wouldn't feel better. He thought that Jack would feel better without the hydration. (I have seen that same statement other places.)

Jack's father came back accompanied by Jack's sister when Jack was within days of dying (mid-August). They and others in Jack's circle took turns sitting with Jack during the last day. We remembered that he never allowed more than one person at a time to visit him in the hospital. We followed those rules even though Jack was no longer speaking. His father was in with him when he died.

When I was looking through things saved from those AIDS years, I found some letters. I wrote condolences to Jack's parents after David died the next summer. They wrote back that David and his partner Steve had come to visit.

The visit was good and healing to all of them even though David was very sick and spent the time in the hospital there.

So many times, people have to choose what sort of treatment to have and if it's worth it. My neighbor Joyce dealt with metastatic breast cancer for at least seven years. She had significant pain with cancer and horrible times with chemo. I wonder if she would do it all again. Joyce went through years of treatment and many good times during those years, including travel and time spent with friends. I don't think she regretted the treatments at all.

In the end, Jack didn't have many, or even any, good days. He had some better times but not what he would have chosen. I was happy that he and his parents ended on pretty good terms. I was happy that the process seemed to bring his parents and his brother together as well. I felt blessed to have known Jack. Still, Jack said he would rather have not gone through those months in Swedish. He would have chosen to die in January if he had known how it would work out.

==========

Jack, 1991

> He walked heavily leaning on his cane.
> His clothing hung loose,
> gray sweatpants and sweatshirt.
> He sat on the couch, asked me to sit beside him
> to lean upon him, to tell him about my life.
> He was dying. My pain, my gift,
> to let him support me. His gift to me, his love

Facing Death or Not

My brother and I recently talked about death (because someone in the extended family was very sick). My brother said he didn't mind not being alive before he was born. He thinks death will be the same. I didn't argue, but I think it's different. And it scares me.

Back when I knew many people living with AIDS, death was almost certain and always quick. Medications weren't effective. The only protection was the natural defenses that some people had. So yes, there were a few HIV-positive people who lived for many years without developing AIDS. Some people died within months of diagnoses. Others took years. Mostly it was quick, and people knew it. I knew it as well and became very conscious of just being in the moment with each person. No future was guaranteed.

Facing death did odd things to people. I remember meeting a young man once (and only once) when he signed up to get a chair massage from me at Madison Clinic. As I kneaded his back and neck muscles, the young man talked about his life. He had worked as a prostitute. He was certain that he got HIV from one of his clients. I listened, amazed at his openness but didn't comment or ask questions. The young man was sure he was going to die soon, and it didn't matter what he said. It was bleak.

Jack was direct about his diagnosis. He anticipated that his life wouldn't be long. He knew the statistics indicating that people with AIDS generally lived less than two years after diagnosis. When I met him, he had already passed that milestone. In the speeches he gave to nursing students, he talked about not having long to live. He heard that death was like taking off tight shoes. To illustrate this thought, he took off his shoe during the talk and wiggled his toes. He also said he had considered suicide when he was young. He saw it as a magical way out from the misery of life (get out of jail free).

Now he thought it was ironic—he was getting what he had imagined. And he chose treatment when he got sick. He wanted to live longer until the last miserable weeks.

Jack gave speeches about living with AIDS. He did it partly for the money. He also did it in hopes of helping others. I knew others (Dave, for instance) who gave speeches for the same reason. Being able to speak gave them a reason for living while they were sure they were dying. Public speaking gave meaning to what they were going through.

Jack also worked hard at healing within. He learned the distinction between healing (emotional and psychological) and curing (physically defeating the disease). Healing even included reconnecting with his parents from whom he was estranged.

Cary was matter of fact as well. He read medical journals and noted his own progress with the disease. In a weird way, he (a doctor) seemed comfortable that AIDS was following its own rules. He made plans for the later stages, including remodeling his basement so that a caregiver could comfortably stay down there. In fact, his brother came from New Jersey and lived there during Cary's last weeks of life.

John didn't want to think about dying. He was angry when any of us brought up the subject. Once he was so angry with me when I mentioned dying that I thought he would stop speaking to me entirely. I learned from the experience and never said anything like that again. He finally acknowledged he was dying a couple of weeks before he did. Then he persuaded the staff at Bailey-Boushay to allow him to stay where he was after dying. Being in place for a day was part of his Buddhist beliefs. It was meant to allow his spirit to leave slowly.

Some of the people John knew and loved died of AIDS long before he did. He refused to ever visit them when they were dying. He thought that they were dying because they had given up on life. Yet he seemed to feel guilty for abandoning those friends and sad he hadn't seen them one last time. He talked often (with his sister) about the man who had been his lover.

Many of us plan for death, especially by filling out paperwork and looking into memorials. Lee (probably with family and friends) planned carefully. His memorial service included invitations to important people, a deluxe meal, and sharing memories. I went to memorial services for other people, all planned by those who survived them. Most of the people I knew didn't have any money or much to leave. John and his sister worked on a list, planning who was to get his possessions. Others may have given instructions to friends or family. I don't think anyone else was as organized as Lee.

All of the people I knew were being treated with the best medications available at the time. Many also used alternatives such as acupuncture and massage. Perhaps some thought they would be cured. Others simply wanted to feel better during the illness.

John fought the hardest of anyone. He chose what to eat, therapies to receive, medications, and meditation. He found many ways to distract himself from the process. He liked when we went out to eat or to movies so he could have a vacation from thinking about AIDS.

When Terry was unable to continue as a flight attendant (missing too many days when he didn't feel well), he looked around for something else to do. He was full of optimism that he could learn to do massage and just do it when he felt well enough. We met in massage school. Unfortunately, he didn't feel well enough to get through school.

Lee was an attorney. He kept working as long as he possibly could. He anticipated losing his eyesight (and did). Even then he learned to find his way around the house and consulted with others. He was able to continue practicing law in this way. Lee shared that he didn't want to keep fighting the disease when he was no longer able to work. Since he liked to plan, he found a nurse who could provide him with a "cocktail," an easy way to end his life when that point arrived. (This was long before death with dignity became a reality in Washington State.) After he went blind, he decided that he would end it all when he got to the point where he couldn't walk. I don't know whether he used the cocktail in the end.

Lee and Terry had been lovers once and continued to be close friends even after they had moved on to other people. Terry got hold of the cocktail soon after Lee did. Since Terry died at Bailey-Boushay, I'm confident he didn't use the cocktail. (I was relieved not to be asked to be present if/ when either one of them actually chose to die.)

Choosing the time to die can be done more openly now. "After being diagnosed with terminal brain cancer in 2014, Brittany Maynard made headlines when she decided to use medication to end her own life at the age of twenty-nine. Now Megyn Kelly TODAY welcomes her husband, Dan Diaz, who talks about his campaign for right-to-die laws. 'I still have good days and bad days' about Brittany, he tells Megyn in an emotional interview" (https://www.today.com/video/brittany-maynard-s-husband-tells-megyn-kelly-about-her-decision-to-die-1246246979998). He talked about her seizures, which caused all of the muscles of her body to cramp causing pain that they couldn't stop. He also stressed that she knew she was going to die within six months. The only question was how she was going to die—peacefully or in terrible pain.

Lee and Terry both wanted to have some say about when and how they died. They weren't willing to give up that control. I guess that people who continue desperately to have treatments to the end of life are also seeking control, prolonging life beyond what it would be otherwise.

Shawn was deeply invested in parenting his daughter Gennie. He also wanted to tell the story of his life, especially of his childhood. He wrote longhand. Later he convinced someone to get him a computer. He never could make it work well (after a short time of sending emails). I have a box of his writings. They are so scrambled that they are not usable, I think.

When I first met Shawn, he began telling me the story of his childhood. He described being the family scapegoat, the one who was punished simply for existing. He said he was locked in closets for hours and hours. The other children weren't allowed to interact with him. I felt privileged by the telling. I later learned he told everyone the same stories. He said that his brother Patrick would vouch for the truth of those stories and that his other brother who lived nearby also agreed. Patrick agreed with Shawn, but I didn't hear the other brother say anything about it. Shawn longed to have his mother acknowledge the abuse. She wouldn't.

Shawn related that Gennie was the child of a woman he knew in the Midwest. When she discovered her pregnancy, she was frantic because the father had abandoned her. Shawn stepped up to marry her and claim the baby as his own. When the woman became erratic, he took the child and moved out. He went to court to get full custody and then moved across the country.

During his most stable time, Shawn saw himself as not only the father of a little girl but also the protector of his friends, most of whom had AIDS as well as issues with substance abuse. He allowed various people to live with him. He cooked for them. They stole his food and his possessions. He always said that he couldn't let someone else be hungry if he had anything to share.

Shawn fought to keep Gennie until he saw his own life unraveling. After being evicted and losing most of his possessions, he finally agreed to send her back to her mother and the mother's family. Before that, people who had been his friends tried to get custody away from him. They may not have known how to contact her birth mother, but they didn't think the child was safe with him. He became terribly angry with all of those former friends.

Shawn was convinced (or tried to convince himself and others) that he lived so long (at least sixteen years) with AIDS because methamphetamines somehow overcame the effects of HIV. Some of the time, he thought that HIV wasn't the cause of AIDS. He had a number of theories about the disease and the course of the disease. Those ideas seemed to give him hope.

Shawn went from place to place even more after he let go of Gennie. He lived with friends in Bremerton for a year or so and participated in a harm-reduction drug group. When he became disillusioned with that group (or they with him), he began to say they were just drug pushers. He later lived in an apartment in Seattle. He came to see me, and we walked a long way while talking. By then, he swore he wasn't taking drugs.

I last saw him when he was living at Bailey-Boushay. He didn't acknowledge that he was dying, but he no longer talked about what he was going to do next. Our conversation was halting and sad. He didn't ask me to come by again, and I never did. I wonder now if he died from the effects of drug use rather than from AIDS. He lived so long that he could have had partial immunity to HIV.

I learned from observation and even more from people who worked as caregivers for people with AIDS that people who are dying have some kind of control. They seem to be able to choose when to die even without any sort of medications. More than one person relaxed and died after being told goodbye by those who loved them. Michael was able to let go when his sister assured him she would be okay without him. He had been sticking around for her benefit. He also accepted increased amounts of morphine toward the end, knowing it might speed his death while protecting him from pain.

==========

Marking Time
(For Jack S.)

> His doctor suspected dementia, so he went in for tests
> The next day told me they'd found proof   .
> Jack, so bright and proud, how would he take this?
> He smiled and said slowly,
> "Now I don't have to feel guilty about forgetting"
>
> Then one day he really couldn't walk anymore
> We went to see Rosehedge; he was ready to move in

He said, "I didn't plan for my life to be this way,
But this is my life,"
And it was time to end

==========

Waiting
(For Jack S.)

We often talked of people who were no longer daily in his life
Jack didn't expect them to come
He'd avoided his friend
When he got very sick and looked like E.T.

==========

Truth
(For Lee B.)

When Lee's KS was diagnosed
It was time to tell his parents the news,
From least to most upsetting

That he had cancer
That he was gay
That he was living with AIDS

His dad responded
"Well, nobody's perfect
"You're our son and we love you"

==========

Vision
(For Lee B.)

Bright blue eyes in a face made lean by pneumocystis
Eyes that enabled Lee to continue

Working as a lawyer
Driving his Mercedes
Enjoying the view of downtown

His eye doctor said, "All you fellows with AIDS are so nice"
His response, "How do you think we got the virus?"

He couldn't die in November, his birthday, or December
Don't want his family to have memories of death
At any holiday,
He wanted sunshine
For his memorial service

In February, blue eyes looked from a portrait at the crowd
Gathered to honor the man who loved to party

==========

In His Own Words
(Shawn)

a referral to hospice for pain management
even though he knew it was coming
has hit him hard
left him incredibly angry
unfair how hard this life has been for him
he knows we all suffer
all have tough breaks
death is hard for almost everyone
but damn, for him, it's been a punching match
from the time he can remember
now the fight continues
even though he's lost the fight
must keep getting up until the final blow

==========

Fighting the End
(Lee)

handsome and robust despite the virus
going about life as long as he can
this life is worthwhile

weeks in the hospital back to work
thin and easily tired
pain a constant presence while working

still handsome, life is good
purple spots betray him
don't stray far from a bathroom

vision beginning to fade
his friends, his work he wants to stay
stumbling in the dark

finding ways to continue living
seeking small pleasures
quality of life becomes a moving target

==========

Easing Out
(Jack)

This man once able to track every event and person
with the sharp sarcastic tongue and active mind
eyes bright with curiosity and malice.
                                                    Today
knows me but unsure of my place in his universe

Today worries about his laundry getting done
unconvinced when told no need to worry

Today lies curled in a new bed, in the hospice
dozes and then speaks again of his apartment

Today his words linger without reproof or correction
eyes look into the distance, almost on his way

==========

**Whatever Comes
(Lee)**

Each week. he outlined the changes.
His body failing
under the onslaught of the virus.

He measured his loss of vision.
Wondered how long he would walk.
Fear ruled his future.

Until the day,
until he held in his hand, the pills.
His way out when it got to be too much.
Never spoke of his fears again.
Knew he could handle whatever would come.

==========

Lee (Christine Gregoire)

his old law school classmate
running for attorney general
he was wasting away
almost blind
exultant about his friend
joking he let her know
had the blackmail photos
from years ago
when they were young
now he is close to death
she is becoming somebody

Three Tied Together:
Susan, Shawn, and John

Three people whom I met during height of the AIDS epidemic (Susan, Shawn, and John) were connected and had history together. They had been young together not long after Woodstock (1969). Now they were all living with AIDS (1991). They got help from various organizations.

Knowing one person leads to another and another. Often a community forms. When people in a community have AIDS, much of the community dissolves when the people die. AIDS decimated the arts community. The AIDS community included helping organizations. Many of them have disappeared over the years as more people with AIDS are living longer and healthier lives.

I trained to be part of the Chicken Soup Brigade in July 1990. CSB focused on providing meals for people living with AIDS and rides to medical appointments. It became part of the Northwest AIDS Foundation, aka Lifelong AIDS Alliance, at some point.

People with AIDS signed up for rides. Volunteers were available to provide rides (or do other tasks). Volunteers and clients were permitted to arrange rides on their own and to notify the agency. Volunteers were encouraged to be warm and friendly. Family and friends often abandoned people with AIDS or simply kept their distance. Most people were terrified of the virus at that time.

I gave several rides (to appointments with her doctor) to a woman named Susan. I was surprised to meet a woman with AIDS. She told me that she was infected from a needle. Her husband was a drug user, and so was she. They shared drugs and needles with each other and with friends. Her husband was gay and died of AIDS years before Susan and I met.

Susan lived in a building called Capital Park, one of the Seattle Housing Authority buildings for low-income people. This was the first time I was ever inside one of these cement-block buildings. I didn't know anything about them before that. Since then, I learned that there is no minimum income to live there, and anyone there pays about a third of their income for rent. (It was fairly easy to get in back then. As of 2019, the waiting list is about nine years except for people who are homeless.)

Susan was morbidly obese and had low self-esteem. Her father told her she was ugly and worthless. She was grateful to have the community of gay men (including her husband) and cared for them. She didn't believe anyone else would want to be close to her.

Catholic Community Services sent a volunteer, Sister Sheila, to help Susan with housework. She was quiet and devoted, according to Shawn, who lived with Susan for a time (completely illegally). I met Sister Sheila once or twice when I was visiting, but we never had a conversation.

Susan admitted to several suicide attempts and still wanted to die. That seemed hard to argue with. She had AIDS and not a lot to look forward to. She had seen her husband and friends die awful deaths.

Susan had me drive her to an event, a fundraiser put together by her friend Shawn, featuring a lesbian singer, Rebecca. Susan told me ahead of time that Shawn was the handsomest man she'd ever met. He was there at the concert with his two-year-old daughter. He no longer lived with Susan. He had moved into a different low-income housing place, next to the convention center. She introduced us saying he was her best friend. Yes, he was handsome.

Besides providing rides, I talked to Susan on the phone most days. I wanted her to feel my caring. When she was depressed, she stopped answering her phone. Then she didn't answer for two days. I asked her manager to check on her. We discovered her body. She had committed suicide.

Her address book was on a table. I took it with me so I could call her friend Shawn. He kept me updated on his process, cleaning out her apartment and arranging cremation. He kept, donated, or sold almost everything. She had no one else to take her stuff. Later he gave me a little block of wood with the Robert Indiana love stamp (1973) attached to it. That era was part of their connection.

Shawn and I kept in touch. He lived with his daughter, two-year-old Gennie, in transitional housing. He complained that the management was rude to him. He had fixed the studio apartment up with plants in one corner. He acquired plants by stealing them from other people's yards or apartment buildings. He had many photos and things he'd written over the years. He was the editor of a tourist newspaper in Florida at one time and was proud of his ability to do that since he had very limited education.

Shawn talked about the people in his life. He described former friends who were part of an organization designed to help children affected by AIDS. He complained that the women had been very nice but then tried to get custody of Gennie and accused him of abusing her. He claimed they abused her. (The organization lasted for years, and the woman who founded it was honored when she died. I didn't believe that they abused Gennie. But I just listened.)

Shawn told many stories about abuse from both his parents back in the Midwest. He said his mother tried to kill him. He described being shut in a closet for hours at a time without food or drink or being allowed to go to the bathroom. He said he was locked up in a mental institution from the time he was eight to eighteen, which is why he didn't go to school much. He had a brother who lived in the area (also HIV positive) another brother lived south of Seattle but didn't have much to do with him.

Shawn told other stories about people who were supportive of him although inconsistently. A couple of them were local LGBT singers back when very few were out. This included the singer at the concert when Susan introduced us. Shawn's stories often involved drugs and alcohol. Sometimes he owned up to his own consumption (especially of speed). Other times he talked about the problems of others.

Shawn wanted to be remembered and wrote pages and pages about his experiences. He tried to get someone to agree to publish them, but no one was interested.

Another person who spent a lot of time trying to help Shawn was a social worker at the Northwest AIDS Foundation, Pat. She stuck around while he was mostly not cooperating.

Pat found Shawn an apartment on Summit. It was a lot bigger, with two bedrooms. He furnished it by dumpster diving, especially in the nicer part of Capitol Hill. He often got food that way as well. He also went to the food bank. I bought food sometimes partly because I was worried about Gennie. Shawn cooked for me a couple of times. He was a good cook. He had a collection of dysfunctional friends (all on drugs) who stayed with him, sometimes for weeks.

Another social worker after Pat had moved on volunteered to drive Gennie to childcare at an in-home daycare. After a month or two, she opted out. Shawn was often too out of it to get Gennie ready and didn't answer his door or phone. I did some of the driving to daycare. When I asked for a key to his place so I could get in even if he was sick or asleep, he got angry and didn't call or respond to calls. He was evicted from one apartment and another, eventually ending back at the transitional housing.

Shawn taught me a lot about crystal meth and about addiction. He really tried a number of times to stop using, and it was terrible for him since he got so sick. He seemed manic when he was high. It took me a long time to identify that state, but I was finally aware. Then he sunk very low the next day. He couldn't get out of bed and felt like he had a bad flu.

One time when we were still getting along, Shawn asked me to go with him to the dinner at SASG. This was free for people with AIDS and family or friends. We ate there a couple of times. They had a dinner every Friday night.

Even though Shawn took a lot, he also gave occasionally. He loved Gennie and tried to be a good father. He was a big fan of women singers (such as Judy Collins). He made me a mixed tape of his favorite songs by many women singers.

Shawn introduced me to his friend John, who lived at Capitol Park, a low-income housing where Susan had lived. Shawn and John knew each other for years although John didn't use drugs (except pot) as far as I know. Shawn wasn't interested in massage (because of childhood trauma, he said), but he told John that I was good at massage and could help with his pain. This was at the very end of 1991.

When John called me, I needed a project for massage school. We were supposed to do a series of massages on one person and track improvement. He agreed to be my project, knowing that I would write up what I found and turn it in. I began giving him weekly massages.

John talked a lot during massage and pulled me into helping him with transportation to other therapies. Most of the therapists were volunteers, including a chiropractor, an acupuncture practitioner, several massage therapists, and an energy practitioner. He also had helpers who came to the house, including someone from Shanti (spiritual support for people with AIDS), a chore worker, a case manager from the NW AIDS Foundation, and a massage person from an organization that provided free massage for people with AIDS. If help was out there, John found it.

His volunteer massage therapist (from In Touch) had an office in the U District. We sometimes went over to nearby Tubs to relax in hot water before he got a massage (to make the massage more effective). Her studio was at the top of a tall staircase. As the weeks went on, I had to help him more and more to navigate the stairs. Eventually we just couldn't do it anymore.

John talked about his experiences as he was growing up. He described himself as a freckled farm boy from Eastern Washington and a complete innocent when he moved to Seattle. He indicated some discomfort among family members about his being gay and his HIV status. However, his sister who lives in Seattle was always completely supportive. Over time I met her and other people in his life. All of them helped him with his life. He didn't pay anyone. Many were official volunteers for organizations.

John had several friends who were serious about Buddhism as was he. They arranged for him to be invested as a Buddhist monk. The ceremony was held in his apartment. Some time before that, the Dalai Lama came to speak in Seattle. John convinced me to take him to the event (at the convention center). Because he was in a wheelchair, we got to sit down front in the handicapped section. I don't recall how we got tickets or if I paid for them. Probably. Or else someone else gave them to him.

The two of us drove slowly through the neighborhood when we were headed out to eat (usually at Broadway America Grill since one of the owners comped his meals) or for one of his appointments. John really got on my case if I hit any potholes (hard to avoid). Once we passed a yard sale in which a large Buddha was displayed. John convinced me to buy it for him. I also bought him some music and videotapes. I bought him several massage wands that he used on all his painful muscles. Through him, I learned about Buddhism for the first time and was glad of it. He went for counseling to a therapist he knew through the Buddhist group.

John was devoted to his dog Mo, a Lhasa apso. He made sure I understood that *dog* is *God* reversed, and *Mo* is *om* reversed. Mo generally was in the car with us. John made sure Mo noticed all the dogs we passed just as he noticed all the attractive gay men. John knew that a nearby vet had one day a month when he provided free treatment for pets belonging to people with AIDS. He also gave out free food for the animals. Mo got lots of that food.

Movies provided an hour or two of vacation from AIDS. John pointed out that I had a vacation whenever we weren't together. He didn't get to forget so easily.

He wanted to record his memories. He didn't want to be forgotten. Several people had given him tape recorders and tapes. Somehow it was never the right time to begun the process.

I took John to the Gay Pride celebration at Volunteer Park in 1993. We saw Shawn there. John and I had talked so much about Shawn's drug use and lying. We withdrew from him. Both of us found little to say to him and hoped he would go away. He eventually did.

In the end, John moved to Bailey-Boushay (skilled nursing facility for people with AIDS and others) in October 1993 and died there in February 1994. Shawn lived there later and called me after not being in touch for years. I came to visit him there. We had coffee and found we didn't have much to say to each other. He died there in 2004.

==========

Shawn's legacy

          one box holds the writings
          page after page
          rambling back and forth
          through the life he remembered

          the life as a little boy who was beaten
          the child who was locked in a closet
          the one unwanted among the children

          written in scrawling letters
          unfinished sentences
          words wildly misspelled
          entrusted

          during the years when he moved
          from one apartment to another
          before he lived in the hospice
          before he died of AIDS

          forgotten or forgiven over time
          as he will be
          as he has been by most
          a hard lump, in the corner of my house

==========

Shadow Breath
(For John)

Incense
Piercing my soul
With longing and memory
John surrounded by candles
Buddhas and pictures
A white orchid
Fabric draped.

He's not here.

==========

Daily Diversion
(For Shawn)

he shares his story of the day
racing up the hill frantically
desperate to get home
before the diarrhea
to change clothes
to go to bed
to cry

a little

before
he calls me
shares the details
much bigger than life
astonished others staring
finally it's all too much for me
his goal to get me laughing with him

==========

Survival of the Fittest
(Shawn)

large pieces of bread scattered on the sidewalk
pigeons pecking oblivious to people passing
arouse memory, stories of his childhood

a hungry child, no food from his mother
punished for being bad
sent to school without breakfast

saw birds eating scattered crumbs
dove into the middle of the flock
claimed the crumbs for himself

==========

Black-and-White Photo
(Shawn)

a scrap of his childhood saved through moves;
__the little boy I never knew sits on my shelf,
an odd gift from the man I loved and hated
for all the days we laughed and cried
for all the times he begged and lied;
so little left of his life, but this remains.

==========

Beside Wilting Flowers on the Porch

"Margaret, dear. You have no idea
how inconvenient it is for me
to have to knock down fences
and piss off so many people
just to bring you flowers.
And your not even home.
Alas . . . Love, love, and more Shawn"

Alternative Treatments

Hanging out with people with AIDS was pretty much my introduction to alternative treatments. I had heard of them previously but never experienced them (except a couple of massages).

I took Jack to acupuncture appointments when we first met in January 1991 (before I started massage school). He asked the acupuncture practitioner about the difference between alternative medicine and Western medicine. That practitioner preferred to talk about complementary treatments (any of a range of medical therapies that fall beyond the scope of scientific medicine but may be used alongside it in the treatment of disease and ill health. Examples include acupuncture and osteopathy.) He told Jack that complementary treatments strengthen the body of the person while Western medicine attacks the pathogen. From that perspective, they fit together very well.

Reiki (energy treatment) falls within the definition of complementary treatments. I had mixed results with Reiki. Eric was convinced that Reiki greatly diminished his problems with neuropathy. He also thought it enabled him to stop taking medications for bipolar disorder. Eric appreciated Reiki so much that he learned how to do Reiki on himself. Lee asked me not to do Reiki after one experience. He felt miserable afterwards as if Reiki spread pain through his body.

The first time Denise saw me (1992), I was with John trudging up the stairs of Crossroads Center on Twelfth where she volunteered. I was escorting John to free acupuncture. John used a cane to help him walk. I had a walker and one leg in a cast (for a broken ankle). Denise noticed us because we were such an odd combination. She couldn't figure out who was helping whom. John provided me with an education in alternative treatments: acupuncture, chiropractic, massage, energy work, ground gemstones, and acupuncture. He was always willing to ask for help. He was happy to try anything offered.

As far as I recall, John was the only person I knew who thought sitting in meditation could help his body to fight HIV. It seems logical to me now that meditation could be helpful in making the body stronger and more able to resist any disease. I have seen scientific studies that investigate the physiological effects of meditation as well as the mental, physical, and palliative benefits that meditation can offer patients. People who regularly practice meditation have unique EEG patterns, lower respiratory rates, stable blood pressure, and better immune responses. Mindfulness meditation can help those battling anxiety, depression, substance abuse, and addiction. Meditation can also decrease pain. Meditation was part of John's Buddhist practice and part of his hope to overcome AIDS.

Shawn also liked to try or imagine trying different treatments, often those that seemed ridiculous to me. He picked up on every imaginative theory, including the idea that AIDS was really caused by drugs or by syphilis. He didn't want to think HIV caused it. However, he liked the idea that one could somehow exchange all the blood to get rid of the virus, introduce oxygen into the blood to kill the virus, or use methamphetamines (his favorite) to heal. He talked about the blood exchange and adding oxygen to the blood but never could come up with any specific examples of where it was being done. I liked the ideas but assumed there were practical reasons they wouldn't work.

Lee liked to save money and to try one miracle cure each year. One time it was shark cartilage. I don't know if this was in an injection or eaten. It was available in some other country, so the cost of treatment included travel and a hotel room. It didn't seem to have any effect. Other than the yearly test of a miracle cure, he stayed with more traditional treatments, including massage.

Eric dreamed of living in Kentucky and staying healthy by chopping wood and carrying water. For him, this would be a kind of meditation and a way to get close to nature. He thought that his body would then be healthy enough to survive attacks by HIV. He thought that he could coexist with HIV. He didn't expect to get rid of the virus. I guess having all of his teeth extracted (to get rid of heavy metals) was also a kind of complementary treatment. He thought heavy metals were making him less able to resist opportunistic diseases. It didn't work completely since he died from meningitis (an opportunistic disease). However, he was healthy and happy for years. He was able to travel across the country. He was able to do physical work (including helping Rebecca and Pedro when they moved to

Seattle in 1997). He lived with AIDS a lot longer than many people did until he died of meningitis.

John got medical treatment from Country Doctor., a clinic for low-income people. In addition, he had a team of helpers providing complementary therapies: chiropractic, acupuncture, massage and energy work. He had several caregivers from each specialty. He had at least one and sometimes two or three treatments in a day. He had a Buddhist group to chant with (who chanted for him when he was at Bailey-Boushay). He had people to help with walking his dog. He had people around him all the time, including family members and friends. He didn't like to be alone.

John had a device called a TENS (transcutaneous electrical nerve stimulation, the use of electric current produced by a device to stimulate the nerves for therapeutic purposes.) He often had me help with placement on painful spots. He was sure it helped. (I had a tiny one that seemed to help with arthritis pain. Thinking about this sent me online, and I was somewhat tempted to buy a bigger one for myself.) John also had a collection of electric massagers to help with pain. He was determined to keep going up until a few weeks before he died after living with AIDS for a number of years.

During the '90s, people living with AIDS had many opportunities to get free or low-cost complementary treatments (much more than people living with other life-threatening diseases).

One of the organizations offering complementary treatments was called In Touch. Volunteers from that group offered free massage to people living with AIDS. They aimed for relaxation and also for healing through touch. Many people living with AIDS were not touched by anyone after they got sick. I recall that both Lee and John had volunteer massage therapists from the organization. If In Touch tried to recruit volunteers from my massage school, I wasn't aware of it (seems odd that they didn't approach us). I had never heard of it until John and Lee mentioned it when I was already out of school. I don't know how people living with AIDS knew that it existed. Possibly case managers from NWAF told clients about the service. I don't know why or when it folded. I didn't want to volunteer but would have donated money if asked, but I never was.

Many people living with AIDS developed neuropathy (nerve damage and pain) in their feet. Albert told me it felt like his feet were going to sleep or getting too cold and then tingling and pain. One of the people I knew who was living with AIDS asked me to take him to get acupuncture at the clinic run by Bastyr in Wallingford. When we went into the waiting room, eight men were sitting in the chairs around the room. I knew several of the patients from my volunteering at Madison Clinic. Another alternative was the acupuncture clinic at Crosswords. An acupuncture teacher and practitioner organized this clinic (where Denise saw John and me two years before we met each other).

Not everyone got help from acupuncture clinics. A man named Doug M. clearly had neuropathy. As a former drug addict, he didn't get as much pain medication as he wanted. The doctors weren't allowed to give him much in the way of pain medication. I remember seeing Doug trudging in comfortable slippers on the way to a nearby convenience store to buy his cigarettes. He couldn't get enough of standard pain medication to be comfortable. At the same time, he didn't explore alternatives. He seemed passive and resigned to his fate when I gave him rides a few times.

Many people living with AIDS were quite poor. This limited their ability to buy nutritious foods. They also might not have a way to get to a store or the ability to cook for themselves. SASG hosted dinners on Friday night, a way for people to get at least one good meal in a week.

Chicken Soup Brigade food deliveries helped as well. The food deliveries came once a week with meals in containers that could be frozen. Those living with AIDS had positive contact with people delivering food. The food was meant to be nutritious, which would have helped with physical health.

Joseph did not have food delivery. He was subsisting on instant-breakfast drinks. Empty, crusted glasses sat all over his apartment, but there were no other signs of food.

Shawn and others got food from food banks. Once, Shawn asked me to drive him to a food bank at a church in the central district. They didn't seem to mind that he didn't live near it. He complained about the lack of fresh fruits and vegetables but was pleased to have things like cheese and bread. He didn't have much money for shopping and used the food bank for basic supplies.

Another time, John asked me to drive him over to SASG. He thought they had cases of Ensure, which were available for anyone living with AIDS who asked. The person at the desk walked us back to an area near the kitchens. They had a stack of cases of Ensure. The drinks were expired, but only just recently. We were invited to take a case. This was a simple way of making sure people got necessary nutrients.

Some people who couldn't eat enough (or any) food the normal way had IV feeding tubes (especially Raymond). The disadvantage, he said, was that it made him feel bloated and uncomfortable. Even so, he thought it was better than not getting nutrients.

John was prescribed Marinol to control nausea, but it didn't seem to work for him. Even though marijuana was illegal at the time, he knew how to obtain it, and it did help with the nausea. He kept a joint in the glove compartment of my car and had a couple of puffs before we went to a restaurant.

Steve had a problem with diarrhea. He read that dried blueberries could be used to treat the problem. He liked that idea better than using medications but couldn't figure out how to make it work right.

Without the right food, the body wouldn't be strong enough to fight back against disease. (This is also true for people with cancer.) Everyone I knew who was living with AIDS used whatever medications were available to fight HIV and opportunistic diseases, and they wanted to improve their chances by eating nutritious food and staying strong.

Many articles about the health of old people point out that those who have social contacts do a lot better intellectually and physically than people who are isolated. I suppose that the groups at SASG helped people in that way, and also the Friday-night dinners. Some people who moved to Bailey-Boushay or Rosehedge lived much longer than expected.

John, for instance, was much better for several months before getting worse and dying. He had many friends, but that is not the same as living surrounded by others and having the opportunity to eat or do art projects with others.

The most isolated person I met was Joseph. He didn't seem to have friends or anyone in his life. It sounded like he did better when his family took him home (Texas?), but I don't know how long he lived.

After I had been doing massage at Madison Clinic for a number of years, I heard that the doctor who headed the clinic and other doctors agreed that massage and acupuncture are complementary treatments that they believed were helpful.

I think the situation is more complicated than was explained by Jack's acupuncture person. Sometimes problems are caused by side effects of other medications and not by the disease. Sometimes a complementary treatment helps partly but not completely. Both kinds of treatments are used to treat symptoms such as pain, swelling, itching, etc.

==========

**I Hate Her
(John)**

>   he had careful instructions for me
>   after I helped him to my car
>   we drove along the waterfront
>   up a long ramp
>   to another part of the city
>   to a small faded house
>   flanked by short dry grass
>   he leaned on my arm into the house
>   had me leave for an hour
>   Reiki for pain
>   we never returned to that house
>   she forbade, a drain of her energy
>   that woman, never mentioned again

==========

**Hooked
(For A)**

>   Vajra, a special store
>   For incense and Buddhas and such
>   Behind the counter
>   An attractive woman
>
>   The customer mentioned
>   That he did body work
>   Caregiving is her real life
>   Vajra just helps to pay the bills
>
>   She had a good friend
>   Living with AIDS
>   He agreed to help out
>   Not that he saw much of her later

==========

Carol Glenn (RN) on Facebook asked, "I have a question for all you old HIV folks—around 1993 I watched a home treatment of ozone therapy delivered intravenously. Writing about this experience in a chapter for my book but can't find a reference to it anywhere. Know I'm not disremembering 'cause it was pretty horrifying both as a concept and to witness. Anyone else seen or knows of IV ozone? Thanks for your help."

Bob Wood (MD) said, "Carol—I recall people proposing ozone as a treatment for AIDS, and vaguely recall that someone mentioned it being given IV, which I took as unlikely and possibly deadly. When I did a summer med school fellowship at Cambridge back in '69, docs were experimenting with radiating blood. They ran the blood of patients w/ leukemias through a coil inside a lead chamber that contained a radiation source. I thought one could run blood through a coil like for dialysis and bubble ozone through the dyalizate fluid as the only way O_3 could be applied to blood. Lot of crazy proposals to Rx."

Terry Found Training for Caregivers

Many groups worked to help people with AIDS twenty-seven years ago. All of them employed many caregivers. All had volunteers. Together, we had a community.

When I became part of the AIDS community in 1990, I began to learn about the organizations making up the community. Meeting so many caring people was wonderful. One group (In Touch) offered free massage to people with AIDS. Another one (Multifaith Works) offered spiritual support. Rosehedge was a hospice. Bailey-Boushay (skilled nursing, like a hospice) opened soon after. Chicken Soup Brigade provided rides to medical appointments and meals. SASG provided spaces for support groups and served meals on Friday night. The Northwest AIDS Foundation provided counseling, case management, and help with finding housing. Other groups provided acupuncture and legal help. There must also have been groups I never heard of.

One group, the AIDS Caregivers Support Network worked out of the American Red Cross building in south Seattle. I learned about this organization through my friend from massage school, Terry. He asked me to attend a class with him and his parents after he had dropped out of massage school because his health had gotten so bad. The class offered an overview of information and advice for caregivers. I think this was in the summer of 1992.

I met Terry and his parents at the Red Cross building on the night of the class. No one else was in the building at that time except twenty to thirty people who were taking the class. Most were parents, and some were partners.

Terry's partner D was not there. (D didn't know his own HIV status. He preferred not to know as long as he felt healthy. I don't know what happened to him in the end.)

Terry and I became friends when we began classes at Seattle Massage School in the spring of 1991(February?). He was a flight attendant and said he wanted to change careers (as he said, to deal with one asshole at a time rather than a whole planeful). I think Alaska Airlines was aware of his HIV status and willing to work with him to some extent (giving him time off), but the job required too much energy, and that was the real reason he decided to try massage school. Terry, Josh, and I soon became good friends at school, sitting together during lectures and hanging out during breaks. Others were more casual parts of our group. Marilyn was one, and Jessie was another.

Jessie was very young, just out of high school. The rest of us were all looking for a new career after doing other things. In my case, I had been a teacher for ten years and worked in Mike's business for ten years. Jessie revealed soon into the course of studies (to everyone in the class) that he had been diagnosed with obsessive-compulsive disorder. He was afraid of touching people and things. His big fear was germs (especially HIV), enough that he would cross the street rather than get close to a dropped Kleenex. He hoped to get over his fears by learning to do massage.

Terry and I went for a walk alone during one of the breaks between classes. He revealed during that walk that he was HIV positive. He hadn't told the staff at the school and trusted me to keep it quiet. He didn't hide that he was gay and had a partner. I told him before that day about being a volunteer for Chicken Soup Brigade and wanting to offer massage to people with AIDS. Terry shared his HIV status with Josh a few weeks later. (I think that was after Josh, who is straight, talked about having a gay best friend.) We learned much later that Jessie figured it out (maybe guessed because he knew Terry was gay) and chose to hang around as a way of defeating his fears.

One day, D came over to the massage school to go out to lunch with Terry and me. Terry wanted us to know each other. We went to a place near the school. When we were driving to the restaurant, Terry pointed out the raggedy seatbelts. Their wild black Lab had tried to eat them.

Terry had difficulty keeping up with the academic work at the massage school. We had to memorize muscle names and function. We had to know the names of bones and where muscles connected to them. We had frequent tests. Terry and I talked at length about his difficulties. Josh and I tried to help him to learn the material. Terry blamed his problems on AIDS and yet wanted to continue. He finally told the school about his HIV status and asked for accommodations. According to him, they were angry at his earlier deception and forced him to drop out several months into the yearlong program. He and I sat in his car for an hour or more while he talked about the situation and cried. He was bitter about having to leave, and yet he really didn't have the stamina to stay in school. I don't know whether they gave him his money back or if he asked for it.

Cousin Mickey took me to the wedding of Terry and D on Bainbridge Island. (Same-sex marriage wasn't legal at the time, so it wasn't a legal marriage, but it otherwise was a lovely wedding.) I wasn't comfortable taking the ferry on my own. I think this was in May 1991. Terry and D were dressed in matching hot-pink shirts, white shorts, pink socks, and white tennis shoes. They both had flowers. They were handsome. Both had dark hair and mustaches. Terry's family members were there and supportive.

I met his best friend, Lee, there. Lee was also a handsome man. Lee looked a lot different by the time I got to know him as his massage therapist (since he had lost weight as he got sicker with AIDS).

Mickey and I sat through the ceremony, ate at the reception, and then left soon after. When I look at the photos from the day, I see that Jessie was there as well. He is hugging Terry in one of the photos.

Terry came to massage school graduation, looking very thin and tired. This was in the spring of 1992. By then, he had given my name to his friend Lee, and I was doing massage on Lee at his house. I also went over to do massage on Terry at the house he shared with D. Their tiny house had 670 square feet living area (on a 4,800-square-feet lot). I discovered online that Terry and Lee owned the house as of 1990. (Lee was an attorney who described his father as richer than God.) Lee and Terry had been in a romantic relationship at one point before Terry and D got together. Their friendship remained, including wicked dark humor about living with AIDS.

When I did massage on Terry at that time I observed that his feet were contracted into a shape as if he was wearing high heels. This seemed to have happened since he got AIDS. He also reported he had shingles. Before that, I didn't know it was common for people with AIDS to experience that painful condition. I guess people with AIDS are vulnerable for the same reason older people are vulnerable—impaired immune systems.

When I did massage for Terry at his house, he made a point of helping me to get better at doing massage. He wasn't comfortable with my draping technique. He said I needed to tuck the sheet more carefully around him so he wouldn't feel exposed. We couldn't figure out any way I could help him with the contractures in his feet. When he had shingles, all I could do for him was Reiki. Any kind of touch was terribly painful.

Eventually Terry wasn't able to manage living in the house. I visited Terry a couple of times after he went to live with his parents. They lived in a mobile home park in Auburn (now I'm amazed that I was willing to drive that distance). Once when I was visiting, Terry seemed disconnected and sleepy. He barely spoke to me. And then an uncle came to visit, someone Terry hadn't seen for at least a year. Terry sat up in bed and chatted in an animated way. As soon as the uncle left, Terry collapsed onto the bed again. It was as if he'd used up all his energy talking to his uncle.

At the end of his life, Terry moved to Bailey-Boushay, which had been open for about a year. I went to see him there. I guess it was just once. He only lived for a week after going there. He was thirty-eight years old when he died in May 1993.

When I was visiting Terry at Bailey-Boushay, a doctor came in to insert a catheter into his penis to enable him to empty his bladder. I was going to leave the room, but Terry asked me to stay. I held his hand and talked to him through the painful process. I kept eye contact so that I didn't have to look at what was happening, and neither did he. Terry said it was excruciating, but having company helped.

His parents planned a traditional memorial service at a hall in Auburn. Jessie wanted to attend, so I picked him up on the way, and we went together. The parents had set up many photos at the front of the room. People took turns speaking about Terry and his exuberant spirit. He was always the life of any party. He was also known for changing his hair color frequently.

I guess that the class we took helped Terry's parents once they became his caregivers. The class met for several weeks and was extremely practical, including teaching ways to help someone who couldn't walk or stand by themselves, suggestions about food, and other day-to-day concerns. The teachers were matter of fact about the kinds of opportunistic diseases the caregivers might have to deal with. They talked about medications. They discussed IV feeding and hydration and universal precautions. Most of what they discussed would be ahead for these people who still looked somewhat healthy. The changes tended to happen in a year or two. AIDS was not a long process in those days.

In some ways the class was harsh. They didn't shrink from the realities. At one point, they taught us how to help someone to get out of bed or a chair and into a wheelchair. The person in the bed had to be assisted to sit on the edge of the bed. Then the helper puts arms around the patient's waist while the patient puts arms around the helper's shoulders. The instructor joked, "Shall we dance?"

Then the helper counts, "One, two, three" before lifting up while the patient assists as much as possible by trying to stand. I used that lesson later with John and with others who were close to death (but not with Terry).

I received the quarterly newsletter from the AIDS Caregivers Support Network for a number of years. They offered community education about caregiving to churches and civic groups in the Seattle area. I read in the newsletter when they made the decision to shut down the organization in 1996. By then, people were living longer on protease inhibitors, and fewer people needed to learn to be caregivers. Before shutting down, the organization created a booklet *Circles of Care*. This included many of the important pieces of information from the class I attended with Terry and his parents. I always wondered what happened to the founder of the group. He was a long-term survivor, having lived with AIDS for at least ten years by the time of the class. He was charismatic and energetic.

That AIDS Look

A sudden death is a huge shock and trauma. A slow decline from someone who has been active and energetic is a long loss. Knowing someone who is already dying before you meet is totally different. You never see the strong and healthy person. You don't experience the biggest losses. Meeting as a professional is again different. It's not the same kind of personal loss.

Terry and Lee seemed healthy when we met, Jack and John not so much. Susan committed suicide. None were part of my life for more than a few years some only for months. I guess Shawn lived the longest—perhaps fifteen years.

During the time when many people were dying quickly of AIDS, we watched people get thin and skeletal. We said they had the AIDS look. Muscles in the butt became slack, like old people's. Hair thinned. Eyes seemed big in the face, almost like a child's. I would see strangers on the street and know. Many people also had AIDS stigmata. Michael had obvious Kaposi's sarcoma on his face. Steve was painfully thin like many people with AIDS. (There was a diet candy called Ayds. I think it went out of business after people knew about AIDS.)

When I let myself think about it, the idea that the same person I am now has been in the body of a baby, a toddler, a child, a teenager, and so forth boggles my mind. I think of this as a very obvious kind of reincarnation. The spirit is connected with a new body.

I remember sitting next to Michael as he dozed at Rosehedge. His hair was fine and soft. His hair seemed to me to be like that of a very young boy. He opened his eyes and looked at me. He seemed to me to have the innocence of a small child. But his thinning hair and boniness were also like a very old person. By then, I knew him so well that I didn't think about the KS.

Many people note that old people in some ways regress. Often, very old people can't walk. They may have to wear Depends. They sometimes have trouble with cognition. They may sleep a lot. As I looked at Michael, I wondered if AIDS was causing him to rapidly age as if he became ninety-five years old instead of the reality, forty-seven years old. I began to look at that in other people with AIDS.

Michael was already close to death when I met him. I never saw him healthy (although I saw photos of him at his memorial service.) Lee and Terry both looked good when I met them. They were both handsome young (thirties) men. No one would have guessed that HIV was working in them when we met. Lee was still working as a lawyer. Terry was attempting to transition from being a flight attendant to doing massage. AIDS was not visible in either one.

Terry and Lee were both dead within a few years of when we met. I watched them both as their bodies changed. As I've said, one of the most common effects of AIDS was weight loss. Even today when I see someone young who is skeletally thin, I wonder if they might have AIDS (or cancer). Both Lee and Terry eventually were down to skin and bones. Some very old people (including Mom) get very thin as well. Mom used to feel full after a few bites of food. Having no appetite is common among the elderly, and it was common among people living with AIDS. I also have seen old people who eat but don't seem to benefit from eating. It's as if their bodies no longer know how to process food.

Kaposi's sarcoma was another thing I often saw with AIDS. Kaposi's sarcoma causes lesions to grow in the skin, lymph nodes, internal organs, and mucous membranes lining the mouth, nose, and throat. It often affects people with immune deficiencies, such as HIV or AIDS. Purple, red, or brown skin blotches are a common sign. Tumors also may develop in other areas of the body. Lee had KS lesions on his legs. He told me they didn't hurt and not to worry about them when I was doing massage. Jack's doctor told him that he had KS in his lungs, which cut off his breathing. I see online that another kind of KS is sometimes seen on older men (who also may have an impaired immune system).

Terry had a painful bout of shingles. He said shingles were common in people with AIDS. They are also common in older people (over fifty). This has something to do for both with the impaired immune system.

Old people often have problems seeing or hearing. I don't remember any hearing problems with people I knew who had AIDS, but vision problems sometimes came with opportunistic diseases. Lee knew that he was going to go blind because of his CMV (cytomegalovirus). This is a disease that goes along with an impaired immune system and can also cause severe diarrhea (which happened to Steve and Doug). A recent article links CMV to older people (in whom the immune system is often less active). It can be connected to type 2 diabetes, autoimmunity, cancer, and cardiovascular disease.

A cane is often a symbol of a very old person. It seems odd to see a cane in the hand of a young person unless the person obviously has some disability such as cerebral palsy or multiple sclerosis. A cane is a kind of marker for old age.

Some time after we met, John began using a cane when he walked. Later, I began offering my arm as support when we walked together. I looked twice at other young people who were using canes. This echoed my experience with old people.

Albert went one step further. He managed to obtain an electric wheelchair. This was while he was staying with his friend's family. He and the children of the family had a great time riding the wheelchair up and down the block. It wasn't so good when he wanted to bring the wheelchair inside at the end of the day. There was no elevator. He couldn't get it up the stairs. I think it was too heavy even for the man of the household. Albert eventually gave the wheelchair back. This was unfortunate since he could have used it when he moved back to his apartment at Jefferson Terrace.

Once, when I was chatting with someone about the various symptoms people with AIDS had, the other person (who had AIDS) expressed the opinion that AIDS knew exactly how to hit the person the hardest. The person who was known for good looks ended up with KS on his face. The one who was an athlete ended up unable to walk. The brilliant person ended up with dementia.

I've thought about this conversation often. I wonder if we can say the same thing about old age. Do people fall apart most quickly in the parts they care about most? Or is it just that they notice the places that hurt most? Roger Ebert talked about how hard it was for him after his cancer made it impossible for him to eat the foods he loved most. Perhaps it would have been even worse if he had no longer been able to enjoy and evaluate movies?

Raymond wanted to cook for all of the people who helped him as he was living with AIDS. He loved cooking and loved eating good food. He wasn't able to make that feast. He wasn't even able to enjoy eating food at the end and had to receive food through a tube.

I have seen that it is a great loss for an older person who delighted in baking and canning but no longer has the energy to do those things. She feels she has become useless, at least in this one way. Not to mention that baking done by others can't live up to what she used to provide.

Shawn gave me some tapes that he got from Susan. In the tapes, Susan was talking to her husband who had AIDS and died before she did. The husband said that the only part of his body he liked now was his right leg. The left leg had KS. He had other symptoms on other parts of his body. The right leg looked like it always had. He treasured that perfect right leg.

John was proud of creating colorful outfits for himself, not quite drag but unusual. I knew this but never really saw it. By the time we met, he spent most of his time in comfortable loose clothing. Sweatpants were perfect for his unhappy body. Sweats, moccasins, and scarves were typical of anyone who was nearing the end of life while living with AIDS.

This is not far from the clothing I choose for myself as I age. I remember the days when I liked a little heel and a nice outfit. Now, I want my shoes to keep my feet from hurting and my clothing to be easy to put on and take off and to move in.

Shawn had me laughing when he talked about pushing Gennie in her stroller and trying to get home before diarrhea took over his body. He talked about racing across streets and up hills. It doesn't sound funny now, but he made it so. He wasn't the only one who suffered from diarrhea (or constipation). All the body parts were not working right. People living with AIDS routinely accepted the need to wear adult diapers and didn't even argue.

Many older people are faced with the same battles with incontinence but often are not so philosophical about the need for adult diapers. I wonder if I will accept adult diapers if I need them. It seems easy when it's far away, but not so much now.

I used to notice that Mom had the heat on in her house even in the summer. It amazed me, but as I age, I understand how the internal thermostat doesn't work the same way.

Similarly, the homes of people with AIDS were often extremely warm. Often the individuals were very thin, so this makes sense. Even in the summer, they would wear sweatpants and sweatshirts, maybe with a jacket on top and a hat.

Many of us especially fear dementia as we age. And it does correlate with advanced age. Sophie (as she approached one hundred) told me that she was having trouble remembering names and details, but she had discovered that they would come to her if she waited. I hope that I am like Sophie but am not optimistic since names and details come slowly even now.

There is such a thing as AIDS dementia as well. HIV was often linked with mental decline and worsening motor skills. When the virus attacks someone's nervous system, it can damage their brain and cause HIV-associated neurocognitive disorders.

John showed some signs of dementia toward the end of his life. However, his PCP carefully explained to us that John was still competent. He was thinking a little more slowly, but he was able to make decisions. He wasn't hallucinating or otherwise irrational. So his cognitive impairment at forty-six (and near death) was similar to that experienced by Sophie as she approached a hundred.

Another part of aging is facing the need to pare down and get rid of possessions. Many people reach that point when they have to move into a smaller place or assisted living. The process continues if the person ends up in a nursing home where very few possessions are allowed. Some of the people who were living with AIDS still had their homes and all their possessions (for instance, Lee). Others had very little toward the end. Michael still had everything in his condo but not much at Rosehedge.

Someone, maybe it was Lee, told me that he used to have rheumatoid arthritis prior to AIDS. He no longer dealt with that issue. I guess this would be a very small silver lining. (I think perhaps my allergies have diminished some with age.) My theory is that his impaired immune system no longer responded the same way (mine too).

Like old people, people with AIDS in the early years (before more effective medications) had to think about end-of-life issues. They had to decide what sort of care they wanted at the end. If they were lucky, like Michael, they were in a place (Rosehedge) where they could decide to have more morphine for pain even if it hastened death.

In Seattle, we had a pretty good system for caring for people with AIDS at the end of life whether they were in Rosehedge, Bailey-Boushay, or a hospital. They didn't have to worry about running out of money. Many had very little money to begin with. At the time, low-income housing was available without waiting for years. Chicken Soup Brigade helped with rides and meals. The Northwest AIDS Foundation (aka Lifelong AIDS Alliance) provided counseling and other support. Very little of this support is available to old people or people with diseases other than AIDS.

==========

Silver Lining
(Lee)

> He confided lying on the massage table
> Once he had terrible arthritis
> The kind with redness and swelling
> He got AIDS, and arthritis went away
> This the good side
> Of living with a failing immune system

==========

January 1994
(John)

Three weeks ago, he walked with difficulty,
supported on both sides,
demanded presence,
talked of the future as if it would arrive for him.

Now, I am back from my travels.
He seems smaller, still beneath the blanket,
but his voice creaks out a greeting,
he is still here.

I expect him to be here tomorrow and the next,
always a little bit of life left for me to hold
in my hands and heart, half and half and half again,
still leaves a little of him here.

==========

I've faced Kaposi's sarcoma on bodies and faces of emaciated men who
were dying of AIDS, yes, and still found beauty.

End-of-Life Planning

When I spent time with people who had AIDS, I began to learn a little bit about the kinds of decisions and plans required at the end of life, which often came very rapidly for a person who had AIDS. I wish I had known more about these things at the time and could have helped to guide the people I knew.

I think most people assume end-of-life paperwork is for old people. There also is the understanding that it might be wise for those with a life-threatening disease. Even in those cases, death may still be a long way off. Before protease inhibitors, people with AIDS had a pretty clear idea death would be soon. Most died within a couple of years. End-of-life paperwork should have been crucial. I didn't know it at the time and never discussed it with people I knew unless they brought it up. I only know odds and ends.

Nobody likes to think about dying (most don't anyway) or getting old. I think it's better to be prepared for old age, for the process of dying, and for what happens after you die.

I mentioned a client bringing up end-of-life papers when I was talking to my supervisor at a mental health agency. She immediately jumped to DNR (do not resuscitate). She seemed vague about the various terms and paperwork. How can that be? She had been with Older Adult Services for about fourteen years. She worked with her elderly parents and went through the death of her father. She definitely didn't want to discuss with clients. I talked to a manager above her, and he didn't want to touch it either.

Most people wish to be independent to the end. They want to die in their sleep without any extended illness. Very few achieve this unless they die young. I've been around many people who were dying over the years. I've seen what came before and what came after. Many times, paperwork was sloppy and incomplete. Things were done by chance or not at all.

When I became a hospice volunteer, we were told not to call 911 if the client died. At that time, the EMTs were required to try to bring the person back even if they saw the DNR order. I believe that has changed, and they are now required to honor the DNR. It gets complicated if family members (or the doctor) argue against it even when paperwork is in place. Best to have someone who will defend your wishes.

I thought about questions I should have asked and that I have attempted to answer for myself. Many of them are painful, but I think they are important.

==========

What if you died today? What would happen to your remains?

1. Your body: cremation or casket, memorial service or funeral, buried or scattered, obituary where?
2. Do you want your organs donated? Organ donation registry?
3. Your belongings: clothing, books, photos, furniture, and music?
4. Your loved ones: pets, children?
5. Your home?
6. Your money?
7. Do you have an executor? A will?
8. Reb Zalman asks, Are you saved (what you learned)? Ethical will? What if you were likely to die soon? What treatment do you want?
9. Do not resuscitate?
10. Hospice?
11. Comfort or cure? Advance directive, POLST?
12. Powers of attorney for health care and financial?
13. Death with dignity? What if you can no longer live fully independently?
14. Make sure you have people around?
15. Alarm system for problems?
16. Grab bars and other helps? Assistance with self-care?
17. Moving into another situation?
18. Important paperwork, passwords, friends' contact information, bank accounts?

==========

Independent living gets complicated with age and frailty. Mom had a medical alert device, but I don't think she ever wore it and certainly never activated it. She also wouldn't wear her hearing aids. She sometimes didn't get her phone hung up correctly (and no one could call her). Transportation can be a huge issue when the person is too frail to drive or take public transportation. Ride services help but may require a note from a doctor. People often need help: food, medications, cleaning self or home. Mom's friend had live-in help for years. Assisted living, a nursing home, or family may provide a home.

I guess Mom told her friends and all the family when she moved over here. We did our best to notify people when she died (and there was the obituary). I suspect many people didn't know when she moved to Scott and Valerie's house. Mom didn't have the energy to contact people. I guess no one else thought about it. She wasn't seeing many people during the last couple of years she lived downstairs from me.

Back in the days of AIDS, end-of-life plans weren't often well formalized. In some cases, family and/or friends stepped in to plan a funeral or memorial service and divide up the things the person left behind. This was true for many of the people I knew, including Albert, Jack, Michael, John, and Raymond.

When Bobby knew he was dying, he gave me instructions. He told me to take what I wanted from his apartment. Then his friend from California was to take what she wanted for herself or her family. Everything else was to go to Northwest AIDS Foundation (Lifelong AIDS Alliance), including his car. I was in charge of notifying NWAF. Most of the items were suitable for their thrift store, which often received donations from estates of people who died. The apartment building put his possessions into a storage unit, and I had to remind NWAF to take care of it when the apartment manager called to let me know the stuff was still there. Luckily everyone accepted my authority on the subject, and no one objected. I asked about a funeral. He wanted cremation. His friend took care of the funeral, and I placed a free obit in the *Seattle Gay News*.

John and I agreed I would use his address book to call people when he died and let them know about any funeral plans. I don't remember how people were notified when he moved to Bailey-Boushay. I guess there were enough connections among people that everyone found out. BB was strict about giving out any information and wouldn't have told anyone who called to ask. In fact, they generally wouldn't let anyone go up to visit if their names weren't on a list or if the resident didn't give permission in the moment (except John gave them instructions to allow in anyone who wanted to visit him.)

Albert wouldn't move into a hospice when he was no longer able to walk. He told his family he had cancer. He feared they would totally reject him if they knew he had AIDS. He knew he might die alone if he stayed in his apartment. That was okay with him. He left it to them to deal with his possessions and his funeral however they wished.

Jack had me take a photo to give family and friends. I think he mailed it to various people after I made many copies. However, I don't know whether any of those people knew when he moved to Rosehedge or when he died. It seemed to be just a small circle of family and caregivers who sat with him during the last days and came to the small memorial organized at his brother's home.

Michael wrote thank-you notes and bought gifts in the last month of his life. His sister inherited everything he owned and decided how to dispose of the things and, I guess, his condo. By living at Rosehedge, he had put in place most of the end-of-life issues. I mean I suppose Rosehedge and Bailey-Boushay required people to fill out necessary paperwork.

John gave me the power of attorney for medical matters. Someone else had power of attorney for financial matters. Toward the end, John experienced some slowing of his thinking and some confusion. His doctor explained to him (and to all of us around him) that he was still competent. It just took him a little longer to think things through. He was angry with me after I went to Israel and changed the power of attorney to someone else. Well, I guess it made sense since someone had to be there to make decisions when I was out of the country.

One man told me about his partner dying without a will. The family immediately threw this man out of the house he had with his partner. The family claimed everything in the house. There was no will and no other protection in those days (long before same-sex marriage.)

The first time I was named as executor was for my friend Dick. When he died (1988), I did not want to take on sorting through his house and his possessions. He had named an alternate (his estranged wife), so I gratefully handed it all over to her. I was more prepared when Mom died (2013), and I was again the executor. And it was a less daunting task since she and we had dismantled her house and taken care of most of her possessions already. All I had to do was go through her finances and distribute money as designated in the will. This involved some letters and phone calls plus providing copies of her death certificate, but it wasn't too bad (and Susie helped me with some of it).

Lee planned his own memorial service long before he died. He arranged for the rental of a docked ferryboat. He planned food and the gathering. His family knew to send out invitations. Most of the funerals and memorial services for people who died of AIDS were left to the survivors.

John's sister promised to take care of his dog Mo after he moved into Bailey-Boushay and later. She did, into Mo's old age. I don't know what happened to Steve's pug (when he went into the hospital and died) or to Rick's dog and cat (when he went into Rosehedge and later died). One of Cary's dogs died before he did (put down because of hip dysplasia and extreme pain). Cary's brother came out to care for Cary so he could die at home and took the other dog back home after Cary died. Dick had four cats inside and another six or so who were fully feral. He found people to take the inside cats, but the others went to a shelter and likely were put down. I guess that Cary's brother inherited his house and possessions. The brother gave me a framed poster (Gauguin).

I think some of the end-of-life paperwork has been clarified in the last thirty years (or maybe I just have finally learned what it's about).

One distinction is between power of attorney (medical and financial) and executor. The first are used when the person is alive but not competent. The other kicks in after death. The executor supervises the disposal of the estate, following the will if any or laws if the person doesn't have a will.

DNR (do not resuscitate) is for an acute situation when the person is likely to die without intervention. This has to be filled out and signed by a doctor and generally is used when the person would qualify for hospice (thought likely to die in 6 months or less). Basically, the person is saying, "Let me go if I have a medical crisis." The form should be prominently posted in the person's home and carried in a wallet. At the end, Jack wished he hadn't gone into the hospital with his second round of pneumonia. He would rather have gotten to the acute situation and then slipped away. He died within the six months that would have qualified him for hospice.

Some doctors don't like to put a person on hospice. They may want to think they will somehow cure the person. They want to keep trying to extend life, which often means extending the dying process. Some people don't want to be on hospice. They want to think they will be cured. A person on hospice has additional decisions. The hospice doctor and nurse are the major parts of hospice. The patient also has a chance to request a chore worker, a spiritual counselor, and a volunteer. People who understand hospice can plan ahead. They may decide that six months of this kind of support is what they want for themselves and for those they love.

The directive to the physician (POLST) is filled out by the person and witnessed by two people (not medical, not family, and no one likely to benefit from the person's death). Here the person answers questions about treatment they want while they are dying. Interventions such as hydration, tube feeding, assistance with breathing, and so forth prolong life (or the dying process). Pain medications help to ensure the comfort of the patient. Each of us gets to choose what we want. I saw these questions answered informally by people with AIDS where they chose not to have hydration or other efforts.

In addition to these forms, many people plan their funerals, including whether they wish to be cremated or buried. The executor may ensure wishes are followed with the help of family and friends.

In retrospect, I think other documents need to be added to the above. There should be names and contact information of those people who should be notified if/ when the person moves, is on hospice, and dies. Other paperwork includes financial records and other information about the person's estate.

I wish I had known all this when I spent time with people who had AIDS and could have helped them to figure out what they wanted except, somehow, it all seemed to work out.

Madison Clinic
and ACTU

Even now, the AIDS Clinical Trial Unit (ACTU) continues. AIDS is treatable now but by no means cured. The focus now is on prevention. Madison Clinic continues as well.

When I first encountered these clinics in 1990, they were temporarily located in a building (now gone) on Broadway and Madison. Harborview Hospital was in the midst of renovation of the old building and construction of new buildings at the time. Madison Clinic (named for the street) was the AIDS clinic for Harborview while the ACTU is a UW research unit.

I learned about Madison Clinic when I gave rides to people with AIDS as a volunteer for Chicken Soup Brigade. The Harborview Madison Clinic offered medical care and social services for persons living with HIV/AIDS, regardless of sexual orientation, gender identity, race, or ability to pay. They also had mental healthcare professionals (generally social workers) to provide psychiatric consultations, medication management, and recommendations for continued psychiatric care.

The staff at Madison Clinic includes nurses, doctors, social workers, medical assistants, and office workers. I think they use the Harborview Hospital pharmacy for prescriptions. There was some overlap of staff between Madison Clinic and the ACTU. At the beginning of this time, in the early '90s, doctors worked hard to treat opportunistic diseases while AZT was pretty much it for attacking HIV, and not effective in the long term. Once a person officially had AIDS (low fighter T-cells and/or an opportunistic disease), the immune system continued to decline and little could be done.

Sometimes blood transfusions slowed the decline temporarily but not much else helped.

During and after massage school (graduated spring 1992), I wanted to provide massage to people with AIDS and caregivers for people with AIDS. Volunteering at an AIDS clinic (doing chair massage) seemed like a good way to meet people. In addition, I offered Swedish massage (not at those clinics) at very low rates to people within the community. After I had been volunteering at Madison Clinic for a couple of years, I was enticed into extending my volunteering (with additional hours) into the ACTU. I spent six hours on Tuesdays at Madison Clinic and four hours on Wednesdays at the ACTU until arthritis forced my retirement in fall 2000. (I rationalized adding the extra hours by saying they were in honor of John who died in February 1994. I had a lot more time for doing other things when he was gone, and it helped my grieving process to fill the time.)

The ACTU is the AIDS Clinical Trials Unit for the University of Washington. The ACTU conducted clinical research to learn how HIV functioned in the body, including disabling the immune system. They looked at complications and opportunistic diseases. They worked to develop new treatments and to evaluate the effectiveness of treatments already in use. They also worked to educate about the need for clinical trials.

They provided access for all, including minorities, women, and drug users.

The ACTU has its own pharmacy. Staff includes doctors, nurses, physician's assistants, statisticians, and support personnel. Their budget depended (and still does) on grants for various research studies. The ACTU competes with other trial units for funding to test new drugs. They have to write up proposals and then recruit trial subjects. Any study includes an experimental group and a control group. Neither the clinicians nor the subjects can know which group subjects are in. The person might get to try a new drug. Then they might benefit but also would be facing possible side effects. Or they might not benefit. The control group would receive neither benefits nor the negatives of the drug being tested. However, all experimental subjects might be restricted from receiving standard treatments.

In late 1991, I approached the nurse manager of Madison Clinic about doing massage. He approved and made sure I had a room to work in each time (examining room). The front desk staff in each clinic made the sign-up list available at the beginning of each week. I welcomed patients and staff members to receive massage. I liked having the mix. Staff people were aware of the need to take care of themselves in their stressful jobs and also encouraged patients to use the opportunity. After people got used to having me there, my list was full each week, usually with one or two standbys in case I had an opening. Since chair massage is focused on back, neck, arms, hands, and scalp, twenty minutes is an adequate amount of time for each massage. Thus, I saw eighteen people on Tuesday and twelve on Wednesday.

(I signed up as a volunteer in the Harborview Medical Center volunteer office. When the clinics moved to the hospital, I was allowed to park for free in the employee parking there. I don't recall any interaction with the volunteer office after the first time and when I got the parking pass.)

I brought my massage chair and other equipment with me each week, using a free parking lot, which was connected to the nearby Baptist church. The building that held both clinics had small dark rooms. This seemed to be a defect in the building and the reason it was eventually torn down. The reception area at Madison Clinic was like a large living room with chairs all around the periphery. In those days, people with AIDS generally were thin and gray and slumped in their chairs. Almost no one lived long. Most of the patients were gay white men in those early days. The population changed by about 1998 with many more women and many more people of color (including immigrants).

When the clinics moved to Harborview (1995?) in a new wing, everything was lighter and brighter. It seemed more formal and less like home to me. People in the waiting room sat far apart from each other. The division into offices was a little odd because it didn't match the windows. Sometimes a wall was in the middle of a window. An odd detail—the paper towel dispenser was across the room from the sink, making it likely that someone would drip across everything on the counter (in my opinion).

At first I used paper bouffant caps (available at the clinics) to cover the face cradles. Later, I found flannel covers at a massage supplies store. I bought a large number of them so I could change them with each massage and still have more for the next day. I used them at home as well. I kept notes about each person on index cards so I could remember key points, such as if someone loved or hated hand or head massage. I reviewed the cards when I had a minute.

Some of the people I met at those clinics became paying massage clients. These included Bobby, Raymond, Cary, Randy (who kept forgetting to bring money when he came for massage at my house), and others among patients. Through Madison Clinic, I met Robin, who was a beloved elementary school teacher. Many of the teachers and his former students came to his memorial service (which was packed). I met a friend of Robin, MM, who got AIDS in his one experience with another man. He later married a woman and was horrified to find out about his HIV diagnosis. His wife stood by him throughout his sickness and death and is still in touch with his family. I met Joel, who worked at the ACTU through my experience there. A number of other employees (plus their friends and family members) also became massage clients in my private practice.

I got to know people working in other parts of the AIDS community, through referrals (such as NW AIDS Foundation and AIDS Education Project). The AIDS community was fluid. People in various agencies often knew each other. One of the NWAF case managers, Paul, died in the plane crash coming from San Francisco in early 2000 (Alaska Airlines Flight No. 261). It was a terrible shock to all of his friends, and it was scary to realize that the crash probably was caused by poor maintenance of the plane. One of the staff people at the ACTU knew a woman (a doctor) whose children were on the same plane with her ex-husband. It sounded like the woman was suicidal afterwards. I met relatives and friends of staff and patients. These people made up a good half of my client base. Some are still in my life (at least on Facebook). I met my close friend Donna through her daughter who was courier for Madison Clinic.

Staff people talked while receiving massage. One of their most beloved patients died early on during my time of doing massage at Madison Clinic. I never met the man, but I heard a lot about him. Before he died, he had a birthday in the hospital. Several staff people put on costumes. They brought food and balloons and music. They gave the man a beautiful sendoff. A social worker told me that story. A patient told me while he was getting massage that he had been a prostitute. That was how he got AIDS. I heard about annoying or inspiring patients from staff people. I heard about conflicts between staff people. I didn't talk except to ask about the massage.

One caregiver who never signed up for massage was a PA named Frank. Once he banged on the door of my massage room and demanded that the patient inside come out immediately (almost at the end of the massage). The patient was intimidated. I was angry. Frank was unpopular with his colleagues. Frank left Madison Clinic some time after that and went to work at Country Doctor. He was a caring PCP for John when John was at Bailey-Boushay, and I came to appreciate him.

In the early years, Madison Clinic staff included a courier, a person to carry medical records, lab samples, prescriptions, and other items between the clinic and Harborview Hospital (about half a mile). In 1992, that person was a young straight man not many years out of high school. Even though he was young, he had learned a lot about AIDS enough that he was frightened after a drunken evening in which he almost had unprotected sex. He was worried about himself and also astonished by his peers who seemed to know nothing about AIDS. I think he stayed safe over time. Once, he came in with a bad hangover. The nurse manager of the clinic hooked him up to an IV to rehydrate him.

Despite constantly dealing with pain and suffering and death, nurses and other caregivers were devoted to their work and stayed at Madison Clinic for years. Some of the same people are there even now, including the doctor who heads the ACTU. Most of the staff was there throughout the eight years I volunteered. Many became deeply attached to the patients despite knowing they would probably die soon.

Some friction developed between nursing staff and social workers because of differing ideas about appropriate boundaries. For instance, one nurse hired patients from the clinic to work in her garden. Some social workers disapproved of this choice. I heard that part of the computerized records were off-limits to nurses because of social work rules about boundaries.

One of the nurses at Madison Clinic later had a problem (and got fired) for giving patients medication that had been left behind when another patient died. In her mind, she was simply helping people who couldn't afford to buy certain medications.

In retrospect, it seems to me that the atmosphere at the ACTU was more upbeat than at Madison Clinic. The staff had the optimism of hoping they would find a new miracle drug to cure AIDS. The patients had the hope that they would receive a new drug that would be much better than otherwise available. The people in studies got their medications for free.

At one point during the time that I was volunteering to do massage, I was nominated for recognition as a volunteer who had given many hours to Harborview Medical Center. There was some kind of ceremony, and I got a plaque with my photo and a tribute.

Some time after that, the powers that be decided I needed to be credentialed since I was providing treatment to patients. This involved filling out paperwork and getting letters of approval from several people, including the doctor who was in charge of Madison Clinic. I kept on doing massage while this was going on, and the credentials were finally approved (late 2000). Unfortunately, the credentials didn't do any good since arthritis in my hand had already forced me to give stop doing massage. Still, it was nice to have approval.

Nowadays, Madison Clinic and the ACTU continue their expanded missions. According to the Madison Clinic website, they "also provide medical care to HIV-negative persons who might benefit from having an HIV/AIDS expert involved in their medical care, including those who are interested in pre-exposure prophylaxis (PrEP) for HIV prevention." Madison Clinic also provides treatment for other STDs, infectious diseases in general, and primary care.

I heard (2018) about a new study at the ACTU of people who have just seroconverted. They start them on medications immediately when the HIV diagnosis is confirmed.

I donated a couple of posters of Alfredo Arreguin's art to Harborview. They had one on display in the waiting area of the AIDS Clinical Trial Unit. My friend who volunteers at the ACTU enjoys seeing them when she is there working once each week. I've never been back since I stopped doing massage abruptly in late 2000 because of arthritis. It didn't feel comfortable once I wasn't doing massage anymore. I no longer had a role there. But I miss those days.

==========

In Memoriam

> a drag queen to the end
> John B., pictures taken
> dressed in drag
> week after week
>
> as his body faltered
> destroyed by HIV
>
> displayed by a friend
> after his death
> in memory and celebration
> still and always a queen

==========

Tomm, Perhaps Gone

> an aide at Rosehedge,
>   gently helping dying men
>
>   one day he waited
>
>   silent at Madison Clinic
> a patient with AIDS

==========

Healing Our Lives
(Madison Clinic)

> as my warm palms pressed down his back
> outlining his spine on both sides
> he spoke of his life, memories
>
> of embracing other men for money
> loneliness that walks with him
> through the battle with the virus
> his daily farewells to the body slipping away
>
> my hands probe muscles
> offer assurance
> he is still someone who matters

==========

A Vignette
(For MM)

> Singing shouting whispering laughing lamenting
> Under her hands the cello pours
> Sound into her heart

One hand gently presses the strings
The other holds the bow
Commands, cajoles music into their home
The cello a welcome lover

Her husband
Resolutely resisting the Virus
While it pushes pushes pushes him
Toward the edge

And she gives care, grieves, loves
Holding his fragile bony body close to her
As she sits with the cello in front of them
The strings offer comfort
Pouring into their bodies
A prayer filled with vibration and melody

==========

Madison Clinic

having babies in this clinic
one after another of the young women
working, caring
where so many die of AIDS
nurses and social workers pregnant
rounded bellies
denying the power of death
finding a way to give power to life

==========

Repayment
(For RF)

He owes me money still
Fifty dollars
I know I'll never see it

It isn't so much
He was one of my first clients
Gave me confidence
When I needed it most
Gave me a reason
To say no
I wouldn't schedule with him
Until he paid me
He introduced me to a fine man
Whose friendship I treasure
After all these years
Fifty dollars
I got a lot for the money

John in Bailey Boushay House

Many AIDS organizations have shut their doors over the years since better medications arrived. Others have helped to improve healthcare in general.

Even in the days where there was a long waiting list of people with AIDS wanting to get into Bailey Boushay, occasionally others who were HIV negative made use of the facility. It was licensed as a skilled nursing facility, not just as a place for people with AIDS. When John was there (1993–1994), thirty-three of the thirty-five residents were gay men with AIDS. One of the other residents was a gay man with cancer. Another was a young straight man with complications from spina bifida.

Even though it was a skilled nursing facility, Bailey Boushay functioned as a hospice. Most patients stayed there until they died rather than coming in for treatment and then moving out again. Some people lived there a very short time. Terry was there for only a couple of days. John lived there for about four months, which was longer than most. However, there was one man (whose name I don't recall) who lived there for a couple of years before he died. He always looked like he was enjoying the place.

Bailey Boushay House was founded June 24, 1992. The facility was named after Thatcher Bailey, a founding donor, and his partner, Frank Boushay, who died of AIDS in 1989.

Nowadays, since there are many fewer deaths from AIDS, the thirty-five-bed inpatient program at Bailey Boushay House serves patients who has a variety of life-threatening diagnoses, such as ALS and Huntington's disease. BB provides long-term care, respite care, and end-of-life care. The outpatient day health program serves patients with HIV who are capable of living independently in the community but require medication management and social support.

I recall hearing about the idea for Bailey Boushay before I was ever part of the AIDS community, probably in early 1990. The neighbors around the proposed site made a huge stink. They suggested drug use would be rampant and the whole area would be trashed. Then one storeowner (I don't recall which) came out in favor of the facility. She put a jar in her store, encouraging customers to contribute to the fund for building the place. In my memory, that turned things around. I admired the bravery of that woman. Wikipedia suggests ACT UP also had a big part in the change of heart of the neighborhood.

One of the first patients to move to BB in 1992 was also a patient at Madison Clinic. Damien had a cancer in his lower back. I don't know if massage helped, but being touched and cared for did. He was a sweet man and a favorite among the nurses and other staff at Madison Clinic. He had a row of photos in his apartment. I recognized all of the faces from the clinic. He knew that he was loved at the end even though his family wasn't around. We heard that he had moved into Bailey Boushay. The nurse manager of the clinic called there to ask what room he was in. The BB stuff gave out no information. They wouldn't even admit that he was there. (This was before HIPAA, which was enacted in 1996). I think they softened their stance about giving information to medical people after that conversation.

The large building (beige brick and siding) on the corner of Madison and ML King is partly surrounded by trees and shrubbery. The first floor houses office space and an area for day programs. Anyone who comes in either the front door or the back (next to the parking for a dozen cars) must stop at the desk before being allowed to progress any further.

The thirty-five inpatient rooms at Bailey Boushay are situated on the second and third floors of the building. We discovered when we attempted to visit patients that we had to get approval from the front desk to get on the elevator (after being buzzed into the building). Each patient was asked to provide a list of people who were welcome to visit. If your name was not on the list, you couldn't visit.

Although this was sometimes annoying, this policy was a wonderful thing for the patients living there. People in hospitals seemed to have no way to protect themselves from unwanted visitors. On the other hand, John wanted everyone to visit. Rather than offering a list, he asked the Bailey Boushay staff to put a note on his chart that anyone wanting to visit him should be allowed to go up on the elevator. They agreed. John had many visitors between family, friends, and caregivers. A Buddhist group came in to chant for an hour or more once each week.

Each patient room is large enough for a bed, a dresser, shelves, a long and wide couch under a big window, and extra space for medical equipment. Residents are encouraged to bring in special things from their homes, including pictures for the walls. There are no visiting hours. Visitors can spend all day and all night if they want. The window couch is large enough for comfortable sleeping.

When John was dying, his friends took shifts spending days and nights with him. He did not want to be alone when he died. Once, when I was spending the night, after a day when John seemed disconnected from people and life, he woke in the middle of the night and called my name. Somehow he knew that I was there, and he would have known if someone else had been there.

Because of John, the staff may have second-guessed themselves about encouraging patients to bring whatever personal possessions they wanted to their rooms in Bailey Boushay. They eventually had to tell John to remove some of the special statues and other items. Staff had to dodge all his stuff when they moved around the room while taking care of him. In that way, he was successful in replicating the appearance and feeling of his apartment although I don't think he planned it to be an obstacle course. He always burned incense and candles in his apartment. He didn't win that argument at Bailey Boushay. He wasn't given permission to use candles and incense (but did it on the sly).

John's dog, Mo, lived with John's sister. She often brought the dog to visit, which was allowed. Pets couldn't live there but could visit any time. Mo tended to bark when anyone walked by. He didn't seem (to me) to be comfortable on the bed with John and loved when anyone would take him out for a walk. I wondered if he was worried about his alpha person being increasingly incapacitated.

John once asked me to take him over to look at his apartment after he had moved to BB. It was a sad place without all his treasures and without him. He never wanted to go back again. However, he insisted on holding on to it (thinking he might get better) until after he died.

Bailey Boushay was (probably still is) staffed at a very high level. I think there may have been more staff people than patients, including one nurse for every five patients. John wasn't able to walk when he moved there from his apartment. The staff at BB helped him with walking, escorting him up and down the hall several times each day. He worked hard to achieve the goal of walking again but was never able to walk independently or any great distance and eventually let it go.

Even with high staffing, visitors still could help out with caregiving. Ukon, a Buddhist monk, began visiting and lovingly caring for John even before he moved to the hospice. He continued to visit, often arriving early in the morning to help John with breakfast. I often got roped into helping with dinner, including ordering and picking up food from a nearby restaurant (Broadway American Grill). One of the owners of that restaurant liked John a lot and comped his meals. They usually sent enough food that all of us who were visiting could eat with him. BB had food, which seemed decent, but John liked to order out.

John also had me go with him into the regular dining room on some occasions. He claimed that I could eat whatever I wanted from the buffet. I was never comfortable with that and didn't investigate the policy of Bailey Boushay. I can't imagine that they were ready to feed all visitors. At the same time, the buffet was generous and many of the residents couldn't eat much, so I guess a lot of food got wasted.

Many of the patients living at Bailey Boushay were devoted to their plants and brought them to their rooms. John especially loved white Phalaenopsis orchids. He brought a couple with him from his apartment and acquired at least one more while he was living at BB.

One of the rooms in the building was devoted to plants and set up as a greenhouse. A table in the middle as well as shelves on the side held a variety of plants. John often asked to be wheeled into that room. He thought being with plants was healing. He could sit quietly and sometimes doze in perfect contentment. I guess that his orchids joined the others in the plant room after he died.

Twenty years later, after Mom died, we needed to figure out what to do with her orange tree. Dad had bought it for her more than thirty years earlier. None of us in the family really wanted to take it on. With the approval of other family members, I called BB and asked if they wanted to adopt the orange tree. This suggestion was greeted with enthusiasm. My brother took it over to the building. I like to think the orange tree keeps the memory of both Mom and John alive.

Another special room, not quite so healing, was available for patients who were smokers. The door was always kept shut. I was in there once with a patient who smoked (not John), and it was extremely unpleasant. Some time after that, they must have changed the rules and smokers stood outside the building. Sometimes the smokers were in wheelchairs and wearing hospital gowns. Now I see on the website that they don't allow smokers to move in to BB.

A room at the end of the second floor was devoted to art, including having many art supplies. I guess that patients were free to use it when the volunteer wasn't there. Once or twice a week, a volunteer came into the building to do art projects with residents who were able to get around enough to participate. John was enthusiastic about the art projects and roped me into taking part a few times.

Another room had lots of windows to let sun in from three sides and from above. This was the room John preferred for his massages (both from me and from others who came in to help him). This was also the room we used when we had a care conference for John. His doctor sat with family members and close friends and let us know that John's thinking had slowed but he was still competent.

I could be wrong, but in my memory, there was another room on the third floor that was designated as a chapel or a quiet room. I don't recall ever going there with John, but I went in there after he died. This is when I saw that various people had contributed memorial items for others who had died. John's sister and I both put up memorials to John. I wonder if that still exists. And I wonder if the wall of photos on the first floor still exists. Since HIPAA, both may have been discontinued.

John, while he was there, took advantage of every possible opportunity Bailey Boushay offered. He enjoyed being there even though he had resisted the move.

When I was a hospice volunteer, I visited one of my patients (had cancer) there. He and his family were grateful for the care there. Bailey Boushay has shown us what end of life care can look like at best. It is part of Virginia Mason Hospital now. I'm glad to know it is there for others who need care before dying.

==========

We Dance

John wanted to see the sunset on that December day,
We started to prepare in the early afternoon.
I dressed him in loose sweats, socks, and moccasins as he lay on the bed;
He was long past being able to dress himself.

The staff taught us the dance we needed to transfer him from bed to wheelchair,
His arms around my neck, my arms around his waist,
One-two-three sitting up in bed and turning to sit on the edge,
One-two-three standing up as I stepped backward,
One-two-three turning together,
One-two-three into the wheelchair.

Next his jacket and hat, checking his mustache for crumbs,
Faces inches apart, an exchange of "I love you" and off we went,
Stopping at the front desk to share our intention and then to the elevator,
Downstairs and out the door to the car, and the dance in reverse.

We drove holding hands and talking quietly about my day,
Down one hill and up another to the top of Queen Anne Hill,
Parked by the side of the road where we could see down to the water,
And the magnificent colors filling the sky.

He wanted to get out, to stand by the car, to see more.
Arms in place, one-two-three, stand and pivot.
He looked fiercely at the glowing sunset and then back to me,
Kissed me hard unexpectedly.

==========

Sweetness
(For Damein O.)

Long curly hair was his pride
I've been told
Tufts and that straight
Were all that survived chemo
All that I saw
He always had rings on his hands
A gentle, seductive way about him

He hired me to do massage

At his home
He lived in a low-income high rise
His possessions were few
With just a few photos
The people he loved, who loved him
Were all employees at the AIDS clinic

Damein died in a lonely bed
At Bailey-Boushay, the AIDS hospice
His legs were swollen
Like those of an elephant
The result of rectal cancer
To the end, he was sweetly gentle
Wanted to reassure me

==========

Ghosts
(For Bailey-Boushay)

Once John P. decorated his room with
Masks
A zebra rug
Artifacts from his travels
Greens and blues and blacks were vibrant

Wide halls are filled with pale sky and earth colors
Gray, brown, beige, sand, cream, blue blend together

Once John N. filled his room with
Gold
Buddhas on posters
Guests coming and going
Always the background sound of chants

Nurses talk quietly behind a desk in the middle
Emerge to answer the call button from a patient

Once Aaron zoomed across the
Linoleum
Dangerous in
His electric wheelchair
Then back to his room filled with rock stars

Patients are all neatly stowed in their rooms
Guests tiptoe and whisper, not many at that

A Buddhist monk was often there
In saffron robes
Helping his friend
Talking with other visitors
Or patients walking eating talking living

Religious books are stowed away in the room
Down the elevator you go for meditation

==========

An Obituary

dead at forty-five after a long illness
in what was once the AIDS hospice

we read of struggling eleven years
while concert master of a local symphony
leaves behind parents and a sister
no name given to the deadly disease

but we who know, who read the clues
have no doubt the virus got him

==========

They Knew
(John)

The rule we know:
no candles
no incense.
If we shut the door
no one will say a word.
Five minutes
of sweet smoke,
time to gaze
into the flame,
to center again,
Limit the time.
No one will notice.
No one needs to know.

==========

Solar System
(John)

at the center of it all, the force that holds us
in place, shifting
pulled by words and demands
lined up
to rearrange possessions
to take him out to eat or to bring food in
holding him,
holding him in this life
breathing hope,
talking with each other
notes to share with the next person
brought together by him,
brought together by his intent
that we should be
a living safety net to keep him with us,
with us in this life,

revolving around him
for the last time at the funeral home
his belongings
his treasures
his ashes
scattered at the end, the center gone

==========

Hospice Months
(John)

He clung mightily to his apartment.
He would not speak of death;
living here he could not die. At last
he had to go, to give in, to accept care.
He would go, go to live, not to die,
to gather a circle of friends, new and old,
to hold court among caregivers,
to fill and shape the space he chose,
over time to loosen his grip,
on all that was meant to save his life.
He was dying, and life was good again

Raymond Learned He Was Loved

A photo of Raymond sits on my bookshelf. He is sitting in his living room, surrounded by Christmas kitsch. (His parents used this same photo on the program for his funeral

Tucked into a corner of the photo is a quote from another Raymond, Raymond Carver. Carver says,

> And did you get what
> you wanted from this life, even so?
> I did.
> And what did you want?
> To call myself beloved, to feel myself
> beloved on the earth.

All Raymond really wanted in the end was the love of his family.

I met Raymond in the fall of '92 when I was still in massage school. He was thirty-eight years old and had full-blown AIDS. He died six months later. During the six months of our friendship, I gave him regular massages, first at Madison Clinic and later at his house.

Raymond's social worker encouraged him to sign up for chair massage when I volunteered at Madison Clinic on Tuesdays. With his permission, she put his name on the list. As was my practice, I went out into the waiting room to look for him when it was his turn. He was thin and quiet, sitting next to an older man. His social worker said that his father brought him to all his appointments. Even though the two men were side by side, they didn't look at each other or talk. Raymond's father politely and definitely declined when I offered to give him a massage as well.

The first massage was quiet and strictly business. Raymond answered my questions regarding the pressure he wanted and the focus. He agreed to sign up again when he had another appointment.

We talked more during the next massage. He used to be a massage therapist. We agreed that I would give him massages at his house in exchange for feedback to improve my techniques. He still had his massage table set up in one of the bedrooms of his house. We talked about massage. He had gotten discouraged with trying to build a practice doing Swedish massage. I came to his house to give him massages every week after those first few times.

Raymond owned a house on Cherry, near Twentieth, not a big house but pretty. I think his house was yellow. It wasn't a large house but dated back to early twentieth-century Seattle. The lot was small and included a little garden in the back of the house. Even though he was very sick, he began planning his garden in the early spring. His father encouraged him to order seeds and tools. I think his father planted the seeds for Raymond before he died in April.

After he stopped doing massage, he had a little store where he sold antiques (or at least secondhand items that appealed to him). I don't know where the store was, but he had given it up when he got sick.

In among my mementos of the AIDS years, I found a pamphlet that Raymond put together in 1992, "a guide to Puget area thrift stores." On the back, he asks people to send $5 to buy a copy of the guide. The address he gives is on Twenty-First Avenue. I guess that was his house. He planned to put out another guide the next year. Inside the cover, he talks about the fun and value of shopping at thrift stores. The booklet starts with a map and then lists stores by area (Snohomish County, Greater Seattle, etc.). After those listings, he notes the various places that stores with multiple outlets (such as Value Village) can be found. He concludes with an index.

Over time, Raymond began talking about his parents and the rest of his family. He said they had rejected him when the learned that he was gay. Being gay didn't fit into their religious beliefs. He belonged to the same church when he was young but rejected the church as an adult since the church rejected him. He changed his name from his birth name. Perhaps he was rejecting his family? Perhaps he was letting them know that people wouldn't realize he was related to them with the different name.

He didn't disappear completely. Somehow he kept enough connection that he told his family about having AIDS. His parents didn't talk about the disease. He was sure they didn't tell any of their friends and neighbors. They lived in the same community all of Raymond's life.

Despite all that, his parents came over to Seattle on the ferry from Bremerton to stay with him a couple of days each week. They drove him to medical appointments. His father did renovations on his house to help him as his health failed. He still had a long staircase. I think mostly his father put in extra storage and probably made sure he had groceries for the rest of the week.

We never talked about how he got HIV, and we didn't talk about any relationships. I guess that he wasn't a drug user and the virus was sexually transmitted. I would have listened if he had talked about relationships, but I didn't like to ask questions. Asking about how someone got HIV seemed intrusive to me. Asking about relationships may have been uncomfortable. I wish I had felt comfortable about asking and especially about following up when anyone brought up the topic. Jack and John mentioned past relationships and perhaps would have liked if I had asked. Raymond talked about disappointment in family relationships. Maybe that was what was important to him at the time. Others, especially Jack, seemed most interested in talking about their families as well.

Sometimes Raymond and I spent time together in addition to the massage dates. Once, he introduced me to his favorite sandwich shop on Madison (George's Sausage and Delicatessen). The owner is Polish, and the shop has been there for years. When we went there, we picked out sandwiches, which Raymond paid for. We took them back to his house to eat.

When we talked, I expressed my opinions. I thought his parents showed their love for him by their actions, even if they had rejected him with words years before. Spending time with him, fixing up his house, and driving him to appointments was a clear sign of love, in my opinion. When Valentine's Day came around that year, Ray made beautiful valentines for his parents and his sisters, thanking them for caring for him. He also made one for me.

I looked for and found the Valentine card he made for me. It is on pink paper with a silver heart on the front (signed Raymond, '93). He had cut out a pattern of squares on the heart. No, actually, the foil is woven with the pink paper of the card. Inside, he wrote, "I've learned a thing or two—about accepting love from you—but I'm not finished yet. Happy Valentine's Day. Love, Raymond."

Not long after that, he came up with the idea of hosting a dinner to thank all the people who were helping him as he struggled with AIDS. He put together his favorite recipes into a booklet as he planned the event. I still have the booklet he gave me, although I've never made any of the recipes. I looked for the booklet and couldn't find it, but I'm sure it's here somewhere.

Then Raymond had a crisis and ended up in the hospital for several days. I have another note, probably from right after he was in the ICU, dated March 23: "Dear Margaret, just a friendly thank you for all you've done for me. I've learned love and patience that I didn't know I experienced. As serious as this episode has been, I trust that I'm not expiring just yet. And you'll remain an important part of my life. I feel that I have to remind you that I'm still limited in how much I can accept from the world—you know that. But my acceptance has escalated. Bless you. Love, Raymond."

I don't remember now in what way I may have been pushing him at the time. I appreciated the gentle warning along with his warmth.

As it turned out, Raymond actually was expiring, less than two weeks after that note. He wasn't able to eat much even when I first knew him. Later, he depended on a nightly IV food delivery. When he died, his father found him in the morning still attached to the IV.

Raymond worried about his death. He wasn't worried about dying or even about being dead. He was worried about what sort of funeral service his family would put together. He was brought up in a fundamentalist Christian Church. His parents and sisters still belonged to that church. He imagined a funeral service in the church that he had left behind years ago. He imagined being eulogized as a true Christian when that was far from what he believed.

In the end, he had something much closer to who he really was. His parents had paid attention. They invited their minister to lead the memorial service, and they asked various people, including me, to speak at the service (at the Stimson-Green Mansion). The service wasn't particularly Christian, although the minister included some prayers.

As I wrote this, I wished I could remember what I said about him when I spoke at his memorial service. I knew that I didn't say anything about his being gay or having AIDs. I don't think his parents asked me not to. I think I just decided to honor their caring for him and not embarrass them. I knew that many of their friends and neighbors would be at the service.

When I was searching through keepsakes, I found the order of his memorial service, plus notes for the speech I gave: "Friendship with Raymond—time with Raymond—including sitting quietly in the hospital brought happiness and peace to me. Raymond and I came together because of massage and because of his illness. We shared the belief that touch is as important as food and air. (Cats think so too—maybe that's why we both had cats.) I wanted to get better at massage and better at working with people who are ill. He was happy to accept massage and to teach me. That's what we did. And, more important, our souls touched—in growing openness, honesty, and love. His courage and ability to live what was real will always stay with me. He planned a garden, a dinner party, fixing up his house—and a memorial service, disposing of his belongings, choices of treatments. He believed in life and regretted that his was coming to an end. He was extremely happy and peaceful because of the outpouring of love he felt. And because he was free to love all of us in return."

Raymond hadn't lived long enough to create the dinner he planned. However, his parents hired caterers to make the meal as part of his funeral. They also gave away audiotapes of Raymond playing the piano and many photos. They loved him and knew that he loved them. (They used his full birth name on the program and on the tapes.)

As I expected, the group gathered for the funeral included family, as well as longtime family friends. Several caregivers from Madison Clinic were there, including Raymond's social worker and the nurse manager of the clinic. During the social time after the service and during the meal, Raymond's parents gravitated to the Madison Clinic group. I wonder if they felt most comfortable with those who had been there to the end and who knew about AIDS. Maybe they wanted to be close, to make sure we didn't tell the neighbors about AIDS?

After he died, his parents gave me his massage table. I used it for several years until it literally fell apart, with a client on it. Luckily, she wasn't hurt and laughed about it. I tossed out the table, but still have the headrest on a shelf in my office.

I have a thank-you note from his parents, in which they said they found the carrying case for his massage table. They wanted me to have it. And one more letter from them in December 1993, with a Hanukkah card. His mother shared their Christmas plans and reported that Ray's friend marched in an AIDS walkathon. I hope I wrote back to her, but I don't recall.

Since that was twenty-five years ago, I guess his parents must be in their nineties now, if they are still living. I'm glad my friendship with their son helped to ease the end of his life for them. Perhaps his parents were changed even before I came along, by seeing the way the staff at Madison Clinic loved him even though he was gay and had AIDS.

==========

Always Raymond

We met in February

> a wide smile and buoyant manner
> irresistible, full of enthusiasm
> loving my stories of massage school
> where he had gone six years before
> then he disappeared for months

He appeared again in May

> thinner, with dark splotches of sarcoma
> darkening his cheeks, still he smiled
> my heart drawn to such simple joy
> I offered him a gift of weekly massage
> in exchange for careful feedback

He agreed in August

==========

East Cherry (Raymond)

> For months I drove past and thought of him
> craned to see his house as I passed
> noticed the "For Sale" sign out front
> and when it disappeared.
>
> All the memories of seeing his smile
> as he grew weaker over a year
> The early morning phone call
> telling me his life was over
>
> Wondered how his garden turned out
> Thought about his parents and sisters

Going on with life
The house halted my heart

==========

Never Too late (Raymond)

he spoke of grief
separation
from Mom, Dad, and sisters
what kind of healing
for the dying
not much living left
came to know
he was loved
as best as they could
could tell them of his love
no time to go
on, enough to know

Caring for Myself

When I look at my feet, side by side, propped up at the end of the bathtub, I notice how different they are—left and right, bad and good.

I make list and notes of life events and people. On one of the lists, I can locate the year of my broken ankle, the first broken bone of my life, when I was almost forty-eight. I had fallen many times before, as well as banging into walls and tripping over furniture. I broke my left ankle.

(I don't always know where my body is in the world, or where furniture, sidewalks, or walls are.)

It was a beautiful day in September (1992), sunny and not too hot. John asked me to take him and Mo (his Lhasa apso) down to Madison Park. We parked near the beach. John asked me to take Mo down into the park to do his business. John walked with some difficulty and with the help of a cane, so he stayed above as the dog and I went down the wooden steps, sunk into the path down the hill. I slipped and fell, with my weight landing on my ankle beneath me. Nothing hurt, but the foot hung off the end of the leg. It flopped on its own. I knew I couldn't stand on it. I knew the ankle was broken. I guess the step was defective, but I wasn't really watching as I walked down.

John asked for help from the people nearby. Someone stepped up and called 911. An ambulance came to take me to Group Health. The EMTs agreed to take John and Mo home to Capitol Park, just blocks from Group Health. (Possibly they wouldn't do that nowadays, especially taking the dog.)

As I rode in the ambulance, I realized that I was relieved that no one could expect anything of me now. I recognized how overwhelmed I felt by my massage practice, the needs of John and Shawn (both living with AIDS), and home needs (shopping, cooking, cleaning, laundry). I never felt okay about saying no. Now, I had the right. Now people had to accept I couldn't do everything. The sense of relief was stronger than the pain. I decided to remember in the future and limit how much I offered.

Mike was on a business trip. This was in the years before cell phones became commonplace. Somehow I got in touch with Charlie, head nurse at Madison Clinic. Charlie called Jacob (aged fourteen) when he got home from school and later brought him to visit me at the hospital. I guess Jacob stayed alone at the house. Rebecca was away at college. Maybe Jacob would remember.

Even though I couldn't walk, I wasn't in any pain. The examination at Urgent Care included an X-ray. The doctor who read the X-ray determined that I needed surgery. This was scheduled for the following day.

The surgery included putting in a metal plate. When I woke up, I was in excruciating pain. They gave me morphine for the pain. That helped, but by the next morning, I was nauseated and itching all over. Then they began trying out other pain medications. Tylenol with codeine was effective for the pain. Unfortunately, I would get comfortable and then muscles would spasm ratcheting the pain back up. After discussion, Valium was added to stop the muscle spasms. That was effective, and I was pretty happy.

(I ran out of the Tylenol with codeine and the Valium a few weeks after breaking the ankle. Then I realized how much I liked the floaty feeling the medications gave me. And I decided it was a good thing to run out and not have the option of taking more.)

Mom came to see me in the hospital. My brother Scott brought me reading materials. I had never read the *National Enquirer* before. I was pretty dopey from the pain medication. The *National Enquirer* was about the right reading level for my brain on pain meds. My friend Bobby (who had AIDS) also brought me reading materials—serious books about yoga—and was horrified by the *National Enquirer*.

I was sent home from the hospital in a couple of days, with crutches and instructions to keep off the foot completely for a couple of weeks until they could put on a walking cast. The crutches were awful. They dug into my underarms. I was terrified to go up or downstairs on the crutches. A nurse came from Group Health to check on how I was doing. I told her about my problems with the crutches. She then got me a walker that could handle stairs. I liked the freedom of being able to get around my house as well as going down the front stairs to go other places.

(Loaning out crutches or walkers seems to be a thing of the past. People are expected to buy them, I think. Back when Mike and I were dating, we borrowed a wheelchair from Group Health for a class, so he could find out how people treated him when he was in a wheelchair. They wouldn't do that now. We found out that he became invisible in the wheelchair.)

Shawn called and asked if I wanted him to come and help me wash my hair. I agreed. He washed my hair at the kitchen sink. My left knee rested on a chair. I guess I could have done it myself. Having someone take care of me felt novel and comforting.

As soon as I had a walking cast, I went back to doing massage at Harborview and other places. No one objected, as I carried around my massage table and bag with a cast on my left leg. I even went back to driving. Luckily, parking was easier in those days than it is now. I guess I forgot the lesson about not demanding so much of myself.

(I took John to get acupuncture. Denise saw us there before she knew me, as we went up the stairs. I was helping him, but looked like I was in worse shape, she said. Hence she remembered us. We didn't actually meet until two years later.)

The cast came off in six weeks. I thought everything would be fixed, and then I tried to stand up and walk. My leg wanted to collapse. It began to remember how to hold me up even then as I walked down the hall. I recovered quickly without physical therapy. Probably continuing to walk during the weeks I had a walking cast helped. Dried-up skin came off in sheets for a week or two.

The ankle has never fully recovered. It was swollen for years and still is a little. The foot looks different too, with even more broken blood vessels than my ordinary old right foot. I can't stand on that foot as long as the other. Probably the metal piece should have come out years ago, but I won't do anything now.

(To my surprise, the metal plate in my ankle and the metal plate in my wrist have never caused a problem in airports. I guess they see them and know what they are.)

The next time I had a broken bone was in 2000. We went up to Vancouver BC for Mom's eightieth birthday. Many of us took the train. I had a heavy backpack on and was pushing a suitcase. I didn't see that someone had put a guitar on the ground (not watching where I was walking). I tripped and fell on my shoulder, with the backpack adding weight to the event. Gigi and Dolores stayed with me through urgent care there, which took hours. Eventually I had a sling (taking the weight of the arm off the broken shoulder helped enormously to decrease the pain) and Vicodin (also helped).

By the time we were back in Seattle (two days), I was beginning to have a serious side effect from the opiate—constipation. It got so bad that I couldn't walk. It was worse than the pain of the shoulder. Denise drove me to Group Health, and I begged for the liquid used in preparation for a colonoscopy. It was effective at cleaning me out, and I was very happy.

Luckily, the broken shoulder happened after I stopped doing massage and before I did anything else. I had plenty of time for rest and later for physical therapy. The doctor encouraged me to continue activities such as writing or typing on my computer even right after the break while the arm was in the sling and insisted that I work hard on physical therapy to make sure I got back the full range of motion (I did).

You would think I'd learned my lesson by then, to watch where I was walking. But no, I forgot again, twice in one year (2006).

The first time, Mom and I were walking together, down on Federal where wet leaves had been allowed to stay on the sidewalk, blurring the edges. I stepped off the sidewalk, slipped, and ended up banging my knee hard enough to break the patella. I couldn't walk home, so Mom walked up the hill and got Denise to take me in to Group Health. I could walk enough to get from the car into Urgent Care, with lots of pain. I chose not to have opiates this time and just to depend on Tylenol. I didn't want to get constipated. The pain wasn't terrible once I got the splint.

After an X-ray, they provided me with a splint, designed to keep the leg straight from groin to ankle. I was allowed to take it off for showering but was told not to bend the knee. The parts of the patella were lined up and would heal properly as long as they stayed that way. I was supposed to keep the splint on while sleeping. Walking wasn't much of a problem, but lying down was. That shifted the splint just enough that it dug painfully into my groin. After a week or two, I went back into Group Health and asked for a shorter splint to ease that problem. They had one and it worked.

The doctor prescribed physical therapy after six weeks. This partly meant learning to get up off the floor without using my hands. The physical therapist also told me to stand on one foot, each foot, for a minute. That was way too hard and I still can't do it, but I'm still working on it. Balance and getting up from the floor without holding anything are both part of my regular yoga routine. I told Jacob at the time, and he showed off how he could stand on one foot for much longer than a minute.

Not long after my knee was back to functioning, I went to a lecture at the Seattle Art Museum in Volunteer Park. It had something to do with a relative of my friend Kumi. After the lecture, Mom, Denise, Rebecca, and I walked down the curving sidewalk from the museum. I wasn't watching and stepped off the edge. This time, I put my hand out to protect my knee from the fall—the classic way, I now know, to break a wrist. At least this time I was able to walk over to Group Health on my own, accompanied by Denise.

As with the broken ankle, I had surgery and then a piece of metal inserted. The wrist is not as good as it was originally, but it works. I have a scar down my inner arm. Again, I had physical therapy. Before that, I learned to write with my left hand (barely legible) and to use my left hand on the computer.

One of the odd things, I think, is that I broke my left ankle and knee, but my right shoulder and wrist. I've thought I might be right handed and left footed. Maybe.

Someone told me that a car is never the same after being in an accident. Seems that the body is the same way. Mine carries the history of falls caused by inattention. I had a scar on my forehead for years from a conflict with a toddler friend and one on my knee from running into a packing box in college. Probably if someone looked really closely, those scars would still be visible. I don't mind.

I keep hoping to remember to care for myself as I move through life. I thank John for pushing me to the point that I had to realize self-care is important. I remembered this lesson later when he wanted his sister and me to be his full-time caregivers. I thank Bobby for recognizing that a broken ankle was a big deal, even if not as bad as AIDS. And I thank Shawn for stepping up and helping me when I needed help. And I still forget to watch where I'm going sometimes. However, I know a little more about saying no and am more willing to do so.

Caregivers beyond Doctors

When I spent time among people with AIDS, I saw many helpers beyond the doctors. The doctors are important and are far outnumbered by other caregivers.

Pain relief is more than medications. John was an advocate of every kind of alternative treatment for pain. On his own, he used vibrators and Tenz units for pain. He got chiropractic adjustments, massages, and acupuncture. He also got energy treatments (such as Reiki). He didn't pay for any of those treatments.

Not every alternative treatment was readily available for free. Lee liked to save money and try one "miracle cure" each year. One time, it was shark cartilage. I don't know if this was in an injection or eaten. Shawn also was drawn to miracle cures. He especially liked the idea of exchanging blood to reset the immune system. He also thought that extra oxygen added to the blood would kill the HIV virus. He wasn't able to access either of these alternative treatments. He insisted that methamphetamines kept him healthy. He found ways to keep taking meth (and lived a long time with AIDS). He speculated that the government deliberately infected gay men and got them addicted to speed.

The first time Denise saw John and me was when we were headed up a long flight of stairs so that he could get a free acupuncture treatment. This was in a building on Twelfth and Union (long gone) that hosted a variety of New Age practitioners. At the time, John used a cane. I had broken my ankle. I had a cast and was using a walker (happily, one that worked on stairs). Denise noticed us especially since she wondered which one of us was helping the other. I think this was in the fall of 1992. The volunteer who did the treatments was a longtime practitioner, who also brought students to help. Denise and I didn't meet until 1994, after John had died in February of that year.

The acupuncture clinic moved at some point to the Forty-Fifth Street clinic, in Wallingford (or perhaps that was a different group). They still offered free or low-cost acupuncture to people living with AIDS. Acupuncture seemed to be especially helpful for neuropathy (which was common in the feet and legs of people with AIDS). I remember driving another man who was living with AIDS to that clinic. While we were sitting in the waiting room, a couple of other people I knew came in for treatment. (I see online now that acupuncture is recognized as a treatment for diabetic neuropathy.)

John also made use of the free massage offered by one of the organizations functioning at that time, "In Touch." I think the patients were offered massage every other week. Patients generally went to the massage practitioners. I drove John to get massage from his volunteer over near the UW. Her massage room was up a long staircase. John climbed those stairs as long as he could and eventually had to stop seeing her when he couldn't make it up the stairs. Lee also got massage from a volunteer with that organization. I think his volunteer came to his house. I didn't hear about anyone else who accessed those services. Unfortunately, the organization didn't do a good job of advertising who they were. I don't know whether they had many massage therapists available. I would have volunteered or donated money if I had ever been asked, but I wasn't.

I never heard about any organized effort to provide chiropractic adjustments to people with AIDS. I think John simply found several practitioners and persuaded them to volunteer their treatments. He was always willing to ask. I thought he felt people were lucky to work with him. One person he saw was in a clinic on E John (about Boylston). Luckily, they had a parking lot. Parking was already difficult in that neighborhood. The other was near Swedish Hospital, just off Broadway on a steep hill. Parking was easier there, probably because Swedish Hospital has its own parking.

John also went to someone who provided energy work to him. I am certain that he didn't pay her anything either. This was also true, I think, of the people who advised him about Ayurvedic medicine (and using ground-up gems for treatments).

Shanti provided John with spiritual support. He liked his volunteer and commented that she was very young (a college student, I think). He was in his forties and thought she sometimes didn't understand his world very well.

Individual agencies offered massage, spiritual support, acupuncture, and other services. For instance, the Red Cross provided training for family (and friend) caregivers. SASG offered support groups and a weekly free dinner. Other times, volunteer assistance was consolidated in various organizations. For instance, the Northwest AIDS Foundation offered assistance with housing, help in qualifying for SSI, counseling, and other help. NWAF case managers told people about other assistance that was available. Chicken Soup Brigade provided food delivery and rides to appointments.

Having transportation to appointments is a huge part of living with any kind of disease, especially for people who don't have much money. It's even more difficult for people with AIDS since there was, and still is to a lesser degree, a huge stigma. Some patients connected with a volunteer and ended up getting many rides from the same person. In the end, I drove Jack to all his appointments. And there were others who depended on me for most rides. At the same time, I made some one-way trips, simply taking patients to appointments (or home). I didn't have a sense of connection with those people since someone else drove the other part of the trip. And I never heard from them more than once.

I have a vivid memory of taking Rick to an appointment at Swedish. I found parking and then walked him into the hospital. We were waiting for an elevator with a group of people. Rick talked loudly about having AIDS. He was defiant of anyone who might look down on him. Having someone with him may have helped him to feel supported and that he wasn't alone.

Many people volunteered services in an unofficial way. They were often members of the same community, and some were themselves living with AIDS. One of the local veterinarians was living with AIDS and provided low-cost and free care for the pets of people with AIDS. He also often had free pet food available. That service ended when the vet who had AIDS died. Often volunteers knew many people who were receiving services. The volunteers who were HIV positive knew that they might themselves need services someday. They saw the losses of those who were sick, saw them close up, and often invented ways to improve the quality of life for those who were sick.

One person remarked that AIDS was the best thing to have, if you were going to have a fatal disease, because of all the services available. It seemed to me that this might have been leading the way to improve life for all people with fatal diseases. Unfortunately, many of the services have gone away since AIDS became more of a chronic disease. Some have remained. People with other fatal diseases can now access Bailey-Boushay for end-of-life care. Hospices offer many of the supports that were available for people with AIDS: spiritual support, chore services, and volunteers.

Lifelong AIDS Alliance website says, "We also realized over the years that the unique care we have provided to people living with HIV could be crucial to those battling other serious illnesses and poverty. Lifelong expanded in its areas of core competencies to enhance the quality of life for other communities disproportionately affected with health risks and challenges. We now provide a wide array of services to people living with a broad spectrum of illnesses like diabetes, cardiovascular disease, renal disease, cancers, multiple sclerosis, and conditions of aging affecting health and independence." (Interesting that they kept the same name.)

People who were living with AIDS generally lived independently as long as possible (and sometimes beyond that time, when they really shouldn't have been living alone). Some had family and friends who helped them to manage living alone even when they were weak and sick. Others, those who had no one, needed places where they would receive care. Already existing nursing homes were often reluctant (or worse) to accept people with AIDS. That need led to Rosehedge and Bailey-Boushay.

The caregivers at Rosehedge and Bailey-Boushay were mostly paid (although they did have many volunteers). These people (paid or unpaid) cared passionately about the people they cared for. Jayme was a nurse at Rosehedge. She was as likely to sit and play checkers with a patient as to give medical care. She said she had watched hundreds of people die and loved every one of them. She worked at Rosehedge for many years, perhaps until it was closed not too long ago.

My friend Bob (who worked for Chicken Soup Brigade) developed a close friendship with one of the people served by that group. The man was alienated from his family and depended on Bob to bring him food and medications, allowing him to stay in his apartment. Bob drove him to appointments and spent many hours just keeping him company. Finally, the man became extremely weak, and it was clear that he was close to the end of his life. Bob came over to see him one day and found that the family had swooped in and taken over the caregiving. They would not allow Bob to come in. Bob thought that the friend had chosen family over him when the family was finally willing to be there. I was sad for him but not surprised. The same thing (pretty much) happened to me when Steve's family showed up at the end. I guess people most want love and acceptance from family.

The caregivers at the AIDS Clinical Trial Unit were working (still are) to find better treatments and perhaps a vaccine against HIV. People who were associated with the ACTU went to bars and bathhouses to recruit subjects to take part in clinical trials. Subjects hoped to get the new best treatment for free. They took the risk that the treatment wouldn't work. The volunteers also distributed condoms and education about protecting oneself from HIV.

There are many doctors and others who have spent their entire professional lives treating people with AIDS and looking for cures. Others, such as Dr. Abraham Verghese (who wrote an eloquent book about his experiences), worked in the field for a few years and then moved on to other specialties. I felt privileged to know so many strong and caring people, those who stayed in the AIDS field and those who moved on.

Another group of people work in the area of AIDS education. Beth was a social worker at Madison Clinic when we met. She was (and still is) a beautiful woman with long and thick curly hair and a big smile. She loves travel and hiking in her free time. Over the years, she has worked for various groups, sometimes educating people in other countries about AIDS and treatments. Many countries don't have access to treatments or to ways of preventing transmission of HIV.

Beth introduced me to Robin, one of the AIDS patients she cared for. I went to his house to do massage. He lived in a tiny house in Wallingford with his partner, who, as far as I know, did not have AIDS. The only space for setting up my table was in the living room. Pothos vines were supported up the wall and all around the molding by the ceiling.

Beth, like many people who cared for people with AIDS, believed in Western medicine supplemented by complementary treatments to make life better for people living with the disease. I felt a sense of community among all these people and felt fortunate to know them.

Of course, most people weren't interested in all the things John tried. Each person needed to know what was available and make use of the opportunities that improved their quality of life while they were living with AIDS. For example, Shawn had been beaten horribly when he was a child. He wasn't comfortable with any kind of touch by a caregiver. He did accept food and case management, and he lived his last months at Bailey-Boushay.

==========

Addict, Labeled (for Doug M)

Doug alone, on the steps outside the clinic
Head down, smoking a cigarette

I said hello, what's wrong?

Pain, once an addict, no narcotics given
He limped away, on feet clad only in slippers

Sitting with the Dying

When I was a Roman Catholic, I tried to learn to meditate by focusing on specific prayers or thoughts. I became impatient easily and gave up. I didn't know another way to meditate.

It was only years later I found what worked for me and sort of by accident.

During the years from 1990 to 1998, I sat with several men who were dying of AIDS. Sitting with them became an easy task. I learned to sit. I didn't need to talk coherently. I didn't need to have questions answered. I didn't need to talk at all.

In November 1990, we all understood that Michael was close to death from AIDS. He spent most of the time sleeping on the couch in the Rosehedge living room. I sat next to him working the crossword puzzle. We talked a little whenever he woke up.

When he was able to walk, his friend Jackie took him to a Catholic church. It wasn't what he grew up with, but close enough. We talked about my being Jewish. He wanted some way that we could pray together. We realized that I could read Psalms to him. We approached God together through Psalms.

In December, Michael realized he wouldn't see any of the people in his life again once he died. He said how much he would miss everyone. He wanted to thank us all and to say goodbye. He gathered his energy together. Suddenly he was able to stand and walk (slowly) again. A friend took him shopping for gifts and Christmas cards. I helped him to address the cards, working from his address book. He gave me his favorite pen and a rosary that Jackie had given him.

Luckily, this was all done by the day of the big snowstorm (December 18). Many inches of wet snow fell in the afternoon. Then temperatures went down into the twenties. All that snow froze. Pipes burst, including those at

Rosehedge. The loyal staff stayed the night and made do in rough conditions. I walked the two miles there since my husband Mike drove my four-wheel drive to work. Michael was subdued and barely seemed aware of the situation.

When I came in to visit a few days after Christmas, Michael was no longer talking or interacting in any way. I sat down next to him and held his hand. He was going to die that day or soon. There was nothing more to be done. All I was aware of was our connection in the moment. For me, our connection was a living being. It was God. I felt sure that the connection (God) would continue even after Michael died. For once, I didn't feel any need to plan or think about anything. Sitting quietly was enough and peaceful.

One of the staff people came in and said that possibly Michael couldn't die just yet because he was worried about his sister. If she came in, would I ask her to tell him not to worry, to say she would be okay and it was all right for him to die? I said I would and I did. I left Michael's sister in the room with him. She came out in a couple of minutes. She reported that she had given him the message. He started shaking and frightened her. She left. Michael was dead when I went back into the room.

I went back into the room with the intention of staying until other friends of his arrived. I didn't want to leave his body alone. I guess I didn't want the day to really end for me. I didn't want him to be gone forever. I sat next to him, my hand on his leg that no longer felt anything, for another hour. The time seemed endless and very brief.

When Jackie arrived, she told me that Michael wanted me to have the chain and cross he always wore. I took it home with me. I knew I would never wear the cross, so I found another chain. I put my Jewish star onto Michael's chain and the cross onto my chain. I gave the cross and chain to Jackie. I think Jackie and I still have a connection, many years since we saw each other last.

When Michael was dying, sitting with him was not meditation to me. At least I didn't think of it as meditation. Now I think it was the first time I ever meditated. I was focused on something other than thinking. I brought myself back to focus on him many times, but the feeling was so intense that it didn't seem difficult. I just was present with him and in those moments without any words.

Six months into our friendship, in the spring of 1993, Raymond's parents called to let me know that he was in intensive care at Harborview. I headed over to the hospital and to the unit. The parents took a break from the room when I arrived. They encouraged me to go into the room. Neither the parents nor the staff said why he was in the hospital. Raymond was lying quietly in a bed and didn't respond at all when I quietly stood next to him and said, "Raymond, it's Margaret here."

There was no chair in the room, so I sat down on the floor near the bed. Again (like with Michael) there was nothing to do. I decided to clear a space and just be silent there with him. He might have been dying, but I didn't know. I hadn't brought anything to read (a long time before smart phones). I listened to the sound of his breathing and watched the gentle rise and fall of the sheets. I seemed to drift on the breath and the movement of his chest.

His parents came back into the room about an hour later. They indicated I could stay if I wished. They were heading back to their home since Raymond didn't seem to be dying. In fact, he wasn't at that time. He recovered and went home in two days, but then died a couple of weeks later.

Sitting with Raymond that day in the hospital almost seemed like an extension of all the massages I did on him. He usually was quiet during the massages. All there was between us was my hands and his body. Nothing else was in my mind.

Raymond rejected the church he grew up in and never talked about an alternative. The church condemned homosexuality. He tried for years to accept and be part of that church, but couldn't in the end. However, he was able to accept the love and care of his parents. Love without harsh words was enough. Maybe silent presence brought comfort to him.

When I was first in John's apartment, he showed me a kind of cage that was supposed to be healing for him and a place for him to meditate. It seemed very odd to me, and I don't recall the details. At some point, it disappeared from the apartment, and we never discussed it. (I looked around online just now and can't find anything related to this idea.)

His apartment as a whole was kind of a meditation space. Buddhas, incense, candles, chanting, gongs, and draped fabrics shaped his environment. He loved having white orchids to enhance it all.

John was a Buddhist by choice, not what he was brought up with. He really wanted me to become a Buddhist as well. He talked about the major tenets. He talked especially about the concept that pain is part of life while suffering is optional. He was frustrated with himself since he couldn't maintain that peace of mind. John asked me to read the book *Healing into Life and Death* by Stephen Levine. He then asked me to copy, for him, the chapter about meditating on and isolating pain. I copied it, read it to him, and left it with him. He also introduced me to Ram Dass and his books. Having a common language was good for John and me, but I didn't want to be a Buddhist.

Many of John's friends were Buddhists. They invested him as a Buddhist monk close to the end of his life. A group of them came to chant in his room at Bailey-Boushay during his last weeks. He invited his friends to come and join in the chanting. I never did, and I was glad he had that comfort in his life. John stopped fighting against AIDS and the idea of dying in those last weeks of his life. Perhaps he came to fully accept that he was creating his own suffering by refusing to accept his path? He seemed to be at peace when he died in early 1994.

Talking about Buddhism didn't teach me much about meditation. The times with John that seem the most meditative to me now are the hours we spent in Lakeview Cemetery. John wanted to enjoy the sun. He thought the sun would heal him (and wished he could have moved to Hawaii). He was sure the sun lingered longer in the cemetery than anywhere else in the city. He was perfectly comfortable sitting among the graves. Sometimes we sat together. We often had music playing (mostly Hindu or Tibetan chants). We didn't talk much. Sometimes he seemed to doze. I walked among the gravestones, reading them and feeling the presence of people long gone from the planet.

John died while I was meeting Steve for the first time. John didn't want to be alone when he died. We made sure that people were there with him day and night. His friend Stephen was with him when he died. I went to Bailey-Boushay on my way home from seeing Steve and learned that John had died. He had arranged for his body to stay in place for a day (because of his Buddhist belief that it took that long for the spirit to leave the body). Before sitting with his body, I got on the phone in the dining room, using John's address book to call his friends with the news.

Then I sat in the room with his body and with his favorite Buddhas, candles, and music. I wasn't sure I could feel his spirit, but being there a little longer, surrounded by things he loved, felt good. Some of John's artwork is around my house (including a print of a painting he made of the Healing Buddha of the Hotel Honolulu). Looking at the pieces can bring connection back and a sense of peace. I bought a Buddha about ten years ago. I guess that honors John as well.

Bobby never talked about anything to do with religion, except when I asked him if he had plans for a funeral. He wanted his body to be cremated. Beyond that, he didn't care. He said the ashes could be flushed down the toilet.

Bobby died while in the hospital for a week after his kidneys failed. I sat with him for an hour or two each day. When he began shivering no matter how many blankets he had, I lay down on the bed next to him. Even though he could still talk, we didn't. We might exchange a few words when I arrived and when I left. He was no longer aware or able to talk the last night.

The nurse came in that night and told me I could stay the night with him. I had asked him before he was so sick whether he needed someone to be with him when he died. He said he didn't care if anyone was with him when he died. I chose to leave. I've often wished I stayed.

When I returned in the morning, Bobby had died during the night. I decided that he would have waited for me to return if he had needed company. Still, I sat with his body until his relative arrived a couple of hours later. (She had come up from California the day before and was staying in a hotel.) As I sat there, I was vaguely aware of the hospital around me and briefly considered the life outside the hospital, going on despite Bobby's death. The time slipped away without any other thoughts.

Buddhist meditation was an available elective when I was at Antioch (2002–2005). Choosing a thought or a mantra may work well for some people. However, simply releasing thoughts, like clouds drifting by, is another option, one that works for me. Focus on breath or on some part of the environment (including a dying friend) is another option, which also helps me to meditate.

==========

Bonding (for Michael P)

> When Michael was dying
> We looked into each other's eyes
> Too intense at times
> Frightening
>
> Painful to separate
> At the end of the process
> And yet
> We will never be separate again

==========

In the Shadow

> weaker now
> can't walk
> we hold hands
> eyes join for a moment
> death close at hand
> we flow in and out
> porous to each other
> and to the One
> boundaries melt
> a fierce joy
> fills this room

==========

But, I'm Margaret

> Barbara he said to me
> Barbara bring me some ice
> Barbara hold me, I'm cold
> His eyes looked beyond
> Friendship is far behind now
> All he needs is care
>
> Bobby gently left
> Bobby slipped away
> Bobby died two days later
> Lying in a hospital bed
> Without friend or family
> Alone in the night

==========

With What Is

> being with what is, without an agenda

offering my whole self to all that I see
as I look at the person dying before me
what are the odors found in this place
are there gurgles of machinery or voices
cold water in the hall, for a dusty mouth
reluctant to speak of death as it nears
the soft touch of a hand on a bare arm
leaning against a rough hospital spread
and noting the stiffness of the sheet
a parade of feelings as we see losses

seeking understanding in this minute

Bobby Needed Touch

From birth to death, touch is important. A baby nurses and gets the comfort of contact. A person who is dying may only be able to handle a gentle touch.

Often said, the skin is the biggest organ of the body. It works to keep us comfortable in hot and cold weather. It warns us about danger through pain. It responds to temperature and pressure. In massage school, we were learned touch activates the parasympathetic nervous system, relaxing the person. I wonder if a person who never gets nurturing touch can feel safe and relaxed.

When Bobby (who also had AIDS) was dying of kidney failure, he felt extremely cold. He couldn't stop shaking. I asked if it would help for me to lie down next to him on the hospital bed. He thought it would. I settled next to him with an arm around him. He gradually stopped shaking and went to sleep. His doctor looked in while we were resting like this. He nodded at me and left.

A few days earlier, the doctor asked Bobby if he wanted to go on dialysis. Bobby asked if he would feel better. He had no energy for weeks. All he could do was lie on his bed. The doctor said no. He said Bobby would live longer but would not feel better. Bobby declined dialysis. The doctor then said he would die in a week because his kidneys had totally failed.

Soon after, Bobby was admitted to the hospital. He wasn't able to eat anything and asked me to find root beer popsicles for him. I couldn't find the popsicles. I froze root beer and brought him the ice cubes. He was delighted. He was able to enjoy them for a couple of days. Then he became too weak.

The day I warmed Bobby by lying next to him was midway in his week of dying. By the next day, he was much weaker. He still wanted the comfort of my body next to his. We talked a little. I asked him if he wanted company when he died. No. He said it didn't matter.

Then the night came when Bobby was in a coma. He was close to death. The nurse came in when visiting hours ended. She said I could stay all night if I wanted. I decided to accept what Bobby said. I went home about 10:00 p.m. When I came back at eight thirty in the morning, he was dead. I sat with his body until his cousin came to take over. Perhaps I should have stayed the night.

Bobby died at Harborview Hospital, part of a large medical complex. The hulking building sits in a sketchy neighborhood. It is affiliated with the University of Washington and UW Hospital. The place is not fancy, but I don't believe anyone can get better care at any other hospital.

I met Bobby through the AIDS clinic, which is in another part of the same building. I was doing massage there as a volunteer for patients and staff. People sat in my massage chair (fully clothed) while I worked on backs, arms, hands, and necks. A social worker strongly encouraged Bobby to sign up for massage. He was worried about Bobby who seemed isolated. He thought the stigma of AIDS was particularly difficult for a black man. Other gay men weren't always welcoming. He thought Bobby was ashamed to be known as a gay man and to be known as a man with AIDS.

After the social worker encouraged him, Bobby signed up for chair massage. He showed up on time on the appointed day. He was quiet the first time, aside from answering any questions I had about the massage (what he wanted and didn't want). I didn't know if he would come in again. He showed up the next week and became a regular.

Many of the people who came in for free chair massage also decided to hire me to do Swedish massage (on a massage table). I charged a very low fee for anyone in the AIDS community (person with AIDS, family, or caregiver). At that time, I went to the home of the person since I didn't have my own space for massage. After Bobby had been coming to see me at Madison Clinic for several months, he asked me to come to his apartment. I guess he paid me for those massages, but I don't really remember. (I kept offering free massage to people who were living with AIDS, especially if I liked them.) He lived in a large studio, with a deck, just a couple of blocks from where I live now. (At the time, I was still living in Madison Park.) He must have had a decent income, or he couldn't have afforded to live there.

After a few massages, Bobby began to talk about his life. He worked on cruise ships and traveled all over the world. He referred to himself as a "Mediterranean fruit fly." He never said he was gay, but from the context, I thought he was using that term to mean gay (not how *Urban Dictionary* defines it). He never talked about any relationships. We never discussed how he got HIV. By then (after meeting many people who were living with AIDS), it wasn't something I thought about. If a person wanted to share that information, it was okay, but not a priority. I guess I didn't ask many questions about anything but encouraged people to talk if they seemed to want to.

I don't remember the details of his early life. However, he was estranged from his birth family, or they were no longer alive or both. He had friends (in California) who were like family to him, especially one woman. He thought of her as his sister. I don't know why he lived in Seattle. I think Seattle was known for having good and respectful medical care for people with AIDS, so that might explain it. He didn't seem to have any friends or connections (other than the AIDS clinic and Northwest AIDS Foundation) in Seattle.

People who were clients at the AIDS clinic knew that I knew they had AIDS. In those days, people with AIDS died very quickly. They knew and I knew they were likely to die soon. This was before protease inhibitors. Many people were terrified to be around people with AIDS, much less to touch them. This is one reason I chose to do massage at the AIDS clinic. I wanted to nurture them. I wanted them to know I wasn't afraid to touch them.

When I volunteered to give free massage at the AIDS clinic, I anticipated seeing people who were patients at the clinic. However, I didn't rule out seeing staff (nurses, social workers, doctors, front desk personnel, and others). As it turned out, the vast majority of people I saw were staff. After people got used to me being there (six hours one day and four the other), my sign-up sheet was always full, often with a few extra names in case a space opened up. I divided each hour into twenty-minute increments so I could see eighteen people one day and twelve the other.

I liked seeing staff as well as patients. Nurses, doctors, social workers, and others who worked in the AIDS clinic were in a stressful situation. They loved and cared for patients and watched them die, sometimes in a few months. They needed nurturing. I liked massaging a doctor and then massaging a person with AIDS. To me, this blurred the line between caregivers and those receiving care. We were all part of the community living with AIDS one way or another.

Generally, a staff person referred patients who came in. A few patients found out about me other ways. Some only came once or twice. Others became regulars. The front desk had the list until the day I came in, so they signed up people who called and requested slots. The clinic provided me with an examining room for doing chair massage. The sign-up list was posted on the door when I came in.

Robin was one person I never saw at Madison Clinic. A social worker gave his partner (her friend) my name. I did a few massages at his house, but he was close to death when we met, just able to talk a little. Karl was another person I met only at his house. He had liver failure. This was the first time I had seen someone actually turn yellow.

I was often surprised by the openness of most massage clients, especially the people living with AIDS. I especially remember one man who told me about turning tricks to make a living. He got HIV from someone among those many. Some talked about friends and lovers who had died. Many talked about painful rejections from family. Some lost jobs when their HIV status was revealed.

People were relaxed by massage. They felt safe in the space of my little room (with the door closed and music playing softly). They felt nurtured. The clinic in general, and the staff, was nurturing and comforting to the patients. They felt accepted when they came in. They benefitted from touch.

Bobby told me the crew on the boat socialized together and used a lot of cocaine. This was how they got through the boredom of the long trips. When he learned his kidneys were failing, Bobby wondered how much the cocaine contributed. He also had used a lot of Tylenol for chronic pain after his diagnosis. We guessed cocaine and Tylenol worked together to damage his kidneys.

When I broke my ankle, Bobby came to see me in the hospital. He brought me books about yoga. They were old and well worn. I was too out of it to ask if he did yoga and never thought about it again. (Now I wonder if my decision to learn yoga and practice it faithfully is partly a tribute to Bobby.) He was horrified at the *National Enquirer* newspapers my brother brought me. I didn't tell Bobby that this was the level of reading I was able to do at the time (cognition hobbled by pain medications).

Over the time we knew each other, Bobby called me occasionally. He would leave a message, sung to Hello Mudder, Hello Fadder, "Hello, Margaret, this is Bobby . . ." I wish I still had those voice mails, just to remember him. He was so joyful in those moments. I felt joyful spending time with him.

When he died, he gave me several items and left instructions for his friend to take what she wanted. Bobby gave me a keyboard, which I passed on to Jacob. He also gave me a beautiful basket, which he bought in Africa. I have a couple of balance toys and an African hat he used to wear. I don't know what his friend took.

Bobby wanted all the rest, including his car, to go to the Northwest AIDS Foundation. I was in charge of telling NWAF. His friend and I had several conversations. After she left, I contacted NWAF to tell them his wishes. I had the key to his apartment, and they never questioned my right to give them his possessions. I didn't question it either. The apartment building manager wanted his apartment back but had a room in which his possessions could be temporarily stored. They contacted me when NWAF hadn't moved quickly on it, and eventually it was all taken care of.

The NWAF had a thrift store (and still has one in current incarnation as Lifelong AIDS Alliance). This is where most of his possessions were headed. I don't know what they did with the car. It was elderly and brown. It was Bobby's pride and joy. It gave him freedom. He knew he was ready to die when he could no longer enjoy going anywhere.

In my opinion, the formal nature of the setup at Madison Clinic made touch feel safe to Bobby (and others). Paying for Swedish massage at his home was a continuation of that. Massage from a massage therapist has clear boundaries. People can get the touch they need and no more. I think everyone needs touch, and unfortunately, many do not get it. (The person giving the massage gets safe touch as well.)

Bobby was forty-nine years old when he died, just a little older than I was at the time. I wrote a short obituary for the *Seattle Gay News*, using his driver's license for a photo.

==========

Star (for Robin)

> Flowers bloomed along the path
> Inside Pothos stretched over the windowsill and the fireplace
> Birds startled in their cages, a shy cat slipped away
> Robin's smile filled the room as he greeted me
>
> He was a prize-winning teacher
> Mentor to other teachers, teacher of small children
> Dead of AIDS at age thirty-nine.

A school auditorium was filled at his memorial service
Friends, family, students, parents, teachers
One sang alone, her soaring voice wresting tears from us

Concentric circles join
His work community, friends, family, caregivers
Each in turn left behind during the dying process
Finally his spirit disappeared into the empty center

==========

Echoes (for Bobby C)

"Hello Margaret, this is Bobby," sung to a silly tune
He's off gallivanting, in his new used brown car
To Seattle Aids Support Group for the Friday feast
Or to Bastyr clinic for acupuncture
Giving advice to all in his path, without being asked

Until the day he couldn't get out of bed and didn't
Wouldn't answer the phone or call for help
Finally asked me to take him in to the clinic
They hooked him up to an IV to hydrate him
Temporary respite, a few days at most

==========

The Final Loss (Bobby)

it was small brown and ancient
his car was his pride and joy
he cruised a few miles
he lightened his afternoons

he met others in a crowded room
he sat in comfortable chairs
this was his chance to hold forth
they sat over heaping plates

then one day he couldn't move from bed
then he gave up his car, and hope
then he was done with life

==========

Final Words (Bobby)

He said no to hours of dialysis without promise.
He said no to plodding through long days.
He settled into the hospital bed to wait
for the seven days it took his body shut down.

We talked about endings. We talked about wishes:
Reduce his body to ashes. Do what we will.
Flush them down the toilet. He did not care.
He was done. He said goodbye.

==========

Remembering Bobby

yes, he would consider, hours of dialysis
hooked up to the machine
for just a chance, for life
along these nearby sidewalks
sitting over a meal, driving,
reading, laughing with a friend
yes he would do it, but no
not if he would be left in the same place
struggling to get out of bed
too tired to do anything
no, he will slip gently away
too late, for these last pleasures of life

==========

The Quiet Exit (Bobby)

he left behind his home without regret
he had no need to cling
to the treasures he had collected
he gave his car away
without a second thought
he settled into the narrow hospital bed
his caregivers stopped by to visit
but there were no friends to contact
only one to call to come from a distance
she arrived after he had died
he chose that lonely path
he chose the hospital bed he chose

Couples with AIDS

When I think of couples who lived and died with AIDS, I think first of Charles and Craig. I met them at Bailey-Boushay. I guess it was about 1992.

Back when I was doing massage, I was intrigued by the ways I met clients, mostly through word of mouth. Often it was through a long chain of introductions. Many started with a friend from my old neighborhood. Others began with people I met through my volunteer massage at Madison Clinic and the AIDS Clinical Trial Unit. The AIDS community was small, and people moved around within it, so some staff people gave my name to staff people at the NW AIDS Foundation, Chicken Soup Brigade, and other groups working with AIDS. I have a document on my computer. "Lineage of Clients." I looked there when I began thinking about Charles and Craig to see how I met them. It didn't help. They were listed under "other."

I guess a health provider gave my name to Charles. He was mostly worried about Craig, his longtime partner. They lived together at Bailey-Boushay. Craig could no longer walk and spent all his time in bed. His muscles were painfully contracted, and massage seemed to ease the tension.

It was only when I came for the first time, prepared to give Craig a massage, that I learned about the muscle contractures. Charles said Craig wasn't able to get out of bed and onto the massage table although he still talked and expressed opinions. He let me know where he had pain and whether massage was easing it. He was usually lying on his side. I reached under him to work the muscles around his spine and down to his hips, where he had the most pain.

Since I had brought my massage table, sheets, etc., Charles had me give him a massage as well, that first day and every other time I came to see Craig. Charles was able to get up on the massage table. Months later, after Craig had died, Charles had an IV infusion running, and we had to work around it while he was on the massage table.

The rooms at Bailey-Boushay are set up as single rooms. They are large and comfortable, including a long couch by the window, a comfortable place for a visitor to sleep. Craig and Charles were the only two residents who shared a room. They had two rooms. Both beds were in one room. The rest of their furniture was in the second room. That room looked like storage. I don't think they ever went in there.

Charles had been a ballet dancer. His body didn't appear to be much affected by AIDS since he had kept his physical strength much better than most. He walked with grace. His muscles hadn't deteriorated or grown lax as they did for many people with AIDS. I don't know whether he still did any ballet exercises. There wasn't a lot of extra space in the room.

When I was doing massages on him, Charles liked to talk. He said Craig had been a hairstylist in the Broadway Market. They met when Charles came in to get his hair cut several years before. When I went to the Broadway Market, I thought of Craig and wondered if I'd ever seen him back when he was healthy. I wondered if the people there knew he was dying at Bailey-Boushay.

Charles said both families had rejected them—because they were gay, because of AIDS, and because Craig was white and Charles was black. No one from either family ever came to see them or offered support. They were the only family each of them had. And they had a circle of friends.

Charles was determined to be with Craig when he died. This was one reason they shared a room. Charles hovered when it became clear that Craig was close to the end. Then Craig died and Charles was not in the room after all. Charles said Craig died when he (Charles) was in the bathroom. I had heard (and told Charles) that people have trouble dying when those they love most are present. It was too difficult to leave then. Charles seemed to feel better when he thought about that.

Craig's funeral was at the Stinson Green Mansion. Charles planned the service, with a lot of help from a longtime friend of them both. It was simple and sad. People didn't seem to know what to say. Charles wore a black suit. He seemed smaller and defeated. He was quiet and miserable. Chairs were set up in what was once the living room of the mansion. There were about thirty friends attending.

I continued coming in to give massages to Charles for the next couple of months. He got much sicker and battled some opportunistic diseases. Once, Charles was greatly distressed by moans and screams from another room. He said the person never stopped crying and complaining. Since we couldn't shut off the noise, I hoped we could find a way to make it bearable. We discussed the possibility that Charles could let the other person express his own pain and terror. That seemed to help.

Then Charles died. As far as I know, there was no service. The service for Craig had really seemed to be for Charles as well. They were joined in death.

Thinking about couples reminds me of Sam and Randy, another couple who lived together with AIDS and died a few months apart from each other. I met them through my volunteer work at Madison Clinic. They signed up for chair massage and later paid me to come to their residence to do Swedish massage. Sam also hired me to do massage on his mother and on his sister (one time each).

Sam was short and craggy. He was friendly and chatty when we met. He was the one who arranged for me to come over to do massage on him and on his partner. He paid for the massages. Sam had been in the military. He was thrown out when they somehow found out he was gay. He resented the discrimination. He was quite a bit older than Randy, maybe in his fifties while Randy was in his thirties. Sam seemed to be used to being in charge and making decisions for the two of them.

Randy was tall and skinny. He was angry with AIDS and angry with his mom, who hadn't ever been much support to him. Both Randy and Sam were beyond being able to work when we met (too sick). I don't recall what kind of work they had done when they were healthy. Sam seemed to be someone who would have done construction or some other physically demanding work.

They lived in a remodeled double garage, which was like a large studio apartment. The place was packed with furniture and other possessions. Shelving went up to the ceiling and was filled with more things. There was barely room for me to set up the massage table in the middle of the space and just enough room for me to walk around the table. The kitchen area was partitioned off and usually the person not on the table stayed back there. (When that person was Sam, he generally smoked back there.) No one ever put on any music to accompany the massage.

Sam often didn't talk during massage. Randy always talked. He was bitter that his family had almost completely disowned him for being gay. He didn't expect to ever see them again before he died.

A few months after I met Randy and Sam, Randy's health got much worse. He was bedridden, and he had AIDS dementia. Taking care of him became impossible for Sam, so Sam made the decision to move Randy to

Bailey-Boushay. Randy was angry at the move and angry with Sam for sending him there. He didn't want to see Sam. Sam asked me to do another massage on Randy. This seemed to help Randy, but it didn't stop his anger.

After Randy died, someone at Madison Clinic told me about the memorial for Randy in his favorite coffee shop on Pike. Everyone was supposed to come and drink vanilla lattés (Randy's favorite) in Randy's memory. I went to the memorial. All the others in attendance were gay men, friends of Sam, I think. Sam was polite, but I didn't feel welcome. I declined the latte and left after a few minutes.

I heard a few months later that Sam was at Bailey-Boushay. I didn't attempt to visit him. I heard when he died but not about any memorial.

Living with AIDS was difficult for everyone in those days. Most people died very quickly. Most had to live with pain and disfigurement during the time before they died. Charles and Sam both had the additional burden of watching the person they loved most as he went ahead of them on the path. They dealt with loss as well as the anticipation of their own terrible future.

Bailey-Boushay itself came from a partnership of two men with AIDS. Thatcher Bailey and Frank Boushay were longtime partners. When Frank Boushay died, Thatcher Bailey began raising money for a place for people with AIDS to live and die in peace.

After writing about couples where both were living with AIDS, I thought further. My friend Jack didn't have a partner. His brother David was also gay and also had AIDS. They were both partly estranged from their birth family. David lived in Seattle, while Jack lived in San Francisco.

Jack had a miserable experience in the hospital in San Francisco when he had pneumocystis pneumonia the first time. All the health care workers were afraid to come near him without being gowned and gloved from head to foot. David told him that people in Seattle were more realistic about AIDS. So Jack decided to move up here. I think he had been here about a year when we met.

David worked as a computer techie. He was tall and thin and determined to not let AIDS slow him down. He had a partner, who also had AIDS. Steve was struggling and couldn't get out of bed most days. He lived longer than Jack, but died before David. (Both of them were present at the informal memorial service we had for Jack, looking at old photos and taking more photos.)

As I recall, Shawn's brother Tim also was HIV positive. They had a love/hate relationship, and he wasn't around much. I have a chair that Tim found on the street and gave to Shawn. Then Shawn gave it to me when he moved.

I don't know whether Tim died of AIDS or not. Many, perhaps most, of Shawn's friends were also HIV positive or had AIDS. Probably few of them have survived.

Michael told me a story about a close friend who disappeared when Michael got very sick and decided to move to Rosehedge. He tried to call the friend, but the friend wouldn't call him back. He guessed that the friend, also HIV positive, didn't want to be near someone who was so sick and approaching death. Michael was sad about it, but not angry. I heard the other half of that story almost three years later when John moved into Bailey-Boushay. He was the friend who wouldn't go near Michael. Still, Michael had many friends who visited him at Rosehedge, even though they also were dealing with the virus. I saw obituary notices for a couple of them a year or two after Michael died.

==========

Together in Sickness (for RS)

       Their names were almost one word
       Most days Randy and Sam were at the AIDS clinic
       One young, smiling and gregarious
       The other older, crusty, a loner
       Both angry about the disease

       For the first time in years he was alone
       Sitting in the home they shared
       His partner gone to Bailey-Boushay
       Too much dementia
       Blindness and a failing body

       He talked of dismissal from the army
       Dismissed for being homosexual
       Told them the names of other gay men
       To his great shame
       He avoided me after that day

AIDS Doctors, Diseases, and Treatments

I want to write something about the doctors I've met in the AIDS community. I don't know what it would be like now—these are memories from more than twenty years ago.

The years I spent hanging out with and supporting people with AIDS were a great gift to me. Not the least benefit was the chance to know the wonderful caregivers within that community.

While I was sitting in the hall one day at Kaiser Permanente, with nothing much else to do, I thought about the doctors I met or heard about through people with AIDs. I remember hearing gossip about doctors who were twins. Supposedly they both encouraged patients to use a lot of drugs (painkillers) beyond what was allowed. Susan saw one of the brothers. I don't know of anyone else who did. However, in their defense, they were caught in a tough situation. People who knew they were dying and who were in great pain didn't see any reason not to take any pain medications (generally opioids) they could, and probably their doctors had a hard time defending restrictions.

Once, Lee told me that his doctor was worried about his Dilaudid prescription. Sounded like the authorities were pressuring him to limit the amount of pain medication he dispensed and to make sure people weren't selling prescription medications. Lee assured the doctor that it was all for his own use. His doctor told him to inject the medication slowly. Lee preferred to inject it quickly to get a rush. He figured he could at least have that little bit of pleasure in his life. It seemed crazy to me that the authorities were concerned about the pain medications dispensed to people dying of AIDS (worrying about addiction) although I understand why they might not want pain meds to be sold on the street.

The amount of pain medication also came up with regard to Michael. He wanted more morphine when he was clearly quite close to death. The nurse told him that the morphine might affect his breathing and hasten his death. Michael was fine with that. He didn't want pain, and he didn't mind if he died sooner. The nurse gave him the morphine he wanted.

I'm not sure where Shawn got medical care. He seemed to doctor-shop, trying to find a doctor who would give him the meds he wanted. He wasn't really looking for pain medications. He was addicted to methamphetamine and wanted an easy resource. He explained to me that meth helped him to survive the effects of HIV. He also found at least one doctor (according to him) who bought that story. In the end, he lived a long time with AIDS (at least eleven years). Of course, it is possible that he was one of the people with genetic resistance to HIV. He might have lived much longer without any damage done by the amount of meth he used. He was one who bought into theories that the US government had deliberately infected gay men with HIV and/or with addiction to meth.

Shawn told me about the special pharmacy for people with AIDS. It was behind an unmarked door near Swedish hospital. Pharmacies are often leery of carrying large quantities of drugs that appeal to addicts. Initially, these were drugs like morphine and Dilaudid. Oxycontin was released in 1995. It became popular both with patients who need treatment for pain and on the street. Pharmacies who didn't want to be targeted by addicts and those who sell drugs were reluctant to carry opioids. Many patients also got prescriptions at pharmacies associated with medical facilities.

I heard that prescriptions for opportunistic diseases were often not available in regular pharmacies. Here again the special pharmacy filled in. The weakened immune system caused by HIV made people with AIDS vulnerable to many diseases not found in those with intact immune systems. Opportunistic diseases include CMV, PCP, KS, thrush, toxoplasmosis, TB, shingles, and others. When Terry had shingles, he told me the disease was common among people with AIDS (as it is with elderly people).

CMV (cytomegalovirus) was one of those disease-causing pathogens. The virus (in the herpes family) is everywhere but is only dangerous to people with impaired or undeveloped immune systems (including old people, infants, and others). Once someone is infected with CMV, it stays for life but usually doesn't cause problems. When the person's immune system can't resist, the virus causes very serious consequences, such as blindness, severe diarrhea, and brain inflammation. Antiviral medications can slow the damage but not destroy the virus completely.

Lee had CMV and worried about losing his vision since he was a lawyer. He managed to continue working until his vision was completely gone. Doug had CMV, which attacked mostly his digestive system. Albert learned to run an IV machine at home to get his medication for CMV. The machine got off balance many times during a treatment. Then he had to adjust everything to get it going again. He was proud of his ability to work the machine.

PCP (pneumocystis pneumonia) is another disease that takes advantage of a compromised immune system. A fungus that generally doesn't cause illness in healthy people causes PCP. (According to a source online, most people have fought and defeated the fungus by the time they are four years old.) It is treated with antibiotics (needle or pill) and nebulizers (breathing a mist with medications).

Jack had PCP twice, once in California and again after he moved to Seattle. His lungs collapsed the second time, and he spent several months in the hospital. He recovered enough to leave the hospital but never became healthy again. There were many stories early on in the AIDS epidemic of people going into the hospital with pneumonia and dying soon after. This was before there was a treatment protocol.

KS (Kaposi's sarcoma) looks like purplish blotches on the skin and is a cancer that develops from *cells that line lymph or blood vessels.* A virus in the herpes family causes KS. It can be treated by antivirals like other cancers, but I don't think they had a treatment twenty-five years ago. People with impaired immune systems are susceptible to KS, including old people. Michael had KS on his face. That scared me the first time I saw it and scared others, I think. Lee had KS on his legs.

After Jack came home from the hospital, he continued to have breathing problems. He didn't have any visible KS. However, an X-ray showed KS in his lungs.

Thrush is an overgrowth of the candida fungus, a yeast infection of the throat and mouth. It can be treated with an antifungal antibiotic. John suffered from thrush in his mouth. His sister thought he should cut way back in sugars and dairy, including not drinking wine. He cheated as often as he could.

Toxoplasmosis is caused by a parasite commonly found in cat feces. It can cause dementia. People with AIDS were encouraged to give up their cats, especially if cats were allowed to go outside. There are treatments for the disease although healthy people generally get better without treatment. This makes me wonder how Rosehedge could have had the cat (Mama cat). She wandered in and out of the house whenever she wanted.

TB that is resistant to treatment became a huge concern in the nineties and was found among people living with AIDS. When Joel was admitted to Virginia Mason Hospital with a respiratory problem, the staff worried that he had TB. Anyone who went into his room (staff and visitors) was required to put on masks and gloves. I have a vague memory of the same thing happening, briefly, to John at Bailey-Boushay. Everyone was relieved when TB was ruled out in both cases.

People living with AIDS often had several opportunistic diseases and needed the accompanying medications. People transitioned from HIV positive to full-blown AIDS partly on the basis of having opportunistic diseases. HIV itself was being treated with a variety of drugs at the time. Anyone who was living with AIDS was likely to have a large number of prescription drugs.

Albert's windowsill had a lineup of bottles. Anyone who knew about AIDS medications could have read the labels and known that he had AIDS. When he was in the hospital, he was at Providence, even though he lived next door to Harborview. He refused to get any treatment there. He had a relative who worked at Harborview. He was afraid she would find him in the computer and tell the rest of the family (and then none of them would visit him anymore). I don't know if he hid his medications when people visited.

Jack had so many medications that he couldn't remember what they all were for. He ended up putting them all in a big bag and bringing them to his doctor. The doctor went through them all. He took away some that Jack no longer needed to take. He labeled the rest on the top of the bottle—what they were for and how often to take each medicine.

Jack's doctor had a large private practice. Many of his patients had AIDS, and many of them died very quickly during the nineties. His office was across the street from Swedish Hospital, and that's where his patients were hospitalized. Of my friends, Terry, Lee, and Jack were all patients of this same doctor. Once, I brought Jack to an appointment and saw Terry in the waiting room.

Several people I knew, including Kelly, got medical treatment at Country Doctor not far from my house. Frank was a PA at Madison Clinic. He left and the next time I heard about him, he was at Country Doctor (clinic for low-income people), and John was seeing him. He set up a care conference for

John when John was at Bailey-Boushay. He explained to all of us, including John, how he interprets competency. AIDS had slowed John's thinking, but he was still competent. We just had to give him time to think things through. I appreciated Frank's care in explaining this to all of us.

My PCP at Group Health worked with a group of people who were HIV positive but hadn't progressed to AIDS. He saw many patients, and probably most of them were in pretty good health. I guess that many are still alive today (or would die from other causes).

Eric believed in the doctors at the Pike Place Market clinic and at Bastyr College. Even after he moved to Tennessee, he came back here to see those doctors.

Perhaps the greatest number of people living with AIDS in Seattle got medical care at Harborview, at Madison Clinic, and/or the ACTU. Since I volunteered there, it was odd when I accompanied someone to a medical appointment and sat with them in the waiting room. It felt like a very safe place. Everyone there was dealing with HIV, so there wasn't any stigma or need to hide. I remember taking Joseph to pick up prescriptions at the pharmacy there. My friend Bobby died at Harborview.

The clinics at Harborview were involved with research as well as providing medical care to people who didn't have much money. I met Dr. King Holmes during my time doing massage at Madison Clinic. He was passionately devoted to medicine and research, depending on his assistant to keep him on track. I suppose he is still working even in his eighties.

One doctor who greatly influenced my thinking was Dr. Abraham Verghese. I didn't know him but read his book, *My Own Country*, published in 1995. He talked about being the stigma of being the AIDS doctor in a small town in the South. This made him an outsider. He was also an outsider by virtue of being East Indian (grew up in Ethiopia). The people he described seemed as vivid and real to me as many I met in real life. Reading his stories made me want to equally describe people I knew.

Some of the doctors I met during that time were also HIV positive. Two worked at Harborview. One, Bob Wood, was very open about his HIV status, including writing an article for the newspaper on the subject. He is still alive today. The other, Terry, quietly did his job and then wasn't there anymore. I heard that he had died. My friend Cary was also a doctor (but not an AIDS doctor). He read extensively in the literature and was quite interested in following the process of HIV in his own body and comparing to what he had read.

Forgetting AIDS for a Minute

In all the time I spent with people who were living with AIDS, we talked about dying and death quite often. We talked about our lives. Sometimes we just had fun.

Not every part of time with people who had AIDS was focused on illness. Some parts were about friendship and companionship. Some activities were not about illness, although illness affected how the activities happened. I saw this with others as well as with my own relationships.

Steve, the husband of someone who worked for my husband, was interested in offering services to someone with AIDS. I introduced him to Lee. Lee needed someone to fix some drawers in his home. I guess that Lee would have done those repairs himself before he got sick or wouldn't have needed repairs because he could pull out sticky drawers. Steve was good with tools, so he seemed like the perfect person to help. I think he spent a few hours there and enjoyed chatting with Lee. Then he asked me to introduce him to another person who could use help and companionship.

John was always glad to have new helpers, so I introduced Steve to John. Prior to that time, John had taken the train to Eastern Washington to visit with family. This was becoming difficult for him. He asked Steve to drive him over there and stay with him for a few days. (Steve was a farrier and could make his own schedule.) When they were visiting the relatives, Steve and John stayed in a trailer on the property.

I think they drove each other crazy some of the time, during the long drive and during the visits. It was good for them both as well. Steve continued visiting John after John was at Bailey-Boushay. In fact, he was with John when he died.

John's Buddhism affected our friendship in large and small ways. The biggest thing was when we went to hear the Dalai Lama speak at the Seattle Convention Center in June of 1993. We left John's apartment early in the morning and drove downtown. In those days, parking wasn't as difficult as it is now. I found a place to park a couple of blocks away and pushed John in his wheelchair over to the convention center. We were directed to the elevator. When we got up to the correct floor, we learned that handicapped people were allowed to sit in front of the fixed seats. I pushed John into a good position and then sat on the floor near him. He was thrilled to be so close.

Another time, we drove to the Buddhist Monastery in Greenwood. The doors were open, and we were able to go in and look around at the paintings on the wall. The monastery was new at the time, and all the colors were bright and impressive. The goal seemed to be to cover every bit of wall with pictures. For John, it was inspiring and fit in with his beliefs. For me, it was interesting and odd, but didn't attract me to Buddhism (which disappointed John). After seeing the monastery, we went to see my mom who was living in a small house on Dibble at the time. We sat in her backyard and had tea and cookies.

Susan and I went to a concert planned by Shawn. Susan and Shawn had been friends for many years. She let him (and his daughter) live in her apartment while he was waiting to get low-income housing. She told me he was the handsomest man she had ever met. She introduced me at the concert, but we never met again until after Susan died.

The concert featured a lesbian singer (Rebecca), who made one album that I know of. The concert was at the Broadway Performance Hall. Shawn and I later went up to see Rebecca in Bellingham. I was glad to get a look at Bellingham. Other than that, I felt extraneous. I was just the chauffeur. In connection with Rebecca's music, Shawn talked over the years about his friend Patrick Haggerty (record, *Lavender Country*, 1973). Their friendship began at the time Patrick made his album and continued into the nineties. I dropped Shawn off at Patrick's apartment downtown on one occasion. I think they shared an apartment in Bremerton some years later. Shawn made mixed tapes of some of his favorite singers (all women) for me.

Such times and events made me think that we were building friendships. I hoped that I was valued as a friend and not just as someone helping. I loved that we took time out from thinking about AIDS, even when it was so simple as watching television, going out to eat, going to movies, or other activities.

Albert was thrilled when he convinced some nonprofit to get him an electric wheelchair. Walking was difficult for him. Zooming around in the electric wheelchair was great fun, especially when small friends and relatives hopped on to ride with him. I remember standing outside on a sunny spring day and enjoying his pleasure in his new toy.

John, Patrick (a gay friend of mine who didn't have AIDS), and I enjoyed a trip to the Tacoma Art Museum. Alfredo (my brother-in-law) had a show there, and Patrick (also an artist) wanted to see it. John wanted to see the paintings and was hoping for romance with Patrick. The romance didn't happen, but we enjoyed a whole day that had nothing to do with AIDS.

I have walked through cemeteries with Mom and with Gigi. (Of course, I've sometimes been in cemeteries during funeral services.) We've looked at stones and statues. We especially enjoy visiting the elaborate stone belonging to Evelyn Y. Davis in Rock Creek Cemetery (Washington DC). Going to Lakeview Cemetery with John was different from those experiences. He liked it because it was an open area and high. He thought the sun lingered there long after it was gone from the streets.

John and I went to Lakeview Cemetery often, especially in the late summer. At first, he was able to get out and walk. Later, when he was having trouble walking, he sat on a blanket in the sun. I might sit there with him or wander around reading the dedications. Mo (John's dog) sometimes lounged on the blanket. Other times he walked with me. He was especially happy when I had a ball to toss for him. (This probably wasn't okay with the cemetery management.)

I have been back, walking through the cemetery, with other people since John died. It's different. John was facing the likelihood that he would die. Being there seemed to help us to accept the idea that both of us would die someday (even though John didn't actually accept that he would die soon). When I am in that cemetery now, I remember being there for John and miss him again.

A pleasurable moment that sticks in my mind was when I brought a Japanese pear to Michael at Rosehedge. Japanese pears were new to me, but he'd had them before and was excited that I brought it in. I cut it into wedges. He ate one with great enjoyment, but then he couldn't eat any more. Still, there were a few minutes when we joined in appreciation of the crisp sweetness. We offered the rest to others in the room, sharing the pleasure.

Much of the time John and I spent together was centered on eating. We had many meals at the Broadway American Grill. I would drop him off at the

restaurant and then park across the street in underground parking for Fred
Meyer and stores on the same block. Mo always came with us on those trips.
He had to stay in the car, but was okay with it. I learned the hard way to hide
my glasses after he chewed the earpieces. No matter what else we ate, John
and I enjoyed and shared the fruit cobbler. The restaurant had one every day.
The fruit depended on the season.

I remember going to a movie with John. I don't remember the movie.
He liked it better than I did. He said that a movie (any movie) was the
opportunity for him to have a vacation from AIDS. He said that I could have
a vacation from AIDS any time I wanted while he had to make opportunities.
We were at a movie theater on Forty-Fifth, near I-5. It is still a theater, but has
changed since we were there. Now it has many small theaters. In 1992, it just
showed one movie at a time in a large theater. There was an Italian restaurant
in the same building. We ate at that restaurant before the movie. As usual,
John decided what he wanted to get and then tried to convince me to get his
second choice. That way he could have a few bites. He generally encouraged
me to get a glass of wine for the same reason. He wanted to have a sip or two
without getting a whole glass.

I miss those meals, movies, and conversations. John often talked about
growing up in a farming community and feeling like a country boy when
he moved to the big city. He gossiped about friends and people in the circle
supporting him. He talked about people in his building. He reported that
many were selling and using drugs. He shut the door of his apartment, turned
up the music, and cuddled with Mo. He didn't have to interact with those
others.

Whenever we went out in the car, John liked to take a long slow route
home. We drove through Volunteer Park. He had spent many happy hours
there in the past before he got sick and liked to remember. He and Mo both
looked out the window for interesting sights. John looked for good-looking
men. Mo looked for other dogs. Once, we drove down Fourteenth toward the
park, and John pointed out a huge Japanese quince in a glory of deep pink
blossoms. He said this was how we knew spring was on the way. Every time
I see a Japanese quince even now, I remember John.

My hands don't miss doing massage. My heart misses it. Massage was a
huge part of my connection with people who lived with AIDS.

John loved massage more than anyone else. He got massage from a
woman who was part of an organization offering free massage to people with
AIDS (In Touch). He got massage from my friend Chris, which was how

Chris and I met. He looked for bodywork of any kind anywhere he could get it. And he thought of it as an interactive process. He was always willing to try new things and always gave lots of feedback. We were clearly doing it together.

John and I used to go to TUBS before he got massage from the volunteer. He only liked the hot tub and was happy there while I also went into the sauna. The space was simple. There were no pictures or Buddhas, no books or videos, and no other people around. It was quiet. We rarely talked. It was warm and soothing with bubbling water. Time there was the very definition of being in the moment. I felt some of that at Hot House, but it was different being in a space with many people rather than just one dear friend. I can sometimes recapture it in the bathtub, except that the water isn't hot enough and doesn't cover my whole body so it isn't so relaxing. And John is gone. Those days are gone.

Massage and massage school was my link to Terry. We had friends in common through massage school. We gossiped about the teachers. He encouraged me as I went on in school and the licensing process after he had dropped out of school. Terry taught me about how he experienced being the one receiving massage. Again it was interactive. Mostly it had nothing to do with his living with AIDS.

All the hours I spent doing chair massage at the ACTU and Madison Clinic were rewarding to me, and I miss that time of connection and conversation, as well as helping to ease stress in others. It was an activity I enjoyed. I wouldn't have done it for ten years otherwise. I still have friends from that time.

Times with Jack were low-key. I was in massage school at the time. Sometimes I practiced massage on him. Other times I studied while he watched television. After a while, I would sit with him and enjoy *In Living Color* with him, usually with the sound turned off so he could invent his own funny dialogue. We were deeply connected in those hours.

Stories about John have come up easily in this essay. I knew him for a long time (maybe three years), and he was never afraid to suggest field trips. He expected them and expected me to enjoy the time with him. Friendship with Jack was of much shorter duration (eight months) and yet all those quiet times together built a solid bond. This was true of Michael and Raymond and others. One of us was sick and the other was healthy, but we were equals in friendship. We had tears and laughter.

==========

Rough Roads

14th Ave East is smooth where I live
Farther north tree roots
Snake under the pavement
Cracks and bumps predominate

Remind me of days when John and I drove there
He always shouted "Slow down!"
Every bump jarred his nerves and bones

It was hard to drive slowly
When I felt triumphant
Once again we'd gotten him dressed
Wheelchair in the trunk
Mo, the dog with his leash, in the backseat
Backpack filled with necessities,
Urinal, water, pan in case he threw up
On our way to lunch

Sharing happy times together
Despite everything life was good
I even miss his shouting.

The Last Day, When Death Comes

Sara and I talked about aging and death. She says she realizes (especially as she ages) each time she sees someone might be the last time.

I met Sara after I'd known many people who died from AIDS. Without spelling it out, I had experienced this concept. I had to face it. So many of the people I knew during that time were close to death. I knew I might not see them again each time I left.

In addition, I had experiences even before meeting people with AIDS where I saw the truth of this.

One lesson came from the last week of Dick's life in 1988. He quit doing dialysis because it was too uncomfortable. The doctors told him he was likely to die in a week since his kidneys had totally shut down. During that last week, people who loved him were with him at all times in the hospital.

Dick and I became close friends when we taught together (special education) starting in 1970. He was about the same age as my parents. Before Dick got so sick, he and I talked on the phone almost every day. He was like a surrogate grandfather to Rebecca and Jacob. During that last week, I visited him in the hospital every day for an hour or two. His wife, his children, and many friends took turns spending time with him. We all watched him fail day to day. A day or two before he died, I helped him to and from the bathroom. He couldn't walk on his own.

Then came the day, the last day of the week. He couldn't get out of bed anymore but was still fully present mentally. When I told him I was going home at 11:00 p.m., Dick said, "We won't see each other again in this life."

Yes, I believed him. I hugged him one last time and left. Dick's wife called me at 4:00 a.m. to say that Dick had just died.

When Dick died, we had been through a year of seeing him struggle with dialysis. We knew why he decided to give it up. He was no longer having any good days. We trusted the doctors when they predicted he would die in a week. My father's death, in 1990, was quite different.

Dad had hip replacement because of severe pain. His general health seemed to be good. He was only seventy-one, and both of his parents had lived into their late eighties. We guessed that Dad would get through the surgery and resume his life although limited from living with an artificial hip (no tennis allowed).

My sister came out from DC during Dad's recovery from surgery. (That's my memory. She says she didn't. I guess she knows.) Local family spent lots of time with Dad as well. We watched as he gradually regained strength. He showed his pleasure in being surrounded by those who loved him. He felt well loved. It was good.

Then he died. I don't know whether he had an embolism or an aneurism or something else. I heard various things from Mom at different times. His death certificate suggests that he had internal bleeding after falling (on the stairs) and died immediately.

Dad's death was a surprise and abrupt. For me, there was a lesson in seeing how much we all benefited from the time spent together during his last week. We were fully present and couldn't have done more if we'd known the day he would die.

Like Dick, Bobby (who had AIDS) chose to die with kidney failure, knowing his life would probably be over in a week. He didn't even try dialysis. He didn't notify anyone during that week. I knew because I was there when he made the decision against dialysis (at Harborview Hospital, where he remained). I asked him who he wanted with him when he died. He said he didn't need anyone there. I came in each day, but didn't stay the night when it seemed clear he would die (even though a nurse said I could stay). He was not responsive, and I accepted I wouldn't see him alive again. Except that I had second thoughts when it was too late the next day.

I was surprised when Michael said, after it was clear that he was close to death, that he would miss his friends when he died. He knew he wouldn't see them again. I've never heard anyone else say it quite that way. This realization motivated (and energized) him to shop for gifts and write cards to everyone. I guess people who are close to death must often be aware they are seeing people for the last time, just as the visitors may know they are seeing the dying person for the last time.

Michael was so sick when we met. He was thin. Walking was painful. He had Kaposi's sarcoma on his face. Every day and every chance to get to know each other better was a gift. Just sitting and doing the crossword puzzle with him, or on my own if he was dozing, was a gift. Each day, I was a little surprised to find him still alive and responsive (until the last day, when he was in a coma).

Back in the days (early nineties), when I knew many people who were living with AIDS and mostly dying of it quite quickly, the only way to (mostly) keep some peace was to focus on each hour, even each minute, of every day and give and receive all that the day had to offer. This is the way I learned to be present with people who were close to death. I think it helped me because after my friend died, I know that I had appreciated every minute we had.

When we sat in the late summer sun, John fully appreciated the warmth and healing. We usually had music going. Mo and I played with a tennis ball. Time seemed to stop for us. We reluctantly rejoined our lives when the sun got too low to provide warmth.

That last summer (1993), John stayed in the car. He couldn't really walk anymore. We used a wheelchair to get him from his apartment to the car. He had people with him at all times, except when they didn't show up. When we (his helpers) realized that wasn't working, we finally persuaded John to move to Bailey Boushay in October. His sister promised to keep his apartment as it was so he could move back when he got better. He insisted he would get better.

Moving back to his apartment seemed unlikely, even though people at Bailey Boushay helped him to walk a little. He seemed to be regaining strength. He was able to walk down the hall and back with someone supporting him. He was a small and thin man and not so difficult to support. But this stopped after a week or two. He was no longer able to walk at all.

I took John out once in my car during that time. He was gleeful at leaving Bailey Boushay even for a short time. We drove over to Magnolia. I stopped the car, and we got out to look at the sunset over Puget Sound. John was able to hold around my neck and stand with me lifting as he used his legs. We stood that way for about five minutes, enjoying the view. Then we got him back into the car and headed back to Bailey Boushay. That may have been the last time he left the place.

In the meantime, my children were both heading to Israel. Rebecca was there (University of Haifa) for six months into January 1994. Jacob was there (school outside Tel Aviv) for one school semester, overlapping with Rebecca. With encouragement from Mike, Mom and I planned to visit both of them for three weeks at the end of December and the beginning of January. My ex-husband, Mike, made the arrangements for flights and hotel accommodations in Tel Aviv, Haifa, and Jerusalem. I anticipated John would have died long before I left. I didn't even tell him about the Israel trip until very close to the date of departure, probably in November. I thought I wouldn't have to tell him.

John was angry with me for planning the trip. He tried to persuade me to cancel. I felt terrible about it. I couldn't let down my children and my mother and myself. I wanted to see Israel as well. Neither one of us actually said it, but we both feared he would die while I was gone.

Even though it was expensive, I called John a couple of times while I was in Israel. I spent hours during one frustrating evening trying to get through to him. Among other things, I had to get a new phone for the hotel room since the one provided in our room didn't function. When we finally talked, John said he was okay and wanted to get off the phone.

Despite that distraction, the trip was a success. Mom was an excellent travel companion. We explored the country. Seeing my kids again was wonderful. They both seemed to have grown up through the process of being there where they had a lot of independence. I saved memories that I thought would delight John, especially photos and thoughts about the Bahai Temple in Haifa.

When I got back, I went to see John the same day. He was not very responsive. He talked a little but was past any interest in Bahai or any other aspect of my trip. (He liked a silver ring I had bought for myself and persuaded me to give it to him.) I learned that he had named someone else as his medical power of attorney. He got livelier, more like himself, when he talked to other visitors. John was very weak. He died three weeks after my return.

When John died, I realized that I hadn't really expected him to ever die. I saw him losing strength, yet it seemed he could just wane but never come to an end.

As it turned out, I was not with John when he died. Steve was there. John wanted to stay in place for several hours (in accordance with his Buddhist beliefs), and Bailey Boushay went along with that request. After sitting with his body for a few minutes, I moved to the dining room. I called his friends to let them know he had died and they could come to pay their respects over the next few hours.

While Dick and Bobby chose how to die, I made the choice for my cat Cocoa Puff four years ago, when she was sitting in a pool of pee, not anything a cat would want. Cocoa Puff always was part feral and hated going to the vet. That day, she allowed me to put her in the carrier and sat quietly on the examining table at the vet. I had expected a fight about the carrier and a wild cat at the vet. It seemed to me that Cocoa Puff was indicating her agreement that the time was right. We both knew that was the last time we would see each other (well, I knew anyway). The vet, who was extremely kind, said that the cat was in heart failure and it was time to end her life. Still, even now, I sometimes look at her favorite place on the perch in the window and expect to see her there. I'm glad that I sat next to her, patting her and talking to her during the last few weeks of her life. She seemed to appreciate the attention.

==========

Psalm 23

> He didn't want to die alone
> As death neared we made a list of all
> Who were willing
> To sleep on the couch
>
> I thought that John was confused
> And unknowing that last week . . .
>
> In the middle of the night
> A quiet voice in the dark
> Spoke my name
> Reassured that I was there and awake

==========

February 7, 1994

> Day after day
> changing just a whisper
> sliding toward death

Night after night
we listened for his breath
waited for it to stop

Moment by moment
stretched out unbearably
finally ended

==========

Regrets Only (John)

just two hours away from his side
     then word came that he had died
          he was so close no surprise
               yet deep inside part of me cries
                    he would not have gone would
                         still be here if only I had stayed

==========

. . . John john JOHN John john JOHN . . .

low slow voices
droned
chanted
Tibetan monks
day and night
began to grate
for me
meaning missed
for him, merging
merging with their prayer,
his whole being

==========

Crematorium Moment (John)

past the prim parlor where death is an uneasy
visitor sitting on the slippery couches

down the hall lined with wood paneling
to the back where linoleum and stainless steel rule

together in the elevator to the stark basement
the room where metal doors open onto an oven

big enough to hold the box
big enough to hold my friend's body within

on which we scattered flowers
as we said a few final words of farewell

he probably would have liked a joint as well
to see him happily into the beyond

==========

Vignettes (for Dick G and Jack S)

A measure of a man
Perhaps of a woman too nowadays
Dick used to consider
Whether
He would
Go to war trusting
This person to be beside him

Living with AIDS
Looking forward to sure death
Jack asked
He was getting
Sicker and wondering
Who would be there when he died
Would he be there

Animal Companions, Cary

Seeing the way people relate to their pets tells me a lot and gives me pleasure. Sometimes I remember the animals better than the people.

Cary lived near Northgate on a quiet residential street. He was an anesthesiologist before he got too sick to work. No one at the hospital where he worked knew that he was gay or that he had AIDS, even after he stopped working (early 1994). He thought it was important not to be known. (He also had a good friend, a nurse at the same hospital, who was a closeted lesbian.)

On the other hand, I remember looking at a photo on Cary's wall. This was taken at a Gay Pride parade. The float was from a leather bar. Cary was there with his ex, both looking very macho. I was baffled by the photo, but never asked about it. How is this consistent with staying in the closet? Maybe he didn't really care that much? Maybe he thought that anyone who was at the parade would protect him?

Cary's primary care provider at the ACTU introduced us. The first time I went to see Cary (to give him a massage) I was met at the door by a barking black Lab. Cary came out on the porch to reassure me. That was how I met Lucky, who was young and energetic and very sweet. Another dog waited inside the house. I don't remember her name. Maybe it was Dora. She was much bigger than Lucky. I thought she might be black Lab mixed with something like Great Dane, but I never heard anything like that. She was old and creaky and didn't move much.

The backyard was large and fenced. Cary was not well enough to take the dogs for walks. They could run in the yard if they wished or hang out in the house.

I walked Lucky a few times, the first time I'd experienced a retractable leash. He was strong and lively but obedient, so it wasn't difficult. We never met anyone on the sidewalk as we walked. Cary had trained the dogs to go to the bathroom next to the house, so he didn't do anything along the walk.

Dora had hip dysplasia, which seems to be common with Labs. This caused her a lot of pain, and Cary eventually decided that she needed to be freed from misery. He called a vet who came to the house to administer a shot. After Dora was dead, Cary had Lucky come in to say goodbye so that he would know she was dead and not just missing. Then the vet took the body away.

Cary was both a person with AIDS and a doctor. He was careful and rational. He read about the progression of AIDS in other people and commented on the symptoms he saw in himself. He seemed to be more interested than distressed by seeing what was happening.

During those years, I took one dog to Harborview to see his master. I didn't know if it was allowed, but I guessed no one would question me if I acted like I knew what I was doing. The dog was probably Lucky and the master Cary. Lucky liked me and enjoyed going in my car. All went well until we went into the hospital elevator. The dog was horrified and shaking from fear. I spoke to him and calmed him, and we made it to the correct floor. Cary was very glad to have the visit. No staff person questioned why we were there. I chose to take the dog down the stairs on the way out. Lucky was fine with that.

Cary was bedridden, very thin, and unresponsive for about two weeks at the end of his life. I came over to the house a few times to sit with him. We encouraged Lucky to hang out with his master. The dog was skittish and uncomfortable in the room. He really didn't want to be in there with his unresponsive master. After a couple of tries, we let him be.

Toward the end of Cary's life, his brother Rick came across the country from NY City to be his caregiver so Cary could stay in his house until the end. Sometime before he got sick, Cary had remodeled the basement into a separate apartment. He was so proud of the room set up with a desk and a computer, saying he would work there when he was better (never happened). His brother stayed there (and the brother's wife too when she was able to come out for weekends), and finally the computer was used. I suppose the brother inherited the house. I know for sure he inherited the dog and took Lucky back east to hang out at a store owned by the brother and wife. We wrote back and forth about this. He said Lucky was happy in his new home. He loved greeting customers.

Lucky was not the first dog to seem shy of his dying master. Mo, John's dog (Lhasa apso and terrier mix), seemed equally uncomfortable as his master became weaker and less responsive (about a year before I knew Cary and Lucky). This was when John was living at Bailey-Boushay. John asked him to get up on the bed with him, and Mo resisted, going to the far end of the bed. He barked at people who went past in the hall. Perhaps, like his master, he wanted everyone to visit. Maybe he hoped they were coming to take him out for a spin.

Before that time, Mo and John were close companions. John walked the dog as long as he was still able to walk. When walking was difficult, John made sure his own caregivers also took the dog for walks. (In any weather, day or night, Mo was always happy to go.) Mo slept with John on his bed and was always ready to accept treats from visitors. I took him out in the hall of John's building a few times and threw a ball down the long hall for the dog to chase.

Mo had no issues with elevators, but he was used to them since John lived on the eighth floor of a Seattle Housing Authority low-income building. Mo was always ready to go anywhere we would take him and didn't even seem to mind when he stayed in the car while we were eating at a restaurant. Once, he must have bored and chewed the earpiece of my glasses. Sometimes I took him for a little walk before we headed home. I walked him in rain and snow.

John's sister took care of the dog when John was in the hospice, bringing him to visit most days. Then she kept the dog after John died.

Another dog who came into my life about the same time was a pug belonging to Steve. The dog was very sweet and didn't seem much interested in playing. I don't know how his toilet needs were taken care of, but Steve was able to walk her at least a little during the time I knew him.

I don't know what happened to Steve's pug. Steve's family stepped up at the end of his life. They came around when it was clear he was going to die soon. They had been distant before then and didn't seem to want me around once they began supporting him. I saw him once in the hospital and heard later that he had died. I don't remember what work he did, but he was a good cook and cooked a meal for me once. He described trying to make baba ghanoush and finding it way too complicated.

Terry and his partner had a black Lab in their tiny house (maybe 500 square feet). The dog was young and rambunctious. Once, when Terry and I were at massage school together, I rode in Terry's car. He pointed out that the dog had eaten the seat belts. Another time, Terry told a story about the dog eating the carpet at their house, right by the door, making it very difficult to open the door. Possibly no one had the energy to take care of the dog.

Terry's parents took him toward the end of his life. When I went to see him there, the dog (and the partner, who never got tested for HIV—he didn't want to know) was not around. In fact, I don't remember the dog being there when I went over to give Terry massages a couple of times when he was still in his house. Perhaps he and Terry's partner had moved out.

(Terry was a flight attendant for Alaska Airlines. He seemed healthy when we started massage school and simply wanted a change of career. He joked that he would rather deal with one asshole at a time rather than a whole planeload.)

Joel (office assistant at ACTU) and Clarke (actor, director, playwright) had a young chocolate Lab. That dog was crazy. She had endless energy and wanted constant interaction. I went to their house to do massage. We had to shut the dog out of the room, or I wouldn't have gotten anything done. She might have knocked over the massage table or me. Joel and Clarke were nothing like the stereotype of gay men with the perfect, clean, and orderly house. They owned lots of stuff without much order. I couldn't tell if the dog contributed to the mess.

The cutest dogs I ever met lived with a man I met only once when I went to do a massage. These dogs were dachshunds with long curly hair. They were a little shy but friendly. I remember them but don't remember the man.

Jeff had a dog all the time I knew him. He was HIV positive but never developed AIDS. He worked until retirement age. He spent his weekends hiking or walking in parks with his dog. When his dog got very old and died, Jeff got another young dog. He has no intention of going away quietly.

Fewer people with AIDS seemed to have cats. I vaguely remember conversations with people who had given up cats once they got diagnosed with HIV. They had learned that cats were dangerous since toxoplasmosis could harm a person with an impaired immune system. I think that's mainly a problem with cats who go outside and bring in germs that end up in their litter boxes, but I understand why most didn't risk it. (Toxoplasmosis is also dangerous for pregnant women or for the fetus.)

Rick had a small dog and a cat. I was only at his place once (giving him a ride, not massage related) and met the pets who seemed quiet and well behaved. He said that the cat was much more likely to stay close and attentive when he wasn't feeling well.

Shane described his cat as a nurse cat. Shane had been a restaurant owner and bartender. He was a handsome man with lots of charm. When I drove him to medical appointments, the staff acted like he was a visiting celebrity. He said the cat stayed very close when he was struggling. He thought that cats were much better suited to be caregivers than dogs.

Raymond had owned a small store filled with kitsch before he got sick. He was also a massage therapist. He agreed to teach me more about doing massage in exchange for free massage. After he died, his parents gave his massage table to me.

A skinny and shy calico cat lived with Raymond. She would peer at me from downstairs if I went up the stairs or from another room. His parents came across from Bremerton to care for him one day a week. His father remodeled his house to make it easier for Raymond as his health failed. I suppose the parents may have taken the cat after Raymond died.

Kelly didn't have a pet of his own (living in several different apartments over the years I knew him). He cleaned at my house (how he supported himself) in exchange for massages. While he was here, he and Charlotte (calico cat, the best cat ever) interacted with each other as equals.

After observing nurse cats and aloof dogs, I had a theory. I guessed that dogs (pack animals) shy away from a pack member who becomes disabled or sick. Cats (mostly solitary) may react to a sick or injured human as a mother cat would care for kittens.

Rosehedge, the hospice that came before Bailey-Boushay, had a black cat named Mama Cat. She had wandered in, and they allowed her to stay. I never saw her interacting with residents, but I suppose she did and that they liked having her around.

When I sat with Cary at the end, I enjoyed the framed Gauguin poster on his wall. I was delighted that his brother offered the poster to me after Cary died. It is on my wall inside my door and reminds me of hanging out with him and his dogs.

==========

For Nothing (Cary)

> He clings to the railings as he labors down the stairs
> leads me to see his treasure,

the computer fills a desk and one wall of his office
he finally has it up and running,
he talks of his plans, all that he will accomplish
one day, when he is well

He turns and struggles back up to his couch
never to go back down again.

==========

Lucky (Cary)

happily jumped into the backseat,
an ordinary black Lab,
off on another adventure.

followed willingly on his leash,
stopped in confusion
in front of the elevator
trembled at strangeness,
walked down the wide hall.

shrank from his master
lying in the strange bed,
craned his neck to see this place.

Inheritance

When one person in a couple dies, the other generally inherits when there aren't any children. Or some part may be left to others. Sometimes it gets complicated. Back when I was around people living with AIDS, there was no same-sex marriage. No matter what legal documents were signed, inheritance wasn't guaranteed if the birth family objected.

One of the men who died at Rosehedge had a bitter story. According to him, he and his partner lived together in a house originally owned by the partner. They both understood it to be their house together. Their families were always supportive of the relationship and the mutual ownership. Then his partner died. The partner's parents swooped down, claiming the house and everything in it. They could, since the two men hadn't been able to marry. The remaining man (who was telling this story) was left with nothing. Maybe they thought it didn't matter since he had AIDS and was going to die anyway?

My house (bought in 1993) holds memories of people I never knew and a story that intrigues me even all these years later. I wish I had known them. No, maybe not.

My house is a duplex. The first floor is one apartment. The second and third floors create the other apartment (mine). My apartment had a newly painted and nicely appointed first-floor bathroom. (I added the upstairs bathroom.) The bathroom in the other apartment was shabby and just functional (probably dating back at least twenty years). My kitchen was small and dark. I improved it by having a wall taken out, between the kitchen and dining room, and installing an island with storage underneath and a tiled workspace above. The downstairs kitchen was large and bright, with a butcher-block island, a gas stove, and lots of storage. Mom said she'd never imagined she would have such a nice kitchen. In both apartments, the interior walls (upstairs and down) were recently painted and the carpeting was new. The apartments together appeared to be in the middle of being remodeled.

All I know of the history is what I heard from the woman who rented the downstairs apartment until the time I bought the house. She lived alone down there. The apartment was attractively furnished. She had worked to add edging and lights to the garden. Several medical students rented the upstairs. Furniture was very minimal (beds and a table in the dining room).

According to the downstairs tenant, the previous owner of my house was a gay man who had AIDS. He lived there with his longtime partner. He had AIDS, but his partner did not. In those days, as they both knew, AIDS was a death sentence within a year or two. And in fact he died, leaving his partner behind.

Then came the surprise. The man's will left his house to his partner, on the condition that the partner survived him for at least a year. The partner lived on for a year and then committed suicide, just as the first man had feared, according to my informant. Relatives of the second man then inherited the house. They did not live in this state and decided to sell the house after renting it out for a period of time (a couple of years, I think).

As I write this, I wonder whether the relatives of the first man might have tried to dispute his will. I wonder if it seemed unfair to them when it went to the second man's relatives. I've always wondered about the relationship of the two men. Seems to me that the story of the will suggests their relationship involved a lot of struggles for control, even when facing death. I wonder if the remodeling stopped when the first man got very sick or after he died?

Years later, Jacob and I pulled up the old and, by that time smelly, carpeting in the living room and dining room. We discovered a wood floor, in so-so condition, underneath. Unfortunately, the floor had paint randomly spilled all over. It looked like they had painted the rooms and maybe furniture without protecting the floor. And then they put carpet over it. This seems to fit with the unfinished remodel. (We tried to get up the paint and decided it was impossible.)

Joel and Clarke shared a house north and west of Greenlake, up on the hill, so it had a great view of downtown Seattle. The house was small, a townhouse on half a lot, I think, but adequate for them and their dogs. It looked to be new (I see online it was built in 1984, so it was quite new when I was there in 2000 and before). I guess that Joel was the owner since he had a job at the ACTU (AIDS Clinical Trials Unit), which probably would have paid enough to afford a house. I doubt that Clarke had the money to invest from his work as an actor and director. However, he was the star of their relationship. Joel was proud of Clarke's accomplishments and awed by Clarke. (In real life, Joel was the dramatic one, and Clarke was often cold and formal.)

I went to a play directed by Clarke in the tiny theater at Hugo House over on Twelfth. There may have been room for thirty people in the audience, but not all the seats were filled. In my recollection, Mom and Denise were with me at the event.

From Clarke's obituary:

> Clarke () legit actor, singer and director, died Jan. 30 after battling cancer and HIV. He was 53.
>
> (He) began acting with the Enchanted Theatre Co. at the Bathhouse Theatre in Seattle.
>
> Other Seattle Theatre productions include *The Music Man* and *Bells Are Ringing.* He also co-wrote and performed in the play *The Fool.*
>
> While living in Hawaii, (He) directed several plays such as *Born Yesterday, Love! Valour! Compassion!* and *Master Class.* (He) was also a member of SAG, Equity and AFTRA. His only film credit was an appearance in the Martin Scorsese film *After Hours.*
>
> He is survived by his mother and father, a brother and a nephew. (February 28, 2001)

I don't know who wrote this, but I'm sad that it said nothing about Joel. Joel continued living in the house after Clarke died. He adopted two more dogs to be friends for the wild chocolate Lab. He contributed some money to a pocket park near the house, and it was dedicated to Clarke. I was there for the dedication of the park. Joel seemed lost after this.

Also, Joel and various friends arranged a tribute to Clarke at a theater over in Bellevue. We were asked to contribute money for the production if we wanted to receive a video of the event. I never received the video and don't know if it was ever actually made. I never felt comfortable asking Joel about it.

After Clarke died, Joel and I went out for lunch or breakfast several times in the Greenwood neighborhood. At one point, Joel got very sick and was in Virginia Mason Hospital. The staff feared that it was TB, and everyone was supposed to wear masks when they came into the room (upsetting to Joel). The staff treated it as a joke, wearing the masks on top of their heads or around their necks. That alarm was called off after a day or two. He eventually recovered and went back home.

Joel had a brain tumor (not malignant), which required surgery to protect various nerves. The tumor grew back later, and surgery was no longer possible. His obituary:

> Joel (…) Age 54, passed on Thursday September 8th. He is survived by his family in Ohio, his friends in Seattle who love him very much and his three constant companions Shannon, Zack and Benjamin. In lieu of flowers memorials may be made in Joel's memory to: Multifaith Works A.I.D.S. Care Team, 1801 12th Avenue, Suite A, Seattle, WA. 98122. (Published in the *Seattle Times* on Sept. 14, 2005.)

Nothing here about his partner who predeceased him. I see that his house sold in 2006, I suppose, by some relative and heir.

I knew others who were living with AIDS who also owned their homes. Michael owned a condo on First Hill. He didn't have a partner and left everything he owned to his sister. He worried about her, and from what he said, she wasn't very functional. I hope she was able to hang on to the place and live in it. Lee also owned a house (on Queen Anne Hill). He had no partner, so I guess his family inherited it. This was also true of Cary (north Seattle) and Raymond (Twentieth and Cherry). Cary and Raymond both owned houses and didn't have partners to inherit.

Others who died lived in rented spaces, but not low income. Bobby had an apartment near my house. Dave lived in a rented place in South King County. Joseph had an apartment over on Summit, west of me. Jack lived in an apartment on Mercer and Harvard. I think Robin and his partner (who did not have AIDS) rented their house in Wallingford.

Many people who died from AIDS lived in low-income housing. I learned a lot about Seattle Housing Authority buildings during those years. Albert lived in Jefferson Terrace (by Harborview). Doug lived in Bell Tower (downtown). Shawn, John, and Susan lived in Capitol Park (on the next block from me). Marty lived in Denny Terrace (above the freeway).

John lived in low-income housing. He also rented a garage for storage. He had a lot of stuff. He had books and Buddhas, music and videotapes, special fabrics (for draping his body and his home), incense, candles, electric massagers (for his chronic pain), a television for playing videotapes and tape players for playing music, and much else. His home was an expression of who he was, and he loved everything in it. He always thought that he would record his memories, but he never did.

He absolutely hated moving from his apartment to Bailey-Boushay. The only way he would do it is if his apartment was maintained as he had left it so he could return when he got better. He took a few things with him (too many in the opinion of the staff at Bailey-Boushay since they had to work around the Buddhas and tape players whenever they cared for him).

When John and I went to "Tubs" to relax in the hot tub, we both appreciated the simple surrounding, just the water and a fake orchid. We talked a little about this. I guessed that even though he loved all his stuff, it was also stressful to be around. He agreed and blamed himself for being attached to stuff.

John had a will and an addendum to the will in which he listed who should receive each of his possessions. His sister helped him write the list and distributed things after John died. After John died, his sister got in touch with many of the people on the list and asked them to take the items John left to them. I later saw many of those items at her house. I guess some people didn't want the items once he was gone. They seemed different when they were separate from John's energy and the environment he created. They seemed different even after John moved out of the apartment.

Shawn, unlike John, had very little. This was good because he moved a lot, from one low-income place to another (often evicted). He welcomed homeless friends (who also were HIV positive) to stay with him. Shawn clung to a few family photos, papers from his past, and some art. Other than that, he gathered (through dumpster diving) new furniture, plants, and clothing every time he moved. Much of his stuff disappeared along the way, and I don't think he had much by the time he died at Bailey-Boushay.

And then there was Bobby. He gave a few things to another friend and to me. He delegated me to give everything else, including his car, to Chicken Soup Brigade for their thrift store. This was the simplest solution to possessions after the person died. (The store got lots of donations during those years.) And it seems sad to me that there was no family to inherit or to remember his life.

I have some lasting memories. My own Buddha and Quan Yin remind me of John, also the music of Taizé. Danny made me a tape of music he liked. I had Raymond's massage table (long gone) and his recipes, though I've never used them. I have a necklace Shawn made for me. Michael's gold chain is with me every day. The poster from Cary is on the wall by my front door. Memories in the house also include rocks from Eric, a trailing plant that reminds me of Robin (and Jacob is creating something like that in his kitchen), and music of Enya (I don't remember who played that during massage. I don't think that was the household where the person with AIDS was dying of liver failure). I have Jack's taped speech on videotape, plus a news story about Rosehedge.

Things that gave joy to men living with AIDS included movies and eating out. They were for John a vacation from AIDS (as was Tubs). Eric's paintings mattered to him. Steve and Raymond loved cooking. Dogs were the beautiful part of Cary's life.

Art came from people with AIDS. John painted and combined photos with paint. J writes poetry and has come out as a person living with HIV. Patrick's paintings memorialized his partner who died from AIDS and his own journey as a survivor. The quilt keeps memories on the national level. Several people, including John, wanted to write memoirs. I have a book that includes much art from people with AIDS.

I pointed out to my sister that my night-blooming cereus has five buds. She, our other sister, and I all have night-blooming cereus but never discussed getting them with each other. I told her how I got my plant from cuttings from John's sister, so I often think about him when I look at it. I also inherited a plant from him (I think a dracaena), but it died long ago. Eric left an aloe and a ginger plant with me. They didn't survive the tender ministrations of my cats (mostly peeing in the large pots).

==========

Not AIDS (For Clarke E)

> He told me when we first met
> That his T-count was under 200
>
> > I said brightly
> > Showing that I knew
> > All about that stuff
> > That he had AIDS
> > It wasn't just HIV+
>
> Clarke stiffly declined the label
> But forgave me over time I think

==========

All Gone Finally

       homes where friends with AIDS lived
           everything from houses
              to apartments
                     to low-income residences
                        to the hospice

       looking at layers of loss
       some went through it all
       some held on to the end

                      keeping cars
                or even their jobs
            as if the process of aging
         speeded up by the virus
       months only from retirement to death

Residence or Home

I've thought often about the way my home seems to echo my mother's homes (plants, paintings, pets, music or musical instruments, and many books). I didn't see that combination in any of the homes of people I knew who were living with AIDS.

I remember the apartment Shawn had when I first knew him. It was one bedroom, at the Cambridge, overlooking the convention center. The Cambridge was a place for short-term housing (not sure who ran it, and it may not be functioning anymore). He had moved there after living with Susan in her Seattle Housing Authority low-income housing. He liked to walk through Freeway Park across the street and appreciated being able to see it from his apartment. We walked through it a few times, and it was a pleasant change from city streets. I wouldn't feel comfortable in that park by myself.

Shawn's daughter (aged two) slept in the one bedroom. All of their clothing was there as well. He slept in the living room. The kitchen worked well for him (he liked to cook), but was often overflowing with dirty dishes. The bathroom was small, barely big enough to turn around.

He didn't have a lot of stuff. He had moved many times over the years. He gathered furniture, dishes, and appliances when he got a new place to live. He was an expert dumpster diver and could furnish an apartment quickly. He clung to photos and other memories. Once, he showed me a newspaper he put out in Florida (a brochure for tourists).

Like me, Shawn had indoor plants. His favorite part of his apartment was the corner in which he had a garden. He acquired plants by liberating them from gardens he saw on his way through the city. He justified this when I was with him by focusing on abandoned houses and yards. He dug up bamboo from one vacant lot when we were walking together. He also felt okay about taking plants in front of apartment buildings since (in his mind) they didn't belong to anyone in particular.

Shawn knew how to access food and clothing in each new home. Again, he found many items through dumpster diving. He was amazed at the good stuff people threw out. He also found charities that gave away clothing. He went to food banks. He signed up for food deliveries from Chicken Soup Brigade. He shared food and clothing with people he met on the street, especially those who were homeless. He cooked meals for me a couple of times. His place usually smelled like smoke since he smoked constantly. Opening a window didn't help much (above the freeway).

Shawn had one or two books, but he wasn't much of a reader. He once borrowed a book from me, about women with AIDS, and never returned it. I guess it got lost along the way. His story involved being locked in a mental hospital for years and having no education past about third grade. He had a number of audiotapes of music and usually had music playing in the background. He liked women singers, both lesbians and straight women (such as Joni Mitchell, Linda Ronstadt, and others). He once made a mix tape for me of women artists he liked.

Over time, Shawn moved into various apartments and lost much of what he had. I helped him move to the one after the Cambridge. He kept everything except the plants. The next place had two bedrooms, and he furnished it quite well from what he brought and what he found in dumpsters. He also acquired a circle of friends who used drugs, slept in his apartment, and stole from him. He eventually was evicted and ended back at the Cambridge with fewer things and much less order in his life.

John's apartment is also vivid in my mind. He lived in one place (Seattle Housing Authority building) during the time I knew him until he moved into Bailey-Boushay. I think he had lived there for years.

The apartment was tiny. The kitchen was barely big enough for one person to stand in. I don't think he did any cooking, but some of his helpers did simple things such as making tea or miso soup. The bathroom was big enough. He was able to hand wash items and hang them up to dry on the rod for the shower curtain. He used the (back) room that was meant to be a bedroom as a living room. He had a full-size waterbed (illegal) in the largest room, which was in front, just past the kitchen. Both rooms had so much furniture that it was difficult to walk without bumping into things. He had painted one wall orange, which was also illegal (according to him).

My place has lots of art on the wall, mostly created by friends and relatives, but a couple of pieces are my own (a drawing of a guinea pig and a painting of a windblown tree in Edmonds). John had original art on his walls as well. He created almost all of that art. He painted with watercolors. He sometimes mixed photos and paintings. After John died, His sister had cards made from four of his paintings. I have some of them framed on my walls. I like best the Healing Buddha of Hawaii and one of Mo (his dog) contemplating the view of downtown from John's eighth-floor apartment.

John had statues and pictures, mostly to do with Buddhism. He had plants, including a type of palm. He loved white orchids in bloom. I don't know whether he kept them after they stopped blooming. He had video and audiotapes, again mostly to do with Buddhism. He introduced me to the monks who chant in a deep monotone. He also had a few books. John loved incense and had some beautiful incense burners. He had candles in various sizes, shapes, and colors. He loved fabrics with colorful patterns. When he was healthy, he often turned them into clothing. Later, he had them hanging as decorations in his apartment. Once, I observed one of his helpers, standing on a chair, attempting to drape a piece of cloth in exactly the right place and exactly as John wanted it to hang.

John's dog Mo was important to his life. He cuddled with John and enjoyed walks. The two of us hung out with the dog and took him with us when we went out to eat. He liked being in the car more than staying home in the apartment.

I have a framed poster down by my front door. This used to hang in Cary's bedroom. It is a Gauguin painting of a Tahitian beach scene. Cary's brother gave it to me after Cary died. It reminds me of the hours I spent sitting with Cary during his last couple of weeks since it was in his bedroom at that time. And I like it very much as a painting. I enjoy having something that my friend Cary liked. Cary had other posters and paintings on his walls.

Cary's house was just south of Northgate. It was a two-bedroom house with a large backyard, including a hot tub (that I don't think he used anymore). He hired me to do massage initially, and I set up the table in the living room. It turned out that he wasn't very interested in massage, but he did want to keep me as a friend and weekly visitor. I spent a lot of time in his house.

Cary was a doctor. I know he read medical articles about AIDS and thought about where he was in the process. I don't remember seeing magazines or books, but I was never in his bedroom until he was close to death, so all that might have been cleared out. His dining room table was a sea of mail, probably including journals. I guess his brother went through all that stuff after he came out to be caregiver. Most of our attention when I was at Cary's house was spent on the dogs or running errands. His two black Labs were loyal friends and companions.

Some of the people I met in the AIDS community became friends (including Cary). We spent time together whether or not I was doing massage. I saw the homes of many other people because they often didn't want to travel to my house for massage (or didn't have transportation to do so).

The homes varied a lot. Terry and Dwayne lived in a tiny house in West Seattle. I think it was less than 500 square feet, which was crowded for them plus their black Lab. It tended to be chaotic, with papers and boxes piled next to the bed and in a niche that was meant to be a dining room. The only open space was in the living room, and that's where I set up my massage table. (I didn't try to bring the massage table or do massage after he was living with his parents. Their trailer was much too crowded to even try.)

Lee, on the other hand, lived in a large and beautiful house on the slope of Queen Anne Hill. He had a great view from the living room. The house was furnished just as one would expect (stereotype) of a gay man and always immaculate. He lived alone and had no pets. He had tasteful art on the walls and around the place. I always did massage in the living room area and only saw his bedroom when he was too sick to be able to walk up and down the stairs without a lot of effort. He took a shower once and asked me to stay in case he fell. I was relieved when he completed it safely.

Joel and Clarke lived in a new and narrow house west of Aurora at about Eighty-Fifth. They had a lot of stuff and both were smokers, so their house was not at all the stereotype of gay men—except for the art on the walls (nude men). I did massage in their guest room, squeezing in next to the bed. The room had stacks of books and papers. Their chocolate Lab contributed to the confusion.

Raymond's pretty house was in the central district of Seattle. His living room was decorated in a Western theme. Those were the things he loved and sold in his secondhand store. Everything else in his house was simple and minimal.

I have a vague memory of a beautiful house, perhaps in Ballard, but don't remember the name of the man getting massage. The house had white carpeting, and I always thought that I shouldn't be walking over it, but that was the only way to get to the space where I was asked to do massage. The furniture was like what you would see in a showroom. The walls had beautiful art. The plants all looked well behaved.

Others lived in apartments, mainly low-income places maintained by Seattle Housing Authority. Kelly lived in an apartment building Mike inherited from his parents. The bedroom, which looked out on Greenwood, was fairly big. He had stacks of paperback books. Over the years, he borrowed many books from me and always returned them. His clothes and other possessions were shabby but always clean and neat. The kitchen and dining room were one room. Kelly cooked a meal for me once. We sat at his tiny table to eat. He was a good cook.

Kelly had no pets but had a good relationship with my cats, especially Charlotte. He liked her to help out when I gave him a massage. He also got along well with the dog and cat belonging to Rick when they dated for a few months. Rick lived in a low-income building near downtown (Denny Regrade). Kelly lived in at least three different places during the eight years of our friendship.

Doug lived in a Seattle Housing Authority in the heart of downtown. He had a fabulous view of Puget Sound and beautiful antiques (inherited from his parents) in his apartment. He lived in a different SHA building when we first met. He moved because of conflicts with the manager and with his neighbors.

Jack was living in an apartment on Capitol Hill when we met. He didn't have many possessions. His walls were blank. I bought him a poster (bright flowers) when he was in the hospital, but it never got unrolled and hung on a wall. He had recovered from pneumocystis pneumonia when he moved to Seattle. It seemed that he didn't bring a lot with him. He was hoping for better medical care here. I think he lived in that apartment for a couple of years before dying at Rosehedge.

I guess that people tend to shed possessions when they move a lot (as many did), including moving to Rosehedge or Bailey-Boushay. Old people often let go of stuff, and people with a serious illness may tend to do the same thing. I have no way of knowing how these friends lived before AIDS hit them. Some had pets, and some had plants. Most didn't carry around a load of books (the way I do). Most had some kind of art, and many had music. None of their homes would be mistaken for mine.

==========

Wearing Blinders (for Shawn)

> I was hurrying on my drive home
> Planned to eat lunch and nap in the two hours I had
> Before my next client
> Still my eye was caught by the figure
> Trudging along with his backpack on the cross street
> It can't be him.

I'd been wondering
Why Shawn worked in our garden for a day
And then disappeared,
No word from my old friend,
Who loves me so much and needs to earn money
I turned the corner,
Snuck a peek back as I passed
Yes, it is he.

I hoped that he wasn't headed for my house
Still part of me hoped
He hadn't seen me and wouldn't know
I didn't want to see
Or talk to him
Or give him a ride
Or hear any of his excuses
For disappearing again

==========

Laundry Day (Shawn)

A sea of clothes across the floor
weeks of wearing and discarding
clean mixed with dirty
too tired, can't deal with them
no money for machines

We piled the cart to overflow
wheeled down city blocks
rows of machines waited for us

We filled one two three four five
Put my coins into the slots
waited wearily in chairs, to shift them
into dryers, to fold, to carry back
A chance to start all over again

Support Groups

AIDS is less scary now than it was twenty-five years ago, but it's still here. HIV is a virus and capable of changing over time. There may never be a way to immunize people.

I sometimes feel sad for those growing up now. When I was a teenager, we were afraid of pregnancy and maybe somewhat afraid of sexually transmitted diseases, but never had anything like AIDS hovering over us. Love and pleasure should not bring the danger of death. We hoped for the best and often couldn't access protection, but we weren't afraid of dying.

I thought about this even more back when my children were teenagers (1987–1996). Most of those who were infected with HIV during that time became sick quickly and died within a couple of years. Any sort of sexual exploration had to be attended by fear. I made sure my kids knew about protecting themselves form AIDS even before they dated anyone.

Nowadays, the drugs are better. Many people live a normal lifespan with some degree of inconvenience because of HIV. Others develop bad reactions to the drugs, and some slip through and still die young. But it is different.

The new drugs were not yet around when I was shortly out of massage school (1992–1993) and trying to build a client base. The massage school occasionally notified students and graduates of volunteer opportunities, which might lead to new clients. We were encouraged to bring business cards and other advertising to hand out to those we met at the events. I did a few of those events.

The event that I remember best was at a motel near the Seattle Center (maybe Holiday Inn, just off Denny). This was interesting to me as a volunteer opportunity and even more because the event involved people in the AIDS community. I liked that caregivers, people with AIDS, family, friends, and anyone else who was interested mixed together. This seemed healthy to me.

The event happened over a weekend, from Friday evening through all-day Saturday and into Sunday morning. Some of the sessions included the whole group. Others divided us up into smaller groups. The intention was for the smaller groups to allow individuals to express their thoughts and feelings (generated in the larger sessions) and to support each other.

The massage therapists had the chance to show our stuff during the large group sessions. We put our massage chairs around the edge of the room. People could wait in line or simply hope to grab an opportunity to be massaged on backs, arms, hands, and head. I don't remember whether we had them sign an agreement to get the massage. I don't think so. Many people took my business card. None of them ever contacted me after the event. (This was typical of other volunteer events I attended as well.) The only lasting benefit I got from the opportunity was getting to know another massage therapist, Leilani, who has stayed an email and Facebook friend over the years.

The details of presentations at the conference have disappeared from my memory years ago. I think it was helpful at the time. They provided information about opportunistic diseases, various medications, the stigma of having AIDS, and other topics. I don't remember anything about the organization that sponsored the event.

The smaller groups were set up with a circle of chairs. Twelve of us sat around the circle. Most of us were middle-aged. One was tall and skinny, with glasses and acne. He was eighteen years old and recently diagnosed with HIV. He was frightened and angry. He felt betrayed. He had thought he would be safe if he only had sex with men close to his age. He thought AIDS was a disease of middle-aged and older men. The HIV diagnosis was unfair. He ranted. He cried. He didn't let anyone comfort him.

No one else could talk. The young man dominated all of our small-group sessions. The groups were informal (no one facilitating). I think the others felt as I did—unwilling to shut down the young man's grief. We didn't know what to do. In retrospect (and at the time too), I don't think the venting did him any good. He was just as angry and upset at the end of the conference as he was at the beginning. Listening to him certainly didn't help the others of us in the group.

At the time, I wished that we had a facilitator for the small groups. A facilitator would have put limits on each person's time for talking. We all could have expressed our thoughts and feelings. A facilitator could have prevented resentment of the young man who dominated or his resentment of anyone who tried to calm him. None of us was willing to take on the role of facilitator.

I thought about this recently and then thought maybe the conference was doomed from the start. The idea of mixing people with AIDS, caregivers, family, and friends is idealistic and loving, but I don't know that it was ever going to work. I haven't heard of such a mixed support group anywhere. I'm pretty sure caregivers couldn't feel comfortable complaining about their troubles with caregiving to the people who are receiving care. I also assume people with AIDS wouldn't want to hear about any complaints from caregivers and wouldn't be in a position to help.

The group I know best is the one I facilitated (every other week) for about nine years at Sound Mental Health. The group members were all older adults (over sixty) who were chronically mentally ill. Aside from once or twice, all of them were women. My job as facilitator was to make sure everyone had a chance to talk and received respect from the others. I also introduced topics for discussion and brought food for the break time. The group members felt safe there. They all had lived with the mental illness label for most of their lives. They didn't want people outside the group to know. There they could talk about it safely in a setting where there wasn't the stigma associated with being mentally ill.

AIDS had the same kind of stigma or worse (and maybe still does). Most people with AIDS didn't like to talk about it in public. Many didn't tell their families or friends or employers. They might make up some other reason for being sick or simply choose to disappear. They might be convinced that those who didn't have AIDS, including caregivers, couldn't possibly understand what it is like. Being in a group with other people with AIDS would make it comfortable to discuss opportunistic diseases. One person who had been in a group (just people with AIDS) told me that AIDS knew how to find the way to hurt a person most. The handsome man got Kaposi's sarcoma on his face. The man who loved to work out had wasting in his body. The person who liked to read might go blind. (This was an interesting theory, but I don't think it really worked that way.)

On the other side, I've been in support groups for caregivers as a hospice volunteer. I think we had a lot more freedom to talk freely about our fears and annoyances in a group with other volunteers than we would have if hospice patients had also been there.

I remember a person whose partner had AIDS complaining about the partner. The caregiver was frustrated by the sick man's behavior. He said that his partner wasn't going to die of AIDS because he was going to kill him first. He wasn't serious, just expressing frustration in the safe situation of talking to another caregiver without the presence of his partner.

Still, the AIDS community was never so neatly divided between patients and caregivers. Some of the people who worked as volunteers for Chicken Soup Brigade were HIV positive. As long as they were healthy they could continue helping others. Doctors, nurses and other medical people worked caring for others with AIDS until they became too sick to work. (Of course, some of these caregivers were HIV positive but survived because of their effective immune systems or because they got the right drugs.)

Some people with AIDS were able to look past their own illness and be supportive of caregivers. This was especially true of Jack. He was sympathetic when I had a bad cold. He listened to my other problems. He said that it was good for him to think about someone else.

John, on the other hand, dismissed the problems of those who didn't have AIDS unless he was inconvenienced by their inability to help him. He once said that people like me could take a break from AIDS any time we wanted. The only time he could forget was when he went to a movie. He probably wasn't interested in any kind of support group or spending time with others who had AIDS, especially since he didn't want to hear anything about dying. I don't remember him ever talking about going to a support group. He broke off contact with Michael when Michael moved into Rosehedge.

Shawn got me to come with him to the Friday night dinner at Seattle AIDS Support Group one time. These dinners took place in an old house not far from me. SASG provided this dinner for people with AIDS every Friday night. We filled our plates from the buffet table and then sat in chairs and sofas around the living room. Several other people I knew, including Bobby, also went to the Friday night dinners. The plus part of attending the dinner (I think) was letting people with AIDS know that I wasn't afraid to eat with them and even sometimes share food with Shawn. Still, I was not sure that I belonged there and didn't go again. Many of the people in the room seemed to be looking sideways at me, as if they were wondering why I was sitting among them and eating the food.

Besides the Friday night dinners, SASG had many support groups for people with AIDS. The first time I heard of it was when Jack asked me to drive him to the group. He invited me to come in with him. In retrospect, that was a mistake. I should have waited in another room.

Kelly went to a support group at SASG quite regularly. He liked being able to talk freely to others dealing with the virus. He hoped to meet someone for romance since he was lonely. He complained that people in the groups talked about others who weren't present at the time. He was certain they gossiped about people in the group when they were with others. (This was against the rules of the group.)

Another person who went to SASG groups was MM. He felt a bit out of place there as a straight man, but wanted people to talk to. The hardest part for him was watching others get sicker each week and eventually disappear when they died. He eventually decided that pain outweighed the benefits of attending the group.

Women with AIDS felt so uncomfortable in groups at SASG that they decided to form their own support group (Babes). Women who have AIDS tend to have different health problems and relationship issues than men. Babes is still thriving although the women who founded it died many years ago.

SASG still exists as well. The house where it was has been torn down. I think the woman who sponsored it (and owned the house) may have died or at least gotten too old to continue. SASG is now located on Fifteenth. It has free HIV testing and, I think, support groups.

Thinking about the continuation of support groups made me wonder about people still getting infected. Mostly I think it must be very difficult to be perfect about protecting oneself over the years. I've heard that some think AIDS is no longer a big deal with the new medications. Researchers are working hard to find medications that can protect people from ever getting infected by HIV. They have found a combination drug (to be taken every day) that seems to work well without many side effects.

Nevertheless, in 2016, 39,782 people in the United States received a new HIV diagnosis. The annual number of HIV diagnoses declined 5 percent between 2011 and 2015. (Other sexually transmitted diseases often go along with HIV since people may not be protecting themselves.)

==========

Woman Warrior

Alison, red hair
tall and fierce
seen for years at AIDS vigils

and at ACT UP meetings
founded Babes since women
weren't welcome at SASG

worn down over the years
by opportunistic infections
no longer public
by the time she died
we all thought
she'd been gone for years

==========

Support (Michael M)

For months the group gave him heart
to share the path, to talk with others.
All living with the virus.

Every week on the top of his calendar.
Until one died and then another.

He would not continue,
could not face the news, or
watch the tide ever closer to his feet.

==========

Support Group

we looked into each other's eyes for five minutes
allowed to talk for a few seconds afterwards
and then went back to the workshop
as if looking into each other's souls
me a massage person, him a man with AIDS
but we would kind of check in visually
with each other over the next day
no need to exchange names or anything else
as if we already had our total relationship

Massage on People with AIDS

Stopping massage in October 2000 (after ten years) was difficult. In many ways, I felt that I was finally getting to be good at it. Arthritis wouldn't let me continue.

I guess that I learned from every massage I did, and some people taught me more than others. I met John when I was partway through massage school (summer 1991). He and Shawn were friends. John told Shawn about the pain he dealt with, mostly in his back, and Shawn was happy to introduce us.

John's pain was intense and chronic. He applied Tiger Balm frequently. He always had at least one vibrating massager to apply to painful spots. He introduced me to the "TENS" machine. Online, "Transcutaneous electrical nerve stimulation (**TENS**) is a method of pain relief involving the use of a mild electrical current. A **TENS machine** is a small, battery-operated device that has leads connected to sticky pads called electrodes. You attach the pads directly to your skin." And "**TENS** machines works by sending stimulating pulses across the surface of the skin and along the nerve strands. The stimulating pulses **help** prevent **pain** signals from reaching the brain. **Tens devices** also **help** stimulate your body to produce higher levels of its own natural painkillers, called Endorphins.'" He often asked me to move the TENS unit around to spots he couldn't reach.

When we met, John persuaded me to come over regularly, once a week, to give him massages. I was happy to have the opportunity to practice (especially with someone so willing to give feedback). He loved having me try out every technique I knew, even the ones I barely knew at all. Whenever we learned something new in massage school, I knew I would practice on John.

John lived in a low-income building (across the street from where I live now). I brought my massage table to him. John's apartment was small and filled with furniture, candles, videotapes, Buddhas, incense, plants, and other essential items. By carefully moving some of this to the side, I was able to set up the massage table in the middle of the larger room. I had about eighteen inches of space to move in on all sides of the table. I worried (and John worried even more) that I would run into and break one of his treasures. He shouted at me if I bumped into furniture.

John loved bodywork and took it very seriously. He was completely focused on each massage and on the way his body felt during massages and after. He loved to talk about other things before or after massage. During massage he talked, but only about the massage, often encouraging me to go deeper or stay in one spot longer. He was the only person who was so direct during a massage. He was even better at feedback than my fellow students. His feedback was very helpful.

Some of the techniques taught in massage school seemed a little odd. One of those was Reiki. The idea is to capture energy flow in the massage therapist's body and direct it through the body of the client. We learned that Reiki energy could heal the therapist as well as the client. In fact, people could learn to do Reiki on themselves. Sometimes the therapist lightly touches the client while using Reiki energy. Other times, hands hover above the client. (Hovering was my preferred method.) Advanced practitioners could learn to direct Reiki from a long distance. During class, we experimented with having our hands facing each other and feeling heat between them.

Reiki was difficult to explain to most people. John, however, understood and loved the idea. He happily relaxed under my hands for an hour or more when I was practicing Reiki. Eric also liked Reiki. In his case, he wasn't comfortable with touch, so Reiki was perfect. He claimed that Reiki was extremely helpful for stabilizing his moods (bipolar disorder), for neuropathy, and for Crohn's disease. It didn't seem to help with HIV or with opportunistic diseases.

Deep pressure into the abdominal muscles was another challenging technique. When we learned it in massage school, more than one of the students couldn't handle receiving that pressure, and many were uncomfortable with practicing it. John, on the other hand, thought it was great. I hesitated when I first told him about it, and he insisted that I go ahead. He asked me for abdominal massage many times. I may have been the only student at massage school to ever practice that technique. I don't think I ever used it on another client though.

Learning to properly drape was another challenging task in massage school. John didn't worry about draping, so I learned more about it when I began working on other people. Both Terry and Lee were insistent that I do it right. Both of them always told me if the draping was too loose or if they felt in any way as if they might be exposed. They were kind, noting that I was still learning, but pointed out that I wanted all of my clients to feel comfortable.

I continued to do massage on John after I was done with massage school. He had no money, and I never asked him to pay me. When he moved to Bailey Boushay, John had me bring my massage table to a sunny room that was used for family meetings or visits and also for treatments like massage.

At the end of his life, when he was close to death, John still wanted me to continue with Reiki and also with another energy technique called polarity therapy. "Polarity Therapy is the art and science of stimulating and balancing the flow of life energy within the human being. The term *polarity* relates to one of the fundamental laws of nature, namely the attraction and union of opposites through a balanced middle point." I learned at massage school to hold the client's feet and focus on balancing the two sides. John always liked that and especially wanted it when he was bedridden.

John was close to death for a week at the beginning of February. A nurse at the ACTU had given my name to one of her patients, and I had an appointment to give him a massage. I hesitated and decided to go ahead to meet the new person. I thought that John would wait for me to show up if he needed to be with me one more time before dying. He did not wait, and I learned about his death when I came back from meeting the new person, Steve.

John was gone, but Steve was another person who was ready to give me lots of feedback during massages (over the seven months that we knew each other before he too died). And much of what he wanted and liked was quite different from John.

Steve had exchanged massage with other gay men over the years. This was the way he always got massage until he met me. Then he found he liked getting massage from a woman, where there was no question of sex being involved. Steve absolutely hated being draped. He tried to go along with it when I said I needed to learn to do it right, but finally said he couldn't stand it and did not want the top sheet. I learned to avert my eyes, for my own comfort, and to accept his choice.

Unlike many people who quietly drift into a meditative state, Steve also rebelled against the idea that he would get a better massage if he stopped talking and simply experienced touch. He tried it once, at my suggestion. About halfway through, he announced that he couldn't stand it and had to talk. We talked all the way through that massage and the massages he had in the future.

Steve had a lot to talk about, much of it angry. He didn't talk about what I was doing. He talked about other people in his life. He insisted his parents and his lover had abandoned him when he developed AIDS. They still communicated with him, but mostly from a distance. He was lonely. I heard a lot about all of them and never met any of them. He had other stories of bad treatment from earlier in his life, including the person who infected him with HIV. He was bitter about his former coworkers. Once he stopped working, because of his illness, he never heard from any of them again. He went in to the office to visit once, and they all seemed embarrassed and reluctant to talk to him.

Steve lived in a condo on the lower slope of Queen Anne Hill. He had a dog, a pug, whose name I have forgotten. The dog was sweet and smart but didn't seem to have any concept of play (or any toys). I guess Steve took her out to do her business, but I never saw it and never walked her myself.

After hearing so much about the family who abandoned him, I decided to invite Steve to attend a family gathering with me. I recently looked through my photo albums and found the occasion in the summer of 1994. Gigi and Dolores were visiting from DC, and the family had gathered at Mom's house (downstairs from me). Steve was tall and thin. He had Kaposi's sarcoma on his neck. No one commented, and everyone was warm and welcoming to him. I think he brought a salad to the meal.

Steve liked to cook and cooked for me a couple of times at his condo. He made hummus with pita and vegetables and some sort of dessert. He confided that he tried to learn to make baba ghanoush, but it was too complicated and he gave up. We both like baba ghanoush better than hummus, but the hummus he made was good. Eating together was a nice social time. I treasure this reminder that we were friends and it wasn't just about giving him massage.

A dim memory is surfacing of going to a comedy show with Steve. He told me that he had the tickets and asked if I would like to join him. I agreed and we had an enjoyable evening.

When Steve got very sick, his family showed up. They called me to cancel a scheduled massage. I didn't hear anymore from him or his family although I have a vague memory of possibly visiting him in the hospital and discovering we didn't have anything else to say. I didn't see him at the end. I don't know whether he had any kind of funeral. It was just done.

Not long after I last heard from or about Steve, I met Cary through another nurse at the ACTU. When I got to his house, I set up the massage table in his living room. We chatted and began to know each other during the massage. He made another appointment the following week. I realized after several massages that he wasn't really interested in receiving massage. He was interested in gathering a care team around him as he lived with AIDS. He was a doctor and realistic about what was happening to him. He had a friend across the street and other friends who stopped by from time to time. We talked and I agreed to come over once a week. We spent time talking, and I drove him on errands, especially shopping.

By the time Cary was at the end of his life, weekly meetings with him were just part of my schedule. His brother moved in with him to be his major caregiver, and I continued to visit. I came more often during the last days, sitting quietly in his bedroom with him.

Even though Cary didn't want massage, spending time with him fit in with my learning curve about massage. Accepting his lack of interest without taking it personally was just as important as soliciting feedback from regular clients. None of the feedback was personal. Nor was it personal when Steve disappeared from my life.

Even though Shawn introduced John to me, so John could get massage, Shawn had no interest in receiving massage. He was too traumatized from childhood abuse. He gave his two-year-old daughter Geni back massages. He had discovered early on that massaging her back helped her to fall asleep. He also accepted back massage from her. That he could handle.

==========

Cruising (for Steve S)

Sometimes I think of him as I never saw him
Sitting at the edge of the dance floor at the Timberline
Waiting for someone to approach him

No one ever did and Steve didn't understand why
He was always handsome and popular, with a clever tongue
Never had any trouble meeting people

Now he had the marks of Kaposi's sarcoma
On his thin face, his body far too thin to be gorgeous
His walk painful from neuropathy

==========

Naked Moment (Steve)

No sheet for him.
No sheet to cover his bony body.
No sheet pulled up for modesty.

He chatted as I smoothed lotion up wasted arms.
He laughed as we considered revenge on the world.
He mourned the loss of life and love.

I looked away as I worked.
I closed my eyes and saw with my hands.
I touched him for a moment.

==========

Steve

The virus was kept outside with the storm.
We were simply two friends, sharing,
did not have to remember one of us was dying.

He had promised to prepare this treat for me.

We ate hummus redolent with garlic.
We dipped the pita bread into the bowl.
We talked about food and cooking.

The dog waited and hoped for a bite.

We had twenty minutes,
sitting together in his small kitchen
on a rainy Seattle evening.

A Mind of His Own, Eric

Some believe that the only afterlife is when people remember you. Yes, I remember, and maybe putting it in writing will make the memory last longer.

Denise and I discussed Eric recently. She wrote to me, "Per our conversation yesterday, Eric's ashes were largely scattered at Seven Springs Farm (after Margi's drum determination that all flows downhill to Puget Sound) and a bit in your back yard before the bag was disposed of in the garbage. That's per my recollection from quite some years ago."

I wrote back to her, "Oh yeah, I remember now. Harold sent the ashes to me (without asking, they just showed up). I tried to give them to Jim H. He wouldn't take them and then you asked Margi about taking them to Seven Springs. I should write something about Eric, so this information doesn't get lost."

Denise responded, "The story I remember most about Eric was one time he was staying with us. He would go out on the front porch to smoke. There was at the time a young man living in the Capitola who in the morning would stand in his window completely naked. I happened to be out one morning when both Eric and the young man were out and about, and mentioned the young man to Eric. He said, 'Yes, I've been enjoying it.'"

I asked Denise how Eric's name came up in the first place. She said, "We were talking about *pride*, I think, and I mentioned Radical Fairies, and you were trying to remember who you knew who had been in that group."

Eric Richardson came to me through John. He lived above John in Capitol Park (low-income housing, near me). John heard a terrible racket coming from above. He went to knock on his door to complain, and they met. The noise was from Eric's rock polisher. Eric had a special relationship with rocks. By the time he moved away from Seattle, he had many old coffee cans full of them. He could tell the history (or a history) for each one. I allowed him to give me the cans of rocks, but over the years, I've gotten rid of most of them. I still have a few, sitting on windowsills, but have no memory of what Eric said about them.

Somehow, when John and Eric talked, John mentioned that I did massage on him for free since he had AIDS. (Another neighbor named Peter was involved in this as well. I didn't meet Eric until after John had died. Peter gave Eric my phone number.) When Eric called to make an appointment, I explained that I charged for massage, but a very low price for people with AIDS. He was mostly interested in Reiki. I think I did some massage the first time, but he didn't like being touched and had me just do Reiki after that. He had been around people who think Reiki is the energy of the universe and should be freely available. I said that people pay me for my time, whether I do Reiki or massage. I don't remember for sure, but I think he paid me for any bodywork I did on him.

Eric made paintings, which seemed quite primitive to me. Once, he brought a couple with him and offered to trade them for massage. I didn't want them and declined. Maybe I should have accepted? I felt kind of bad that I didn't like his paintings, but he was philosophical about it.

Eric filled out my usual massage form with health information. He was forty-four years old. He was HIV positive. He was greatly troubled by Crohn's disease. He also was bipolar. He hoped that Reiki would help with all these. There was nothing to be done about it, but he also had Klinefelter's syndrome. He explained that because of a genetic mix-up (XXY), he was intersex. He preferred to be male and had a prescription for testosterone to keep the female characteristics under control. In addition, he was gay. I don't know of any romantic relationships.

Eric was tall, probably close to six feet, and heavy, maybe 300-plus pounds. At the end of his life, he lost a lot of weight, becoming almost skeletal. This happened after he had all his teeth pulled. He was convinced heavy metals were affecting his health. At first he had the fillings removed. Later he had the teeth pulled. Then everything had to be cooked to a pulp. He must have eaten a lot less then.

I probably saw Eric for Reiki sessions about once a month for a year or so. He was confident that the work helped to diminish the symptoms of Crohn's. He also stopped taking medications for bipolar disorder over that time. He thought Reiki cured him.

He always talked a lot during sessions, and I didn't understand a lot of what he said. He was impressed by the philosophy of Ken Wilber. Not only that, but he was attempting to go further and expand on Wilber's ideas. I listened and attempted to understand what he was talking about. I didn't know if the problem was with me or if Eric's theories didn't actually make sense.

When I was at Antioch, I eventually bought and read several of Wilber's books, as well as studying his theories in secondary sources. I sometimes thought I was grasping what he had to say, but then it would slip away. The only book I really enjoyed was *Grace and Grit: Spirituality and Healing in the Life and Death of Treya Killam Wilber*, about his wife's cancer.

Eric talked about his birth family. His said they were embarrassed by his problems, especially the Klinefelter's syndrome. He described abuse when he was young and rejection when he was older. His parents were no longer alive, but he suspected his sister intended to find a way to have him institutionalized. She was on the East Coast, and he made sure she didn't know how to find him.

He also talked about his daughter. She was not his biological daughter. Eric's friend was pregnant and abandoned by the birth father when he offered to step up and be the father for her child. It sounded like the daughter was a young adult by the time we knew each other. The connection may not have been close by then. I think they called or wrote once in a while.

Eric had big hopes that his own choices and Reiki and who knows what else could help him to be healthy, even with HIV. At the same time, he worked with a doctor at the Pike Place Market clinic and went along with their recommendations.

In time, after we had known each other for a year or so, Eric decided to try something different. He had a friend, Harold, living on wooded property in Kentucky. He said Harold (in his early seventies) was a retired minister or else had been a minister until he no longer believed. Harold was willing to have Eric move across the country and live in a cabin on his property. Eric said if he focused on chopping wood and carrying water, he could stay healthy. He could coexist with HIV. He envisioned a community of happy, healthy people living a simple life and surviving the virus. He made some effort to get others to join with him in this project. One or two men were interested, but none ever followed up.

In the end, Eric got rid of most of his possessions and moved to Kentucky. He took Greyhound, which meant he couldn't take much with him.

Besides rocks, Eric also gave me a couple of plants. One was wild ginger in a large plastic box (about two feet by one foot by one foot). Unfortunately, Rosie (cat) thought it made a perfect place to go to the bathroom, and the plant didn't survive long. The other plant was aloe and lasted for a few years. I was worried about telling Eric about the fate of the ginger and the aloe. Eric never asked about the plants or about the rocks. I guess when he gave them away, he really let go of them.

Those were the days when email was still pretty new. I didn't have it, and Eric didn't have a computer, much less email. We kept in touch through snail mail and phone calls. He was pretty happy in Kentucky and optimistic about his health.

Because Eric didn't want his family to know where he was, he asked me to accept his mail and forward it to him. He didn't get a lot of mail, and his family never asked me for his address.

In the meantime, Eric thought I should get to know his friend Jim H. They met when Jim was the president of the residents' council for Seattle Housing Authority. Eric was living at Capitol Park (near me) while Jim lived at Center Park. Center Park was designed for people with severe physical handicaps. The units were doubled so that live-in caregivers could have separate space. Jim was in a motorized wheelchair (quadriplegic because of a motorcycle accident), but didn't let that stop him from an active life, including "rolling for office." He ran for the state legislature as a Republican. He didn't get many votes, but he really enjoyed campaigning.

At the time, Jim and Eric were pressing SHA (Seattle Housing Authority) to put in a sliding front door at Capitol Park to make access easier for infirm people (not to have to push a heavy door). The first time they talked, Jim misunderstood when Eric said he lived at Capitol Park. Jim heard "Cattle Park," and that's what they called it from then on. They thought that described the attitude of people running the building. The new door was eventually installed.

After we talked on the phone, Jim invited me to come visit him. I was interested to see, when I came in, a portrait of Ida May Daly. She (who had muscular dystrophy) was a prime mover in getting curb cuts and other ways for handicapped people to have access (back in the sixties and seventies). She donated the land for Center Park and made sure the building was put up. Years later, in a fitting memorial to her, residents of Center Park pressured Metro to provide better access to buses. I liked Jim, even though his political pronouncements often irritated me. I was interested in learning about doing massage on a quadriplegic and volunteered to give him free massage and did for several years.

Jim and I often shared Eric stories. Eric tried to persuade both of us to move across the country as well. He was convinced that there was going to be a major earthquake and then a tsunami that would destroy all of Seattle. Neither of us took the suggestion very seriously.

Because of his continuing connection with the Pike Place Market clinic, Eric came back to Seattle about once a year after he moved to Kentucky. He stayed with me during two of those visits. I picked him up from the bus and took him back when he left. He still had other friends in the area. One time, he visited for a longer time when he was considering moving back here, and he lived in a building on Third Avenue and about Jackson (The Morrison, owned now, I see, by DESC). I went to see him there, and it was an odd and unpleasant place. People on the street nearby seemed drunk and homeless. A security guard sat inside the door. He held my driver's license while I was visiting Eric.

When Rebecca and Pedro moved into their first Seattle apartment (on Summit) in 1997, Eric was visiting me. They had trouble finding a crew to help with the move. He was happy to volunteer and spent the day lifting and carrying.

Life wasn't so good for Eric when he went back to Kentucky. He had a bout of meningitis. He recovered from it, but the treatment was so painful that he swore he would never go through it again. The infection came back in a few months. He didn't get treatment and he died.

One day, a month or so after Eric died, a package arrived at my house. I opened it. The box contained Eric's ashes, sent by his friend Harold. I contacted Harold and suggested the ashes should go to Eric's daughter. No, she didn't want them. I couldn't persuade Jim H to take them either. Hence, the ashes ended up at the farm in Marysville, owned by Denise's friends Margi and Terry. It seemed like a good place for his ashes, a little bit like his Kentucky refuge.

Friendship with Jim H continued after Eric had died. He stopped asking for massage (after borrowing money from me to finance a new electric wheelchair) and stopped responding to emails about 2001. I went to his funeral in 2007.

Harold and I continued with an email conversation over the years. I often didn't understand his essays, but it seemed good to keep the connection. In one email, he said, "We prefer to illusionalize our being the center of ALL and have therefore invented a god for things we do not understand or are unable to comprehend. This satisfies our basic greed of power and influence and provides ammunition for us to deny our participation in every other aspect of this universe of form expression. This in turn gives us permission to destroy other expressions of the Universe, to deplete them, to desiccate them, to overuse them for our own greedy goals of self-enhancement."

After a long silence, this recently came in the mail about 2016: "Great to hear from you with all the pictures. I am still on this planet. Walk with a walker and no longer drive. Coming closer to 100 but might not make. All speaks great for you. Enjoy. Harold." I had been sending emails, but I guess he didn't get them. We've never talked about Eric.

==========

A Good Life (for Eric R)

> Independence day
> July 4 1998
> Eric Richardson left his body
> And all that stuff
>
> Mixed up chromosomes . . . blurring gender
> HIV . . . lurking in blood
> Manic-depression
> Crohn's disease . . . wrenching gut pain
>
> But he had fun
> Adventure
> Playing with sound, energy, food
> Then a leap into the void

==========

Silent Witnesses (Eric)

> He had rows of coffee cans filled with rocks.
> He took out one rock at a time.
> He rolled them to examine all sides.
> He could tell where he found each one,

whether in the forest or by a lake.

Each rock spoke to him.
He talked about their energy
Some he could not give up.
Others he handed on as he prepared to move
across the country, riding on Greyhound.

Some rocks sit still around my house.
I do not hear their voices
I could not tell you about their meaning.

==========

Eric Returns

days of sitting upright on a bus
three days of being crowded
with all his bags
diesel smell permeates
brief meals at truck stops
to cross the country
on little money
the virus rode with him
quiet and inconspicuous
never allowed to rule his life

==========

Eric, Still Remembered, from July 4, 2010

Twelve years now, since the word came from across the country,
just weeks after his optimistic phone call,
sure that he could beat this thing.

Maybe even come back some day,
to reclaim the plants he left with me when he first moved
across the country, or the rocks, each with a story
gathered into coffee cans, too heavy to carry on the Greyhound bus.

And then he would publish his musings or sell his paintings,
continue with life.

Twelve years ago.

Now all that remains
with me: pages of writing, a few of the rocks, and the memory.

==========

Eric

After years of minor problems from HIV,
finally meningitis
attacked, he was

convinced to accept antibiotics,
unpleasant and life-threatening
would not go on them again

Continued to maintain
"Pain is necessary
but suffering is optional"

He was clear and peaceful
during his last few days
at the home of his friend, where he died

Is God Here?

The High Holy Days got me thinking (trying to remember) about possible religious (or spiritual) aspects of my years connected with people living with AIDS.

When I think about spiritual support for people with AIDS, I think about Buddhism. During those years, I learned (for the first time) something about Buddhism from several people. I learned names of some people who interpret Buddhism for Westerners: Stephen Levine, Ram Dass and the Dalai Lama. I learned from people and also from reading books.

Jack quoted this from Ram Dass: "I have a friend named, Emmanuel. Some of you have met him through his books. He is a spook, a being of Light that has dropped his body. Emmanuel shares a lot of great wisdom. He is like an uncle to me. I once said to him, 'Emmanuel, I often deal with the fear of death in this culture. What should I tell people about dying?' And Emmanuel said, 'Tell them it's absolutely SAFE!' He said, 'It's like taking off a tight shoe.'" Or rather, Jack used the last part, about death being like taking off a tight shoe. He still admitted to feeling afraid. He was also influenced by Buddhist ideas about the distinction between healing and curing. Healing is more of a spiritual thing and between people while cure has to do with the body. Healing is the significant part.

I liked a lot of what I learned from Buddhism. One thought that has stayed with me is related to suffering: "Desire and attachment are the causes of unsatisfactoriness and suffering." My understanding is that all lives bring pain and change. It is attachment to not having pain and nothing changing that causes suffering (on top of the pain). I also learned the distinction between attachment and preference. It is human to have preferences. Attachment is much stronger when we can't accept not getting our preference. Jack always intended to live this way. He would have preferred not to have AIDS. He didn't beat himself up about his mistakes that led to his infection.

I read a book by Stephen Levine, who spent time with people who were sick and dying. He used meditation as a kind of treatment—for healing. John had me copy passages from the book, specifically those that address dealing with pain. I went to Kinko's to copy the pages that gave step-by-step instructions on focusing on painful spots, surrounding them with light and diminishing them. I read the important part to John as I was giving him a massage. I left the pages with him for future reference. He said that the pain meditation helped him.

After reading Ram Dass's words ("When asked if he could sum up his life's message, he replied, 'I help people as a way to work on myself, and I work on myself to help people . . . to me, that's what the emerging game is all about.'"), I looked for ways that helping people with AIDS could actually be worked on myself. I remember thinking that Sam resented any expectation of friendship I might have based on the free massage I did on Randy and him. I recognized that expectation in myself and worked on releasing it.

I used to listen to tapes of Ram Dass speaking when I drove to massage appointments. I like the way Ram Dass speaks of the yoga of service, as opposed to yoga as meditation. That was his path and appeals to me. He says others are simply his guru in drag (when they challenge him, especially the ones that are difficult to love) or the self in another form. I had many opportunities to remember those words when I spent time with people who were angry about having AIDS.

Ram Dass was originally Jewish (and still identifies with Judaism as well as Buddhism). Another person who bridges the two belief systems is Rabbi Zalman Schachter-Shalomi. He applied Buddhist thinking to traditional Judaism. (From *Wikipedia*, "He articulated eco-kashrut as an evolving set of practices that extend beyond traditional kashrut by taking the human and environmental costs of food production and consumption into account when deciding what to eat or not eat." "He also pioneered the practice of 'spiritual eldering', working with fellow seniors on coming to spiritual terms with aging and becoming mentors for younger adults.") This concept of mentoring would also apply to people like Jack who spoke about experiences he had while living with AIDS.

The Jew in the Lotus, by Roger Kamenetz (1994) described a dialogue between the Dalai Lama and Jews. ("The book also made prominent a Jewish mystical response to Eastern spirituality in the Jewish renewal movement, led by Rabbi Zalman Schachter-Shalomi, and Jewish meditation as taught by Rabbi Jonathan Omer-Man.") This helped me to fit Buddhism into my Judaism.

John greatly admired the Dalai Lama and convinced me that we should go to hear him speak when he was in Seattle. (The Dalai Lama has traveled the world and has spoken about the welfare of Tibetans, environment, economics, women's rights, nonviolence, interfaith dialogue, physics, astronomy, Buddhism and science, cognitive neuroscience, reproductive health, and sexuality, along with various topics of Mahayana and Vajrayana Buddhist teachings.) Much of what the Dalai Lama said was difficult for me to grasp, but I tried since John thought it was important.

Another person who was greatly admired by many in the AIDS community was Louise Hay (not a Buddhist). By Hay's account, in the early 1970s, she became a religious science practitioner. In this role, she led people in spoken affirmations, which she believes would cure their illnesses, and became popular as a workshop leader.) Both Eric and John thought they could recover their health or at least live with AIDS if they just had a positive attitude. Eric was sure that he could do this by physical labor and living in a rural place when he moved to Kentucky to live on Harold's land. John thought sunshine and hanging out with his dog Mo could make the positive difference. He thought that admitting he might die would ensure that he did die. (I'm not a fan of Louise Hay. I think her ideas made people feel guilty when they didn't recover from illnesses such as cancer and AIDS.)

Eric and his friend Harold introduced me to the teachings of Ken Wilbur. I found his writing to be difficult and always felt inadequate, as if I wasn't intelligent enough to understand while Eric and Harold were excited about his ideas. Even when the author came into my life again when I was at Antioch (c. 2003), I would almost grasp the concepts and then lose my grip.

Ken Wilbur's theory is based on AQAL. (From *Wikipedia*, "All Quadrants All Levels [AQAL], pronounced 'ah-qwul', is the basic framework of integral theory. It models human knowledge and experience with a four-quadrant grid, along the axes of 'interior-exterior' and 'individual-collective'. According to Wilber, it is a comprehensive approach to reality, a metatheory that attempts to explain how academic disciplines and every form of knowledge and experience fit together coherently.") I don't know how this helped Eric. Maybe it was mostly that thinking about the philosophy that gave him a break from his life. Maybe it helped him to think that everything fit together.

During all the discussions about religion with John and others, almost no one was at all interested in my experiences. I guess most knew I was Jewish, but it didn't concern them. John was mostly interested in persuading me to be a Buddhist. After a couple of years, he let go of that hope. He had a Buddhist community anyway, including the people who came to chant for him. Buddhist monks also offered support to John and others, including caregiving. That was enough.

Michael and I talked some about the differences. We were able to compromise between his Christianity and my Judaism with the Psalms, especially the Twenty-Third Psalm. We read Psalms together. Or rather, I read them to him as he listened. The Psalms had a very personal meaning in this context. We were both aware that Michael was approaching death. We were walking through the valley of the shadow of death and staying strong because of the love between us. We were sure that God was with us. I know that we both felt that and didn't feel afraid.

Some of my gay friends had negative experiences with religion in their families of origin. Raymond was bitter about the church of his family. I think Jack was as well. Their families rejected their gay sons because of religion. Yet both Jack and Raymond had some healing in the relationships with family as the end of their lives. Raymond's parents had a minister (who didn't seem to know Raymond) lead his memorial service, but there was very little mention of religion. I think Raymond would have been okay with that. I don't know whether Jack's parents had a memorial service. His friends had a very secular memorial, just a group of us sitting around sharing stories and photos. John's Buddhism and that of his sister and friends shaped John's memorial service.

Shawn talked about the special masses for people with AIDS at St. Joseph's Catholic Church (not far from where I live). He gave credit for the services to Fr. David Jaeger, whom Shawn said was openly gay. In fact, Fr. Jaeger was gay and later was laicized (after some accusations of molesting seminarians). Archbishop Hunthausen was the prelate who approved of (maybe instigated) the ministry to people living with AIDS. Much of that disappeared when he retired in 1991 (or maybe earlier when he was being investigated for deviating from official church policy). Shawn had Father Jaeger baptize his daughter, but I don't think they went to many masses or maintained a connection with the church.

In my experience, the most powerful spiritual support for people living with AIDS was Multifaith Works. Gwen Beighle was the founder of the Multifaith AIDS Project of Seattle. It was born out of an encounter in 1987 with a friend of her daughter Kate Beighle of Seattle. As moderator of the Seattle Presbytery, the local policy arm of the Presbyterian Church (USA), Gwen Beighle invited her daughter's friend, Kenneth Lichman, to speak at a program on AIDS sponsored by the presbytery. Asked what clergy and laypeople could do to help people with AIDS like him, Lichman replied, "We need a beautiful place to die."

In a 1994 interview, the Reverend Gwen Beighle described her adult life unfolding in three stages: Her first career was as a medical technician/bacteriologist. Her second was raising her children. At forty-six, after many hours of volunteer hospital visits as a deacon and elder at Seattle's Wedgwood Presbyterian Church, she began her third career by earning a master's of divinity degree from the Vancouver School of Theology in British Columbia. As she turned fifty, she was ordained a hospital chaplain in 1982. While working at Harborview Medical Center, she began to encounter patients with AIDS. She saw their hurt from being abandoned by family and church.

Rosehedge House and Multifaith Works both began in 1988, with Rosehedge providing housing for people with HIV/AIDS and Multifaith Works running the Care Teams while Shanti offered emotional support services. Multifaith Works developed its own housing program in 1995, and the two groups merged in 2011. All of them depended heavily on volunteers.

Rabbi Anson Laytner was the executive director of Multifaith Works for eleven years until 2005. On July 14, 2003, "originally founded in 1988 as MultiFaith AIDS Projects (MAPS), MultiFaith Works has grown and changed over the years, all while maintaining its focus on serving the local AIDS community. Included under the MultiFaith Works organizational umbrella is the Shanti program, which is 20 years old this year. Other MultiFaith Works programs are: MultiFaith AIDS Projects Housing (MAPS), AIDS CareTeams, Ariel MS House, and the MultiFaith Alliance of Reconciling Communities (MAPS)." Government funds and other support declined dramatically, and the organization closed at the end of 2013.

Even after all these years, I suspect that many religious organizations still condemn LGBT people and would not be accepting of people with AIDS. But I don't know the truth and hope I am wrong. Bailey-Boushay House offers the support of a chaplain to inpatients.

Sharing Food

One of the subjects sure to generate discussion and disagreement among those commenting on advice columns is whether or not to share food in a restaurant. Food memories are powerful and emotional.

That question reminds me of John, who died of AIDS in 1994. We often went out to eat, sometimes before going to a movie. Movies gave John a brief respite. He could forget that he was living with AIDS. After we looked over the menu, John decided what he wanted to order. Then he attempted to steer me toward ordering whatever was his second choice. He knew that I would let him have some of mine. John never ordered wine. That was forbidden because of HIV and his medications. In addition, he avoided wine and sweet foods because of constant yeast infections. However, he encouraged me to order a glass of wine and dessert. He thought a tiny sip (or two) or bite of mine wouldn't count.

As time went on, meals with John became more challenging. He was plagued with nausea. To avoid disaster, he often took a few puffs of marijuana before going into a restaurant. The joint went into a Ziploc bag and into the glove compartment. I never thought I would have pot in my car. I never protested. I drove really carefully.

The Broadway American Grill (now defunct) was John's favorite restaurant, long before we knew each other. He and one of the owners, Debbie, joked and flirted. I always paid for those meals. When John was no longer able to walk, to go to the restaurant, Debbie offered to comp meals for John. One of his visitors would call in the order and then go to pick it up. They must have known that John wasn't eating everything he ordered, often enough for three or more people. He especially loved a pasta dish with clams and the daily fruit cobbler. This continued when John moved to Bailey-Boushay and pretty much to the end of his life.

I have photos of John and copies of his artwork, paintings that incorporate photos and his sweet dog, Mo. One of my favorites is the Healing Buddha of the Hotel Honolulu. John hoped and believed that the Hawaiian sun (any sun) could cure his AIDS. We sometimes had picnics at the top of the hill in Lakeview Cemetery to get the last sun of the day. I remember stopping at a small restaurant called Cedars to get falafel sandwiches for a picnic.

Shawn (who introduced me to John) cooked for me a few times or shared food that he had cooked for himself and daughter Gennie (three years old when we met). I often bought groceries for him. He had elaborate reasons for not being able to buy food (or pay the rent). Either he lost his money or someone stole it. He didn't admit to buying drugs, except once when he talked about a plan for getting rich by selling drugs. He hoped that I would choose to invest in this business plan, but I wasn't interested. Despite all that, I felt loved and cared for when he cooked special meals for me.

Shawn and I attended, once or twice, a Friday night dinner at a house on Seventeenth and Thomas, Seattle AIDS support groups (SASG). Groups for people with AIDS and groups for caregivers met there. Many people appreciated the support. Others thought people were mainly looking for romance or opportunities to gossip about others. Volunteers brought and prepared the food for Friday nights. Anyone with AIDS was welcome to partake. Once, we were there on a summer day, sitting on the grass with others. Another time, in colder weather, we were all crowded into a tiny living room. At one point, Shawn asked to taste something on my plate. I agreed (and wondered if others were noticing that I wasn't worried about getting AIDS from him). Showing off . . .

I have photos of Shawn from the years that we were friends, mostly including Geni. And I have an odd necklace that he made from natural bits and pieces. This hangs on a bookcase.

Another person who cooked for me was Steve. I met him through one of the nurses at the AIDS Clinical Trial Units. Steve had worked hard, trying many recipes, to master making baba ghanoush, but he finally gave up. When he cooked for me, he made hummus. We had a little party, just us and his pug, after a massage. Our agreement was for him to teach me more about doing massage in exchange for massages. He had traded massage with other gay men over the years and had his own massage table. When I suggested massage might be more therapeutic if we didn't talk, he agreed to try. Fifteen minutes later he was ready to explode and went back to talking.

Steve had a conflicted relationship with his family. They were angry, and he was angry. Because they weren't getting along, I invited Steve to Thanksgiving dinner (or some other special meal) with my family. I think that was in 1993. Steve was gaunt and had obvious Kaposi's sarcoma on his face. (Somewhere, I believe there are pictures.) Steve brought a salad to the meal. He was happy with the dinner. My family members were all kind and welcoming to him. When Steve got sicker and was close to death, his family came around. Somehow that meant I was shut out. I wondered if it was because he had said so many negative things about them to me.

I met Kelly through food, when we were both packaging meals for Chicken Soup Brigade. The routine left plenty of time for conversation, and we became friends. Once, we were waiting for the chef to arrive, and Kelly sat down at the piano. He played ragtime, and very well. He sang in a beautiful bass voice. When we met, Kelly was living with someone he was in love with. Later, that relationship fell apart. My husband had a vacant apartment, on Greenwood, which he rented to Kelly. That apartment shared a bathroom with another apartment. Kelly was worried about germs (and cleaned for a living), so he kept that bathroom meticulous. He cleaned at my house later in exchange for massage.

Over time, I learned that Kelly had a severe problem with alcohol. He called a few times when he was drunk. After getting a DUI, he gave up his car, but he never stopped drinking. He died from bleeding out rather than from HIV. (He was positive but never had symptoms.) Kelly made me a delicious lunch once at his apartment.

Another friend with AIDS fed me (and others) in a different way. This was Raymond, whom I met when he came in for massage at Madison Clinic (my volunteer gig). We talked a lot, and I ended up doing massage on him at his house over on Twentieth and Cherry.

He planned a feast to serve to all who had helped him to live with AIDS. He carefully planned the menu, choosing dishes he loved, and knew how to cook. He put together a pamphlet of recipes (I have a copy somewhere). In the end, he wasn't able prepare the feast. His parents had the food prepared for his funeral at the Stimson-Green Mansion, and it was a fabulous meal. They also gave out tapes of Raymond playing the piano. His parents invited various caregivers, as well as their own friends from over the years. Some were invited to speak (including me). They didn't acknowledge AIDS in the service, and the rest of us respected their choice. It seemed that they felt most comfortable with those of us from the AIDS community at that event.

Raymond was close to his parents, who spent a couple of days each week in Seattle (from home in Bremerton) helping him. His father remodeled his home to make it work for him as he got weaker. Raymond struggled with their disapproval of his being gay. They wanted him to embrace the church they had brought him up in. He was angry and came to believe that they could love each other even with that between them. He made beautiful Valentine's Day cards for his parents and his sisters, and for me.

He had a small shop (featuring his favorite Western-themed kitsch), as well as being a massage therapist before he got sick. We decided that he could teach me more about massage in exchange for receiving massage every other week. When he died, his parents gave his massage table to me. (I used it for a long time until the day it collapsed with a client on it. Luckily, she wasn't hurt and just laughed.) I still have the face cradle from that table, in memorial, as well as the recipe book, the music tape, and the valentine he made for me.

I went to another funeral, with food and memories, at the Stimson-Green Mansion. Charles arranged this service when his partner Craig died. They both had AIDS. I met them when Charles hired me to do massage on them. Craig was in bad shape when we met. He couldn't really talk and was frozen in one position. Charles was the picture of health, compared to Craig. He was a former ballet dancer. He still moved and stretched. Craig had been a hairdresser. Both families seemed to have abandoned them, maybe because they were gay, or because of AIDS, or because Craig was white and Charles was black. One of the shocks of the memorial service was seeing Charles in his black suit, which hung on him. He was emaciated and sick. Craig's death had been a blow. Now Charles was smaller and quieter. He didn't live long after that. If anyone did a service for him, I didn't hear about it.

Sam's memorial service for his partner Randy was low-key, simply meeting for vanilla lattés at Randy's favorite coffee shop. I don't remember how I heard about the gathering. When I went, I felt out of place among the group of friends. I had done massage on both Randy and Sam while I was in massage school and didn't really understand I was a caregiver to them, not a friend. Randy confided in me, but Sam kept his distance.

At the opposite end of the spectrum was the memorial for Lee, who planned it himself long before he died. It was on a ferryboat (no longer in service) and included food, music, and tributes to Lee. I met Lee through my friend Terry (from massage school). Terry died before Lee. His parents hosted a memorial service in south Seattle. I went to that one with another friend from massage school. I began doing massage on Lee while I was still in school. He insisted on paying me once I was licensed. Even though we talked a lot during massages, that memorial service was a little uncomfortable. We weren't friends beyond the professional relationship, though I liked and admired him.

Lee used to save some money for a yearly "miracle cure." One of those involved shark cartilage. I'm not sure if it was eaten or put on externally. He worked as a lawyer almost to the end of his life. When we met, he knew that he had been diagnosed with CMV (cytomegalovirus), which might cause blindness. He arranged with a nurse to have a "cocktail" so that he could end his life if that happened. He did go blind and then began learning to find his way around without seeing. He was able to continue working and decided to put off dying until he was unable to walk. He put it off again when that happened. I don't know if he ever used the cocktail.

I have another food memory, of a sort, with Jack. I met Jack when I (a volunteer for Chicken Soup Brigade) drove him to an appointment. We got along so well that he began calling me on his own for rides and I called to check on how he was doing. Later, I hung out with him a lot (after he spent months in the hospital with collapsed lungs, courtesy of pneumocystis pneumonia). I was in massage school at the time (summer 1991). I practiced massage on him and did homework while he watched television (often with the sound off so that he could invent funny dialogue).

Jack sometimes sent me to the store. He especially liked Dreyer's ice cream bars. Even though he was so thin and weak, he worried about being addicted to sugar and limited how many ice cream bars he ate. He used to go to Overeaters Anonymous because of the self-diagnosed sugar addiction. One day, we went through a drive-through at a hamburger place when he was craving a large burger and onion rings. He was only able to eat a few bites of each and thoroughly enjoyed those bites. When Jack asked me to buy something, he paid me back. When I spontaneously brought him something, I wouldn't let him pay me back. This was our agreement, comfortable for both of us.

When Jack died, his brother (who also had AIDS) invited those who were close (all caregivers) to a memorial service, a potluck. We sat and talked out our memories of Jack. It was sad and hard, and we laughed a lot. Jack's brother died a few months later (also of AIDS).

Bill went to great expense and effort to prepare a Thanksgiving meal for all who lived at the low-income housing near me, Capitol Park. Someone invited me to the meal, and the food was delicious.

After that, Bill and I were friendly. I liked his miniature fox terrier, smaller than a cat and of great interest to local cats. And I liked him, always upbeat. HIV affected his brain, and he ended up (for a couple of months until he died) in a head injury unit near Providence Hospital. Curtains, in a room containing six such cells, enclosed his bed, a small dresser, and a chair. Bill said that the typical meal there was a bologna sandwich. Friends, including me, brought him other foods until he got too weak to eat.

Some small food-related stories come to mind.

Eric was sure that the heavy metals in fillings were making him sick (along with HIV). He had the fillings removed and later had all his teeth pulled. I don't know if it helped. When he stayed with me, a couple of times, he cooked his own food so that it was soft enough to eat without teeth.

Once, Albert asked me to wash and put away dishes and utensils. I discovered that he had only a small assortment of eating utensils. I bought a cheap set of stainless for him. He was overwhelmed and grateful. He was twenty-five when he died and was the youngest of ten children. His mother turned the younger children over to the older ones while she worked. He resented that.

Dave and Phil were a couple, even though Phil lived in England. He came here for long visits to get his AIDS treatments. Both of them were occasional massage clients. Once, they took me out to lunch. Soon after that, they broke up. I kept in touch with them as individuals for a long time. Until I didn't hear back anymore. I don't know if either one is still alive.

Bobby had AIDS and kidney failure. Once his kidneys failed, the doctor told him he would die in a week if he didn't have dialysis. No, he wouldn't feel better if he had dialysis, but he would live longer. Bobby chose to do without the treatment. He was in Harborview Hospital, where I visited him every day until he died. He remembered root beer popsicles from when he was a child. I couldn't find any, so I froze root beer into cubes, and that worked for him for three days until he was no longer responsive.

A powerful food memory came from a visit to Rosehedge to see Michael. I brought him a Japanese pear. He was delighted and said how delicious it was. He was only able to eat two small slices. That was probably one of the last things he ate. After he died, his group of friends from drag queen days had a potluck at someone's house. Another group, mostly family, had a different memorial service in a church. They had a catered buffet. Both events were true to him. Not many people attended both.

Sharing food is more than tasting each other's foods. We share food as a community. We share to honor each other. We share to nurture. So many memories are attached to food.

==========

Just Today, in a White Paper Bag (Rosehedge)

a dozen figs dipped in dark chocolate
to share among the men living here
one for my special friend
just one, no appetite for more
but how lovely the taste of that one
how lovely to sit in the moment
how good to have that time
knowing
that this one may be the last
he may not eat again
death hovers over him
but today dark chocolate on one fig

Gay Capitol Hill

I've lived almost twenty-five years in this house. The house hasn't changed much, but the neighborhood around me has changed enormously.

I moved up here from Madison Park, where I felt surrounded by conservative Republicans. Capitol Hill neighborhood had a reputation. This was where gays and lesbians lived. This was where people lived who challenged rules about gender. This was where AIDS appeared in Seattle.

Mom moved in downstairs while I moved into the upstairs of this duplex. One day, she announced, "Now I've seen everything." She met a man walking his potbellied pig. She even knew the name of the pig. I thought I'd seen everything when I saw two Sisters of Perpetual Indulgence walking down Fifteenth. Their colorful clothing (fake religious habits) and makeup made me smile. I learned later that they performed to raise money for AIDS research. (They still work for human rights and respect for diversity and raise money for worthy causes.)

In 1993, the main streets Fifteenth, Broadway, Pike, Pine (and others) had many older small buildings and many funky businesses, such as Red and Black Books (left-wing books), Horizon bookstore (used books in an elderly house), Bailey Coy bookstore on Broadway, and another used-books store on Pike. City People's Mercantile (like a general store but yuppie) was nearby. There were older supermarkets (all gone or remodeled since then), a funky Fred Meyer, tiny restaurants, and so forth. I saw a prediction that the Pike/Pine corridor would be developed. Nothing happened for years. Things have changed, most dramatically recently (after 2010), when many buildings were replaced with much larger structures including expensive apartments.

Many businesses were oriented toward the gay community and/or people with AIDS. Beyond the Closet Bookstore (gone), stocked books and magazines all aimed at the gay community. There was a Lesbian Resources Center (gone) in part of an old house and (later) a Gay Community Center (gone) in a newer building, plus Lambert House (still present for young people) on Fifteenth. The LRC disappeared after moving twice to new venues. I heard that racism and antipathy to transsexual women caused rifts that couldn't be healed. The *Seattle Gay News* was printed in a part of a warehouse on Twelfth (seems to have moved, still exists) and distributed in stores and restaurants all over the hill. During the nineties, many issues of the SGN included obituaries for men who had died of AIDS. Those obits were printed for free. I don't think anyone checked them for facts. Stonewall (gone) assisted gay people (using "gay" here to mean all sexual minorities) who were struggling with addictions while Seattle Counseling Service (still here) provided mental health counseling (still does). Crossroads (gone) had many services, such as massage, acupuncture, Reiki, and other alternative resources.

The Pride Foundation raises money to donate to other nonprofits, especially those that help LGBT people. They also provide scholarships for LGBT youth. Lee was a big supporter of the Pride Foundation. He planned to leave his estate to the organization since his family didn't need it (his father, he said, was "richer than God"). I've donated to the Pride Foundation for years, in memory of Lee.

The Northwest AIDS Foundation and Chicken Soup Brigade provided practical assistance to people with AIDS (now joined as Lifelong AIDS Alliance). Rosehedge (gone) provided hospice care. SASG (still exists) provided support groups and meals (also slightly expired juices and Ensure). Other groups offered spiritual support and massage. Many of the people who worked or volunteered for these organizations were gay. Some were themselves living with HIV or AIDS until they got too sick to work. Harborview Hospital's AIDS clinic was then located close to Broadway and Madison, almost inside Capitol Hill. It later moved to the hospital, just beyond Capitol Hill, but still very much in the spirit of the neighborhood and convenient for the many who lived in it.

In the middle of all this was John B, who lived in a tiny house divided in two. Part of it was devoted to his massage practice. He and his partner Harold lived in the other part. They had been together for over thirty years (gay marriage wasn't allowed in those days).

The house was just a block off Broadway, convenient for clients. John's side of the building included a tiny front area where samples of his artwork (sweet watercolors) were available for sale. Some were original paintings. Others were made into cards. Each massage client had to walk through that room to get to the massage room. I never bought any art and felt a little guilty that I didn't want to. At the time, there was a monthly art walk along Broadway. John was part of it.

John had been a massage therapist for thirty years. He claimed not to have any physical problems from all the years. However, he didn't do any deep pressure and made up for it by applying heat packs when requested. He talked while doing massage. He was partly estranged from his family somewhere in the South and often told stories about their interactions.

His partner Harold never emerged (in my memory) from the other side of the building. They were committed to each other but not monogamous. Harold was HIV positive. John was not. He worried about Harold, of course, since so many people died quickly from AIDS. In the end, John got prostate cancer and died first. Their relationship seemed to me to have all the best parts of a committed gay relationship. As I recall, they had been together for more than thirty years.

Armistead Maupin says, in *Logical Family*, "Chris (Isherwood) and Don (Bachardy) distinguished fidelity from monogamy, preferring, as my Chris and I do, the durability of the former to the folly of making sex the deal-breaker in a union between men" (p. 255–256).

John talked about his treatments for prostate cancer, and then one day he canceled an appointment and I never saw him again. In the meantime (I learned later), he had begun receiving massages from Wendy. I guess he heard of Wendy through me since I used to alternate weeks between getting massages from him and getting them from Wendy.

John N. B 64. 10/25/04. Partner of Harold. Service Sun. 11/14/04 at 12:45 p.m. at SRF Temple, 1825 Serpentine Pl. N.E.
(Published in the *Seattle Times* on Nov. 12, 2004.)

A comment from Wendy on his obituary: "I am saddened by John's passing and so grateful for having known his sweetness, generosity and enthusiasm for life's twists and turns. He will be missed by so many in his communities." Me "I was sorry to see John's obituary in today's paper. He was a fine man and an excellent massage therapist, as well as creating some beautiful art work. He will be missed."

In some ways, Capitol Park (Seattle Housing Authority building on the next block from me) seemed to me to be the middle of gay life and AIDS in Seattle. The first person I met who lived there was Susan. This was before I moved to my house. I met Shawn through her since he was living with her.

Then Shawn introduced John to me (also in the building), and John gave my name to his neighbor Eric.

Once, John invited me to the special dinner that Bill, who lived there, was cooking for everybody in Capitol Park. He used the kitchen at the back of the common area. Bill was a skinny black man with a huge smile. He often walked his miniature fox terrier around the neighborhood. He said that cats were puzzled by the dog, but not afraid of it since it was smaller than most cats.

I think a family member took the dog when Bill got very sick and lived the last few weeks of his life in a building (for those with head injuries) next to Providence Hospital. I went to see Bill a couple of times when he was there. The room he was in was divided into four parts with curtains. Each cell had room for a bed, a bedside table with drawers, and a chair. He complained about the food there, saying that their idea of dinner was a bologna sandwich on dry bread. Bill convinced various friends to bring food to him.

I met several people who lived in the SHA building Jefferson Terrace, next to Harborview Hospital. Albert lived there and also Damien. Albert had me bring groceries to him. He complained about women who sat in the lobby watching who came and went. He encouraged me to go in the back door. He guaranteed that someone would always let me in—since the really scary people already lived there. He was right.

Shawn's friend Michael lived in another SHA building, Denny Terrace (Marty lived there as well) overlooking I-5, just inside the borders of Capitol Hill. Once, Shawn convinced me that Michael was hungry and sick, so I agreed to bring him groceries. When I got there, several people seemed to be staying in the apartment with him, and they all seemed relatively healthy (except all with AIDS). They also seemed to take it as their due that I brought food. I felt very uncomfortable being there, as if they just wanted me to give them the food and leave. That's what I wanted as well.

Others also lived in SHA housing. Doug lived in two different ones, one in Greenwood and one in Belltown (not Capitol Hill). At least one person lived in Olive Terrace, over by Trader Joe's (also on Capitol Hill).

Shawn lived twice in a building called the Cambridge down by Freeway Park (by the convention center), just barely inside Capitol Hill. He liked looking out his window at the park and walking in the park with his daughter Gennie. It was supposed to be short-term housing. I think he got evicted for not paying rent, but I'm not sure. A different Doug also lived there. I once saw him walking the couple of blocks to a convenience store wearing baggy sweats and slippers, the uniform of choice for many who were living with AIDS.

Some of the men who died of AIDS lived in regular apartments on Capitol Hill. Bobby lived in one next to Capitol Park. It was a pretty building, and he had a large studio. Michael owned a condo near Virginia Mason Hospital. Joseph lived in a studio apartment on Summit. Jack lived in a one-bedroom apartment over on Belmont. Steve's apartment was on Queen Anne. I guess they all had money from previous jobs. Michael had good retirement from being a Seattle bus driver. Bobby had worked on cruise ships. I don't know how Joseph, Steve, and Jack managed.

Raymond owned his own house, over on Cherry. Lee owned his own house as well, on Queen Anne Hill. Robin and his partner lived in a house in Wallingford. Cary owned a house in north Seattle. Terry and Dwayne were in West Seattle. None of them were on Capitol Hill, but probably came here for Gay Pride and social activities.

When I walk or drive around the city, especially in my neighborhood, I sometimes think about the people I loved who lived in the various buildings I pass. I see Capitol Park every day, so I remember those people the most often. John B's house is gone, torn down for new buildings and the light-rail. I remember the days when walking near my house meant often seeing people who had that AIDS look, thin and gray. I miss my friends who died so many years ago.

==========

No Contact (for JB)

Often I wanted to lie quietly
Other times we chatted during my massage
I told him stories from my practice
He reciprocated or talked of his life
Disembodied voices hung in the air
No connection with the bodywork

At the end he left the room quietly
I was ready to get on with my errands
Dressed quickly, wrote a check
He was hidden behind his desk as I left
Took my check, confirmed for the next time
Not much to say, didn't meet my eyes

Some Died and Some Lived On

Many of the men who had AIDs were fully retired by the time I knew them. John, Shawn, and Eric never had jobs when I knew them. Jack had left his last job in California. Steve had retired, and so had Cary. They were all too sick to work.

Others were determined to keep working. Terry was a flight attendant and then a student at massage school before finally giving up. I knew at least one doctor at Madison Clinic who kept working almost until he died. And Peter kept working as an assistant at Rosehedge. Clark kept on writing and putting on plays. They showed that they could keep on living as long as one lives. AIDS didn't have to mean just deciding life was over. Lee kept on as a lawyer just about to the end. He was working part-time as an attorney when I got to know him although he was very thin and in a lot of pain much of the time. He decided that he would keep working until his vision was affected. CMV took his vision in a few months, but he found ways to manage to find his way around his house and to still do some work. So then he said he would stop working when he couldn't walk anymore.

Money was a problem for many. Jack had a PO box for the bills he might not pay and so the debt collectors would have trouble finding him. Others didn't worry because they figured they wouldn't live long enough to be stuck. They didn't often have to pay for extras that enhanced quality of life. Someone said people with AIDS were lucky compared to other diseases. They had food, acupuncture, massage, and other services, including support groups.

But then, what happened to those who recovered some sort of health after the advent of protease inhibitors? They had to find jobs, to rebuild lives, and sometimes come to terms with family who had abandoned them. Thatcher Bailey has had a whole new life since protease inhibitors came out. Dave's ex-partner Phil went to massage school. Cary once said when we were on a shopping trip that he would be poor if he lived long enough.

One of the most significant people I met during those years of caregiving in the AIDS community was a woman who worked at an AIDS organization and was also living with HIV. I don't know whether J officially had AIDS. She kept her HIV status private. She told me in 1997 as part of her health disclosure when she first came to get a massage from me. We never talked about how she got the virus. She is about eight years younger than I am and grew up on the East Coast. She is married and has no children.

J got occasional massages, not regular. She liked to talk during massage, and she gave me a lot to think about during those sessions. This wasn't about massage, but more about her approach to life.

She worked as an AIDS case manager for many years. She counseled people who were living with AIDS and sometimes helped them with financial or housing issues. Her heart was in her work, and she always had a creative practice as well (writing poetry and creating art).

Despite being in some ways part of the system, J was skeptical of Western medicine and preferred to work with alternative practitioners. She thought many standard treatments were toxic, doing far more damage than good. She would not accept them at the time (although she did later). She relied on a woman who provided nutritional treatments for HIV. (I vaguely remember the establishment fighting back against this woman and getting her practice shut down, but could be remembering incorrectly.) They claimed that her creations could be toxic.

J told me about Continuum Movement. Continuum movement classes focused on random and slow movements. Some classes were more about creativity of various kinds. She valued this as an important way to keep healthy. I got curious and looked around online. The organization seems to have drastically downsized since the founder, Emilie Conrad, died (2014). Most classes seem to be in California or in Europe. I don't see anything local. Emilie Conrad was a dancer who also studied various kinds of bodywork. Her teaching combined many areas of movement.

Besides working full-time at NWAF, J was and is a dedicated poet. She talked about writing and talked about writing workshops she hoped to attend.

She wrote about her early life (including traumas) and her experiences as a case manager. She led Continuum writing workshops.

J and I have stayed in touch off and on over the years since I stopped doing massage. We went to lunch a few times when she was still working at NWAF. Many emails went back and forth, especially a few years ago. She was in the process (about ten years ago) of deciding to leave the NWAF. The agency was in a period of instability, and she was ready for a change.

She went to work for another agency and later switched again. She wanted to keep working somewhere until she was sixty-five. At the same time, she decided to start a private practice as a therapist. She had plenty of supervised hours, but needed to study for the test. I loaned her books I'd acquired when I was at Antioch and later when I thought about taking the test to be licensed. I hadn't read much in any of them and had long decided that I wouldn't take the test.

J later solicited my opinion when she was setting up her website as a therapist. With her permission, I shared with a couple of my friends and added their thoughts to mine.

Years ago, she wrote articles about health and healing as well as writing poetry. In recent years, she has had success with her poetry. She has published three books (2007, 2011, and 2017). She writes about being an AIDS case manager in the first book. The second is about her experiences while she was growing up. The third brings together her life as a case manager and her experience of living with the HIV diagnosis and wanting to keep it hidden.

I met J more than twenty years ago. Her admission to me that she had HIV showed her courage in going ahead with a normal life despite that burden. She trusted me to keep it to myself and I did. I learned that I could refrain from telling all that I knew. I could decide that no one else needed to know. Even before her third book, she thought that she had revealed her status when speaking at a bookstore about her earlier books. She was amazed that no one seemed to notice. Perhaps it was at that point that she decided to explicitly discuss it in her third book.

J knew that I was trying to write poetry. She invited me to several poetry readings she was doing. I met Thomas at one of them (2008), and we built a friendship. He mentored my poetry writing and eventually helped me put together a book and get it printed (2011). He was the publisher. I wonder if I sent her a copy of the book. So far, I haven't found any mention in emails, but it doesn't make sense that I wouldn't have shared with her. Odd.

Poetry readings reminded me of Pat R, whom I met in 1999, when she was in her late seventies. She was a poet and encouraged me to write. Pat took me to a couple of poetry readings (a little scary because she got confused while driving). One of those (in Fremont) was actually the first time I saw Thomas reading (about 2001). I loved his poetry and wanted to know him. I see in Pat's obituary online that she died in 2011. Going to the readings with Pat helped me get the courage to share my writing with others, including reading my poetry in public places. I learned that poets are kind to each other.

I am grateful to Pat and also think I wouldn't have wanted to share with her and go to readings with her if I hadn't already experienced support from J.

I sent J a draft of my poem about my sister, asking for feedback, recently. She wrote back quickly with comments and suggestions, as well as encouragement. She has talked often of other poets and her admiration of them. She is generous with her support of others. She commented on some of my AIDS poetry in the past. Most of her suggestions involve leaving out extraneous words. Yes.

Because J loved it so much, I decided to try Continuum as well. I went to a number of trainings. She was there for some of them and not for others. We hung out some during breaks when she was part of the group, but she had other friends there and spent time with them as well.

I loved learning to move slowly and experience gentle changes in my body. The leader had us imagine a slowly deflating balloon under the body part moving slowly. This has worked well for me in trying to deal with a stiff neck. And I have taught it to others.

One training that I didn't like much at the time was helpful for me in the long run. This one had to do with feelings versus thinking. I had to realize then that my tendency is to respond "I think . . ." when asked how I feel about something. Over time, I have focused on identifying emotions and not treating them as good or bad, just as feelings (analogous to feeling a touch or smelling something). That is, I've worked on accepting my emotions—but still have a lot of work to do.

I benefited from the (general) lack of judgment in Continuum trainings. I felt freed by the opportunity to follow instructions as best as I could without anyone coming around to tell me how to do the exercise in the right way. If I needed to, I could stop moving and just wait for the next thing without anyone saying anything. Judging myself against others is so easy for me and so unhelpful. I think I've taken that learning into other situations, such as when sharing my writing with other writers.

I went to a writing training that J gave in her apartment. I don't know if it taught me much although it encouraged me to freely write and express my feelings.

J and I met each other because of AIDS. She was working in an AIDS organization. I offered low-cost massage to anyone in the AIDS community (whether they were living with the disease or otherwise connected with the community). She told clients about my offer. We also came together because she wanted occasional massage for her health. In the long run, the most important parts of our relationship were the friendship elements around writing, which have continued almost twenty years after I stopped doing massage. Still, we have the connection through the AIDS community.

Family of Birth and Family of Choice

We form community. This is a human way to deal with life and especially true when people deal with life-threatening illness.

I began thinking about the communities around several people I knew who were living with AIDS in the nineties. Over time, I became part of those communities. Those communities ended (for the most part) when the person with AIDS died. Of course, it is hard when someone dies. Losing a community and regular activities adds to the loss. Sometimes it is really abrupt. During the long, slow days before someone dies, it can seem like you've always been going to the place where the person is and seeing the same people. Death puts an abrupt end to the whole way of life.

Michael had two communities. His friend Jackie, who took him to church with her, exemplified one community. Michael's sister and her boyfriend were connected mostly with that group. They didn't have other family. The other group was made up of friends who had known him for many years. I met a number of people from both groups when I was visiting Michael at Rosehedge and heard stories from him as well. After Michael died (December 1990), both groups planned memorial services for him. I may have been the only person who went to both services.

The church group had a service at an Episcopal church near the Seattle Center. They brought in food (maybe from Costco) for after the formal service. The service included prayers and songs. I suspected the minister who led the service hadn't met Michael or anyone else involved.

The friend group had a gathering at the home of one couple. The house was tucked between E Madison and the arboretum. The house was small and sparsely furnished. Both people in the couple were also dealing with HIV. I saw an obituary, so I knew that one of them died a couple of years after Michael. Friends from the group supplied food. A bulletin board above the table was covered with photos of Michael before he got sick. He was in drag in many of the photos. He was also roller blading around Greenlake in other photos. He was tall and healthy, just a few years before he died. I wouldn't have known who he was from the photos. He looked nothing like the person I knew.

Several of the people in the friend group came up to me and thanked me for being an "angel." They knew that I had visited him every day for a few months. I tried to argue with this description. I enjoyed being with him. It was nothing about being an angel. I didn't feel like an angel, and I knew I was lucky to have his love and friendship.

Jackie and I stayed in touch for several years after Michael died, but I never had any further connection with anyone in the friend group (or anyone else from the church and family group).

Albert worked hard to keep connected to his birth family and always feared they would abandon him if they knew he had AIDS. Various family members visited him, but I never met any of them while he was alive. I just heard about the visits from him. He told me many stories about his childhood and his relationships with family members. They may have heard about me from him. I met a family (friends) who took him in for a few months. They decided he had to go back to his apartment when it became too difficult taking care of him. I don't believe they ever spoke again.

Albert's mother got in touch with me after he died. (So yes, she had heard of me and knew how to get in touch.) She invited me to ride with them to the funeral (spring of 1991, at a black church) and told me about the viewing ahead of time (at a black funeral home). I went to the viewing and accepted the ride to the funeral. I bowed out of going to the meal after the service. I never heard from them again.

Jack had a community of caregivers. He talked about various people, including his Shanti volunteer (spiritual support) and his NWAF case manager. I learned their names long before I had met any of them. He also had his brother David and David's partner Steve living in Seattle (and the reason Jack moved here from California). He talked about his parents and other siblings, but he didn't seem to expect to see any of them again when we first met.

When Jack came home after months at Swedish Hospital, he made sure his community was ready to help him to be at home. He asked people to volunteer to visit one day or another. He didn't expect to have people with him full-time. He did want someone to stop by every day. In addition, to my surprise, his father came out from the East Coast and stayed with him for two weeks. His mother came for a couple of days, but didn't do any caregiving.

I met Jack's father when he was here. I didn't meet others in the community at the time. Many of us gathered (including Jack's father and sister) when Jack was dying at Rosehedge. We took turns sitting with him during that long last night and sat quietly together otherwise. We knew he would only want one person in the room with him at a time. He always required people to visit one at a time when he was in the hospital (so I hadn't met any of them during that time).

After Jack died (August 1991), we gathered for a memorial service at David and Steve's home. Jack's father and sister had already gone home. I have photos from that last gathering. We talked about our memories. David showed us some old photo albums. Jack's parents later wrote a couple of letters to me, but that was the last part of the community for me. I don't know if the other caregivers knew each other and interacted in their regular lives.

When I met Terry at massage school, he was anxious for me to meet his partner Dwayne. We went out for lunch and laughed a lot. His dog was also part of his support system. Terry's parents always stayed close. Terry persuaded them (and me) to learn to be caregivers. They took care of him at the end. I don't know what happened to his partner. Another person from massage school (Jessie) also continued to support Terry to the end. I got to know Terry's parents a little better when I visited him at their home. They were quite elderly and not in good health.

When Terry died (May 1993), his parents notified various people, including me, about his memorial service in the social hall at the trailer park where they lived. Jessie and I went to the service. We enjoyed seeing photos from Terry's early life. We stayed for a couple of hours. I never heard from Terry's parents, or Jessie, again. Terry was the center. Once he was gone, we had no common interests.

The community around Raymond also disappeared after he died (spring 1993). His parents were his main support. Other family members were less so, but still present. Several friends, including me, helped. I guess we heard about each other but rarely met.

When he died, Raymond's parents put together a memorial service at a historic mansion, including a feast based on favorite recipes of Raymond. They gave out photos of him and tape recordings of him playing the piano. Family, longtime neighborhood friends, and caregivers came to the memorial. We didn't form a cohesive community. Caregivers (from Madison Clinic, including me) hung out together. No one discussed that he died of AIDS. His parents' friends didn't know about the disease, and they didn't want them to know. Raymond's parents wrote to me a couple of times after the service.

John was skilled at convincing people to volunteer to improve his quality of life. He was never afraid to ask for help. He approved of all his people getting to know each other. Both Chris and I offered him free massage. John was pleased when we became friends, trading massage for a few years. Chris and I are still connected through Facebook.

John got to know Steve (husband of a woman who worked for my husband). Steve wanted to assist people with AIDS. I knew John would never refuse anyone who wanted to help. Steve was extremely useful since he was willing to drive John to Eastern Washington to visit with family. Prior to that, John had been taking the train (I met the train once and brought him home). As John's health got worse, having someone to drive him there and attend him while he was there made the visits possible. Steve was with John when he died.

I sometimes drove John to visit his sister Mary. Mary and I become friends. After John died, we traded bodywork for a long time. We are still in touch. I send her my weekly essays. She calls occasionally. Once, she brought me a huge bouquet of dahlias. The people who run the dahlia garden at Volunteer Park were putting it to bed for the winter and gave away all the flowers. Mary told me recently that she had been thinking about the people who supported John and wanted to be in touch. She hadn't been able to contact most of them all these years (twenty-five) since he died. She misses the community.

I also got to know a woman named Roz through John. She gave him talk therapy and supported his Buddhist interests. She was a massage client of mine for a period of time. I don't really know how we lost touch with each other.

People from John's community visited him often when he was living at Bailey-Boushay for five months. Some inspired him with Buddhist chants.

Others made sure he had delicious food (donated by the Broadway Grill on Broadway). We planned so that he had someone with him at all times (day and night) toward the end.

After John died, the community planned a memorial service for him. Per his request, people were offered little red Chinese envelopes with some of his ashes (if they wanted them). Many people talked about where they would scatter the ashes, including Volunteer Park. (Volunteer Park was known as a place for gay men to connect anonymously.)

One indirect remnant from my friendship with John was my later friendship with Eric. He lived in the same building and was sent to me by a friend (Peter) who had known John. Eric moved across the country and died in Kentucky. His friend Harold had his body cremated and sent the ashes across the country to the friend here, Jim H. Then Jim got me to take them. His ashes were eventually scattered in a small forest belonging to other friends.

Jim H and I became friends while Eric was still alive and living in Kentucky. We shared stories about Eric and I massaged Jim, who was a quadriplegic from an accident years before. Jim was extremely opinionated and ran (wheeled) for office as a Republican. We argued a lot and got along anyway.

I met Harold through letters after Eric died. He is a retired minister who had become sour about all religions. He wrote his opinions at great length and shared them with me. I tried to discuss them intelligently, but often didn't know what he was talking about. Eventually, we ended up just exchanging Christmas cards. I think he is in his nineties and not in good health. He moved from Kentucky to Michigan to be close to family. I suppose I will know he's gone when I no longer receive cards (none in 2018).

The people who work or worked at various AIDS organizations also were communities. Some of them became longtime massage clients of mine. I am still in touch (mostly through Facebook) with some of those people. Most of them have moved on to different careers.

When I was writing this piece, I spent about an hour looking for the card Raymond made me as well as the recipe book. I found the card plus some notes from his parents. I couldn't find the recipes. I also read notes from Jack's parents and Cary's brother. I looked at many obituaries and some funeral services. There were photos in there: Cary, Steve S, Shawn, Susan, Robert C, Albert, and others. I feel connected with those who died and with those who loved them. I remember those days well.

==========

Clues (for Arle)

Michael puzzled
Whether his friend was HIV+ or not
Since he'd never said so, but
Mentioned something about his numbers

We didn't find out, but
Ten years after Michael died
I saw signs for an estate sale
At what was once Arle's house

==========

No One I Know (for Michael)

Pictures on a big bulletin board
at my friend's memorial service
I never knew him that way
healthy and strong, smiling

posing in a dress and heels
He used to roller-skate in those days
racing around Green Lake
thought it would keep him healthy

All I knew was skin and bones
able to walk with great effort
bedridden in the last few weeks
Who is this stranger we mourn?

Surprised by the Virus

Many people with AIDS knew how they got the virus and weren't really surprised, especially if they contracted it after the HIV virus was known. Others were shocked.

One person, Henry, was a friend who seroconverted a few years after we met. When we met, he volunteered passing out condoms at gay bars (not his job; he was a techie in his real life). He was close to a woman who had AIDS (from being raped by a stranger). He had other friends who were struggling with AIDS. After a couple of years, he moved away from the area to another state. Somewhere in there, he was unlucky or careless and acquired the virus.

Ten years or more now since then, and he seems to be doing okay and (I think) not taking any medications. I wondered at the time if he had some kind of survivor's guilt and was careless because of grief over friends who had died. When he moved from here, he left those friends behind. Spending time with them as they suffered had become excruciating. He was young, just in his midtwenties at the time. He was attractive and lively and able to get good jobs.

I heard about "Big Dave" long before I ever met him. He was tall (more than six feet) and big around. He had a big voice, a big smile, and a big booming laugh. The nurses and social workers in the AIDS clinic all loved him. (And later loved his boyfriend, whom he met there, Phil.)

Yes, Dave was gay, but that wasn't how he got AIDS. I heard the story of how he contracted the virus before I ever met him. He used to work in a funeral home in LA (after growing up in North Dakota). He was preparing the body of a man who died of AIDS when a scalpel slipped and went into him. After he developed symptoms, he moved to Seattle where he could get better care.

By the time I met Dave (and Phil), the more effective AIDS medications were available, and the two of them benefitted from standard and experimental treatments. At the same time, they had other health problems, some of which were side effects of the medications, so life was not easy.

We met in 1999, when Dave was forty-two. Someone suggested that he sign up for a massage from me at the AIDS clinic. When he came in for the massage, we talked a lot about life in general, not about how he got the virus. Sometime after that, Dave signed up again and got Phil to sign up as well. Phil was a big guy, but not nearly as big as Big Dave.

The two of them came for massage at my house a few times. I wondered if my old and rickety massage table was able to handle these two big guys. I don't know, but it collapsed not long after.

Dave was active as a volunteer and speaker (paid) for the Northwest AIDS Foundation until he got into a dispute about how they were spending their money. When he was my massage client, he still did a lot of speaking for groups in Bremerton. He was living in low-income housing (Cal Anderson House, named for the local politician who died of AIDS).

Dave's boyfriend Phil was an American who lived abroad. He taught at the American school in London for years. He kept the secret of his HIV status for years and believed he was terminated when his HIV status came out. He got care at the AIDS clinic at Harborview when he was here. The two men traveled back and forth between England and the United States, often visiting families in North Dakota (Dave's family) and in Washington State (Phil's family).

I stopped doing massage about a year after meeting them because of arthritis in my hand. Dave and Phil took me out to lunch once when they were in Seattle. Beyond that, we kept in touch by email. No matter what they went through, they always were optimistic and a pleasure to spend time with. They talked and joked no matter what health challenges they had.

Dave and Phil broke up a couple of years later. Dave was extremely upset. He said they disagreed about monogamy. According to him, Phil told him that gay men don't do monogamy (which I have heard from other gay men, but certainly not always the case). Dave then said to me that he must be a lesbian. Phil didn't say much about what had happened, just that he was sorry about Dave's pain. He talked about his life, as well as travels with friends and romantic partners.

Sometime after that, Dave fell in love with another man (also named Dave) and moved to a townhouse in South King County with his new love. (No, maybe my friend Dave was living there already and the other Dave moved in with him.) Denise and I were invited to the housewarming. It was good to see him again, and all seemed to be well.

I was very surprised a few years later when I heard from Dave that he was living at Bailey-Boushay House. When I went to see him, he attributed his current health problems mostly to out-of-control diabetes. I think he may have had diabetes before HIV. He had a stroke as well. He seemed sad and defeated. I continued to send emails for a long time but never heard back from him again and eventually stopped sending anything a couple of years ago. I guessed that he might have died, and I wasn't notified (protecting his privacy?).

I met very few women with AIDS, but did meet a few.

One of my regular clients, a nurse from the ACTU named Dana, introduced me to her friend (Joy?) in 1996. I used to drive to Dana's house to do massage. She lived far to the south, beyond Renton. Her friend lived near her. When I massaged Dana, Joy also came over occasionally so that I could massage her as well. Dana moved away from the area, to be close to her daughter after a couple of years, so I didn't see Joy after that either.

During the few massages I did with her, Joy and I talked. She had AIDS. She had been married for years and divorced when she was in her fifties. When she began dating again, she didn't think she needed to use protection. She had already gone through menopause, so she wouldn't get pregnant. She knew about AIDS but thought it only affected gay men, so she didn't worry about it. None of us knew much about women getting the virus at that time.

When Joy got sick, she thought she had the flu. When that didn't resolve, her doctor began doing tests on her. It took a long time before he did an HIV test. No one expected a heterosexual woman who doesn't do drugs to turn up HIV positive. But she was.

After I met Joy, I looked for books and articles by and about women with AIDS. I learned that women seem to be more easily infected than men (in heterosexual relationships). HIV needs broken skin to access the blood supply. Women are more likely to get slight abrasions or cuts during sexual contact and thus become susceptible. (For the same reason, homosexual men who are "bottoms" are more likely to get infected, or at least that's what people said at the time.)

Many women who got infected with HIV experienced the same issue as Joy—it often didn't occur to the doctor to test them for the virus.

Virtually all women who got HIV through sexual transmission got it from men. Very few lesbians became HIV positive if they had no sexual relationships with men (and didn't use IV drugs).

It also seemed that most, maybe all, research about prevention and treatment as being done on men. No one knew how women would be different. The biggest effort with women seemed to be in finding ways to treat them so they wouldn't infect their babies during pregnancy and childbirth. That effort was very successful. I heard that Madison Clinic had no documented cases of babies being infected.

Aside from IV drug users, women were often thought of as "innocent victims." My friend Henry's friend was raped by a man who attacked her in her own backyard. She was frustrated by the lack of services and understanding for women. She was also frustrated by the press and others who thought she should have different treatment than other people living with AIDS. She didn't like being referred to as an innocent victim. In her opinion, no one deserved AIDS.

There was also a famous case, a dentist who may have deliberately infected his patients. I'm not sure it was ever proved. The woman who sued him was very young and died really quickly. (That case may have contributed to hysteria about whether HIV positive doctors or dentists should practice.)

The other "innocent victims" were mainly those who had received blood transfusions after surgery or because they had a health condition (such as hemophilia) that required transfusions. Ryan White became famous for that and because he had trouble getting treatment.

From *Wikipedia*, "**Ryan Wayne White** (December 6, 1971–April 8, 1990) was an American teenager from Kokomo, Indiana, who became a national poster child for HIV/AIDS in the United States after failing to be re-admitted to school following an AIDS diagnosis. As a hemophiliac, he became infected with HIV from a contaminated blood treatment (Factor VIII) and, when diagnosed in December 1984, was given six months to live. Doctors said he posed no risk to other students, but AIDS was poorly understood by the general public at the time. When Ryan tried to return to school, many parents and teachers in Howard County rallied against his attendance due to concerns of the disease spreading through bodily fluid transfer." He was allowed back in school, but it didn't work well. "Ryan White attended Western Middle School for eighth grade for the entire 1986–87 school year, but was deeply unhappy and had few friends. The school required him to eat with disposable utensils, use separate bathrooms, and waived his requirement to enroll in a gym class. Threats continued." The family moved to another state, and he continued school until he died. In the end, he helped to change attitudes about people with AIDS, partly because of his public speaking and because of the movie about his life.

There are also questions about HIV going the other direction, from patients to health care workers. This initially caused huge hysteria, with workers entering patients' rooms double gloved and garbed with masks and every other possible protection. After more was known about the virus, the understanding was that needle sticks and other exposure to blood was the only problem. Even then, I heard that seroconversion from this sort of accidental exposure was quite low (less than 10 percent). Nowadays, postexposure treatment has virtually eliminated the risk.

One of the health care workers (a doctor) at the Harborview AIDS clinic (or at the AIDS Clinical Trials Unit) was exposed to HIV (needle that slipped) back in the late nineties, and she did seroconvert. She was getting treatment. I don't know how it turned out. This must have been scary for other caregivers in the clinic.

I still have emails saved from Dave. The first was, I think, in the year 2001: "I'm starting a weight lifting program to try and rebuild/stop some of the muscle wasting that has been going on. Also trying to bulk up some so my stomach isn't SOOOOOO noticable. It will be good to get into shape again. Who know's maybe I'll even be able to loose some weight."

I saved a number of emails, mostly with him apologizing for not responding to my weekly notes (poems and other stuff, not personal letters).

In 2008, "I'm leaving town Thursday for a 2 week family reunion and my b'day celebration in Hawaii courtesy of my brother and his family who now live there. The first time we've all been together in 7 or 8 years, and they just bought a brand newly built home near Pearl Harbor . . . so he wants everybody to see it." He talked about getting together when he returned.

The last I heard from him was in April 2010: "Well, here I am still at B & B housing. I'm closing down my apartment the 17th of this month. Will have to be giving away everything as I don't have anyone to place a few of my things. My family is coming the 20th and hopefully will get the stuff given away and the apartment is cleaned up. Hope you are doing well. I do pretty good. Have a hard time with my speaking and will be having dialysis in the next month or so. So will have to be gotten thru that." This was after I had visited him at Bailey-Boushay.

When I first volunteered at the AIDS clinics, virtually all the patients were white gay men. I heard that Seattle was a "second wave" city. By the time AIDS showed up in Seattle, some other large cities (for instance, New York City and Washington DC) were seeing many straight people (often people of color) who had become infected with HIV through needles (drug use).

This also became true in Seattle toward the end of the nineties. In addition, Madison Clinic began to get patients who were immigrants (many from Africa) who were married couples. Some of the women were clearly Muslims. I heard that there was a lot of shame about AIDS in this group. I also learned that a large percentage of the people living with AIDS worldwide were in sub-Saharan Africa, which is still true. Many in those countries are not benefitting from the new drugs even now.

==========

Unraveled (Dave)

He still comes to the clinic. But I'm not there.
Years ago we went out to lunch.
We laughed. We talked about the virus.
He hoped for the best.
The big man brought warmth.
Corny humor arrived by email.
New drugs gave hope for a future.
Months ago he wrote. He wasn't well.
His kidneys might be failing.
He talked of going out for lunch.
Nothing since then . . . I wonder if he is still alive.

==========

My Friend, in the Nursing Home

Each time I drive past this building, I think of him.
Each time I look down my list of emails, I see his name.
Each time I think of him, and wonder when
I wonder when I will stop there.
I wonder when we will talk face to face.
I wonder how he is doing today.
Today I plan to find a plan, to get there.
Today I remember all the years and conversations.
Today I will see him for sure, if there is time

In the Hospital

During those years when I knew many people with AIDS (1990–1998), I got to know local hospitals, far more than I ever expected.

The only Seattle hospital I knew prior to those years was Group Health (now closed), where both Rebecca and Jacob were born. No, that's not exactly true. I visited both Mollie (my husband's mother) and Dick (close friend) at Swedish Hospital. Both died at Swedish (1980 and 1988).

One vivid memory from the AIDS years is from when Kelly was in the hospital (1999). This was at Providence, after it became Swedish Cherry Hill. I hadn't been there for years (since visiting Albert).

Kelly was bleeding out from alcohol addiction. He was not dying from AIDS. He was HIV positive, but his T-cell count never got low enough to qualify him as having AIDS. In fact, it was always quite normal. The CD4 count is like a snapshot of how well your immune system is functioning. CD4 cells are white blood cells that fight infection. The more you have, the better. These are the cells that the HIV virus kills. As HIV infection progresses, the number of these cells declines. When the CD4 count drops below 200, a person is diagnosed with AIDS. A normal range for CD4 cells is about 500–1,500. Usually, the CD4 cell count increases when the HIV virus is controlled with effective HIV treatment.

The hospital called me when Kelly ended up in the hospital. My number was the only emergency phone number they had from his wallet. Kelly was not conscious. I was able to give them a little information about how to contact Kelly's relatives.

When I got to the hospital, I learned that he was bleeding internally and from his mouth and anus. They had him on a machine that was pumping more blood into him. It was bleeding out as fast as they pumped it in. This seemed to me to be a foolish use of resources. I wasn't sure of the value of visiting him either since he wasn't at all responsive or aware that I could tell. I think they kept pumping blood into him until his relatives arrived and then cut it all off. Perhaps they needed someone who was qualified to tell them to stop the treatment (probably his grandmother)?

I never heard whether the relatives had any kind of service for Kelly. Perhaps they didn't have contact information for me, wanted to just do a family memorial, or just didn't want to do anything. Since I didn't know his family or other friends, I had said goodbye in the hospital and didn't need more.

The person who called about Kelly had supplied a room number, so I was able to walk in and find the room without talking to anyone. This seems still to be true twenty years later. The last time I went to see someone in a hospital, I walked into the building and took the elevator and walked down halls without anyone questioning my right to be there. The big difference now is that names aren't posted on doors, nor is there a visible board by the nurses' desk (with names and diagnoses). The board with names and descriptions of diagnoses was very much part of the hospital twenty-five years ago.

After Jack came home from Swedish hospital (1991), he hoped to have more good years in his life. However, he never got back to anything like how he was before spending three months in the hospital with his second round of pneumocystis pneumonia. After some improvement, he began to get weaker by the day (with KS in his lungs). At that point, he wished he hadn't had the treatment.

He wished that he hadn't been treated because his quality of life was so poor. He didn't talk about the cost (to whom?) for all those days and all the medications, tests, and equipment.

When Jack went into the hospital, he joked about all the machinery working to keep him alive. His lungs had collapsed. He had pneumonia. He needed a catheter for urine. He had a diaper for bowel movements. He was getting IV fluids and medications. He seemed to have tubes coming out everywhere. Since he had recovered from pneumocystis pneumonia in the past, he probably thought he would recover again and go back to his life.

Once he settled in and was alert, Jack began organizing all of his friends. He didn't want anyone to visit without prior approval from him. He wanted one visitor at a time. He wanted his door shut at all times. At his request, the staff put a sign on the door, saying to keep the door closed. As far as I know, his friends and caregivers complied with requests for privacy.

Jack managed his friends well but didn't have as good luck managing the hospital staff. He used to get frustrated that no one responded to his simpler needs. He could be waiting for hours before anyone responded to the call button. He wondered what would happen if he were in dire need.

It seemed as if the nurses responded more quickly to phone calls at their desk than to patients' call buttons. I called various hospitals many times over the years and would ask to be connected to the nurses' station on the ward where my friend was placed. They were always helpful in giving information about how people were doing. I'm pretty sure that wouldn't happen now (in light of HIPAA) and probably shouldn't since they have no way of knowing who is really calling.

One thing Jack really enjoyed was the art on the walls of the hospital. We often spent an hour or more as I pushed him in a wheelchair up and down halls on the various floors. Most of the art was high quality. I noticed later (as a hospice volunteer) that art in nursing homes was often bland and pale. I wondered if they were hoping to keep everyone very calm by not offering anything exciting. The Kline Galland has fine art, as well as art created by residents (some of whom were professional artists when they were in good health). As far as I can remember, we went off on those tours of the halls of Swedish without bothering to notify the nurses' station as to where we were going and when we were going back. No one ever complained about it.

We went up and down the halls of Swedish Hospital until I was comfortable finding my way around the building, which had expanded over the years. I took Jack outside on nice days. Some places were very far away from others, but there weren't any parts (that I saw) where you couldn't find your way from one end of the hospital to the other by going from one hall to another or going up or down on the elevator. Harborview, on the other hand, had wings that weren't connected. You had to get to the correct elevator (on the first floor). If you were on an upper floor, you might have to go down to the first floor to get to another clinic (you can't get there from here).

Another person who didn't simply stay in his hospital room was Albert. He was in the hospital for ten days. His hospital (Providence) was at the time (1990) run by a Roman Catholic order. Crucifixes adorned each room and many of the halls. Photos of stern-looking nuns were lined up along walls. Albert mostly wanted to get out of his room and onto the fire escape so he could smoke. They told him he couldn't smoke in his room. No one paid attention when we went down the hall and onto the fire escape with him in a wheelchair and pushing his IV pole. I guess they didn't approve of him smoking, but gave up on trying to change his behavior. I had quit smoking in 1984, but I never criticized his behavior.

Back in those days, many people were in the hospital for weeks or months. I think things have changed now. Patients are moved on in a few days, either to a nursing home or to their residence. This seems to be true even when they are dying, if there is no more need for skilled nursing care.

One of the scary developments in the midnineties was the appearance of drug-resistant TB. This was especially rough for people with AIDS since their own immune systems weren't equipped to fight it. It was also scary to the rest of us since anyone who had TB could spread it to everyone around him.

Joel came down with a respiratory problem in about 2003. He was HIV positive but didn't have AIDS (since his T-count stayed high). He asked me to visit him in the hospital (Virginia Mason). I went in and stopped at the front desk. The person directed me to the correct elevator. The elevator took a long time to arrive. I wondered what would happen if there was an emergency and they couldn't get people out of the building.

When I finally got upstairs, I walked to his room. There was a sign on his door, directing anyone entering the room to wear protective gear. I went to the front desk to ask what that meant. They handed me the necessary gown, cap, gloves, and mask. They were worried that Joel might have TB.

I obediently put on the gear and walked back to the room. I knocked and went in when Joel called out. He was pissed off about the fear of TB. He was sure he didn't have the disease. He hated having to visit with people who were wearing all that protection. I didn't like it either. I felt like I couldn't breathe and was shut off from real communication.

By the next day, the hospital had the test results and knew Joel didn't have TB. We were able then to relax and have a normal visit.

Something similar happened when John was living in Bailey-Boushay (1994), only they didn't require the elaborate gear. They just asked anyone who went into John's room to wear a mask. He was supposed to wear a mask if he came out of the room. The nurses made fun of the orders by wearing their masks—on top of their heads. I followed their example. The orders for masks were dropped in a couple of days.

Back when Jack was in the hospital in San Francisco (1989?), everyone who came into his hospital room was garbed in all that protective gear. They knew he didn't have TB. They thought they needed that level of protection from HIV. He hated having medical care from people who looked like they were wearing space suits. That was one reason he moved to Seattle.

People were a lot more casual in Seattle, especially at Rosehedge. I don't recall people wearing gloves, even when they were drawing blood or inserting an IV. No one ever wore a facemask. It was surprising at the time, but I think was realistic. I haven't heard of any health care workers getting infected from patients, except when they accidentally got stuck with a needle (still a very small percentage).

Several of my friends were hospitalized at a teaching hospital (Harborview). They seemed to get a lot more attention than people in the other hospitals. Sometimes a doctor would bring in a herd of students and describe what was going on. This hospital seemed to have more nursing staff and nurses who came more quickly when the call button was activated. Bobby (1993) got lots of attention when he was in that hospital during the last week of his life, including a visit from his doctor from Madison Clinic. I felt their support when I was at Harborview visiting him.

Cary (1994) was also in Harborview Hospital. He wanted to see his dog, Lucky. I managed to convince Lucky to get into my car, and we drove over to the hospital. When we got there, we went to Cary's room, acting like we knew exactly what we were doing. No one questioned our right to be there. Lucky was a little spooked by the elevator, but we managed that as well.

I also spent time with my friends in emergency rooms, mostly at the Swedish Hospital. Each time, we seemed to spend hours. The hospital didn't make a difference between Jack (whose doctor was affiliated with the hospital) and Shawn, who simply claimed the right to get treatment in a convenient ER. Lots of time waiting seems to be standard with emergency rooms even now.

Jack had me drive him once to the emergency room after he got out of the hospital (when he was there for so many months). When he first went into the hospital, he was very clear about wanting privacy when he was examined. By the time we made that trip to the ER, things were different. I guess all those months in the hospital changed his perception of how much privacy he needed. (This was my experience after giving birth—much less modesty.) Jack asked me to go into the examining room with him. When the doctor came in, Jack had me stay. He wasn't at all worried about what I might see or hear.

==========

Laugh or Cry

> black humor
> This boy isn't going to die of AIDS
> . . . because I'm going to murder him

hospital humor
He doesn't seem to be in a hurry to die
. . . just keeps circling the drain

patient's humor
He enjoyed gentle massage from his friend
. . . oh, she was cleaning him up

==========

In the Hospital (Jack)

Though he could barely speak,
tubes protruding everywhere,
too weak to walk,
might not pull through.
He reserved the right to say no.

No, to anyone he didn't want to see.
No, to an open door.
No, to more than one at a time.
He was still here,
still in charge of his life.

A Different AIDS World

When we were busy at Urgent Care, one of the med techs remarked that it's job security. Organizations and jobs come and go, as needs change in society. Urgent care may always be needed.

AIDS still exists in 2019. The helping world looks vastly different than it did in 1991, when I first began to meet people who were living with AIDs. AIDS is different now. The needs for care are different.

A huge understanding in the AIDS world in the early nineties was that most people with AIDS died very quickly (generally in less than two years, often much less). People who were living with AIDS knew this. They believed they had no future or no reason to plan for a future. People who worked in the AIDS community (doctors, nurses, researchers, case managers, various volunteers, etc.) also knew that the people they worked with were likely to die in a short time. Relationships were deeply affected by this knowledge. People were often brutally honest. Hearts were broken. The world was often cruelly rejecting. Family and friends often backed away. People in the AIDS community (people with AIDS and helpers) became close very quickly in the midst of the plague.

AIDS is quite different now in the United States (not so much in places like Africa where people still die quickly). Medications are much more effective, albeit sometimes with unpleasant side effects. The preventive vaccine is also quite effective. People know about universal precautions. Some people die of AIDS. Many live relatively normal lifespans. The medications may impair them. Many can't work. Many need help with housing. Most still need frequent medical appointments. They still may face rejection.

When one of the AIDS organizations closed its doors, Dan Savage wrote a column in the *Stranger*, rejoicing that the place had closed. He suggested some people counted on AIDS continuing for their jobs and for their ability to feel good about themselves. He said people who worked in the AIDS community didn't want to see an end to AIDS because of what they would lose. He thought the end of these organizations was a good thing. The column astounded me, and my immediate reaction was to disagree with all he said. I called him up (at the newspaper) to argue with him. He engaged for a couple of minutes but then abruptly got off the phone when someone else wanted to talk to him. I didn't get the chance to suggest that the best thing would be if the organizations continued but offered help to people with other diseases. So much of what I saw in the AIDS community could have benefitted people with other life-threatening diseases.

By 1990, a huge community had grown up around the needs of people with AIDS. Many doctors, nurses, social workers and others worked in clinics or hospices offering services to people with AIDS. People living with AIDS were able to get help finding and paying for housing. They could get food and rides to appointments. They had access to free acupuncture and massage, plus the possibility of low-cost chiropractic treatments. They could attend support groups and have someone to help with spiritual needs. Investigators worked to find effective medications. Bailey-Boushay and Rosehedge were far better than any nursing home I had ever seen. I was part of all this since I offered low-cost massage for people in the AIDS community (people living with the disease and caregivers). I offered free massage at Madison Clinic and the AIDS Clinical Trial Unit. I was disappointed when I had to stop (because of arthritis) that no one was around to carry on what I was doing. I would have been happy if someone had stepped in to continue supporting caregivers and people living with AIDS and other life-threatening diseases.

Caregivers in the AIDS community tended to stay in the community for years. Some people worked in one area and then moved on to another organization. People from the different groups often knew each other and supported each other. Events like the AIDS Memorial Vigil and the fund-raising march for the Northwest AIDS Foundation brought people from different groups (caregivers, patients, families, and friends) together. I got to know many of them when I was doing massage. I gave up massage in 2000. I think most of those people have moved on since then, but not all. Some have continued at Lifelong AIDS Alliance, Bailey-Boushay, Madison Clinic, and other places.

Of course, many of the agencies are gone now that far fewer people are disabled or dying from AIDS. The people who worked for those agencies had no choice but to move on. Other agencies altered their mission to suit the changing times. Rosehedge and Multifaith Works are gone. Shanti (spiritual support) seems to no longer be in the area although it continues in San Francisco. In Touch (massage) is gone, as are other sources of support in the early nineties.

Bailey Boushay is one place that changed with the times. It is part of Virginia Mason and was never just a hospice for people with AIDS. Others were able to live and die there. In early days, there were waiting lists and most of those who lived there did have AIDS. Nowadays, they still have day programs for people with AIDS, plus the hospice care for others who need it, but who may not have AIDS. One of my former massage clients died of cancer at Bailey Boushay. I volunteered for a hospice patient and his wife for a couple of years before he died (congestive heart failure) at Bailey Boushay.

When I was still associated with Madison Clinic, it changed focus to include infectious diseases in general. Hansen's disease (leprosy) was one disease that they studied, and patients were served. Even so, Madison Clinic still offers medical care and social services for persons living with HIV/AIDS, regardless of sexual orientation, gender identity, race, or ability to pay. Their mental health care professionals provide a range of services for patients with HIV/AIDS, including psychiatric consultations, medication management, and recommendations for continued psychiatric care. They also provide medical care to HIV-negative persons who might benefit from having an HIV/AIDS expert involved in their medical care, including those who are interested in pre-exposure prophylaxis (PrEP) for HIV prevention. On the Harborview website, it looks like infectious diseases and Hansen's disease now have separate clinics.

I liked seeing the way those agencies adapted to meet new needs. I always thought that Bailey-Boushay was a perfect example of what a hospice could and should be. I approved of all the other services people living with AIDS could access and wished it were true of people with other life-threatening diseases. Jack once said that it was better to have AIDS than cancer because so much more support was available. This shouldn't be true. People with cancer should have support as well. This would be true of people with ALS and other life-threatening diseases.

Do people become stronger from harsh experiences? Are they better off having gone through them, or would it have been better if they had avoided them? How do the helpers balance giving and whatever they get from being in the position of helping?

Jack once said that he had learned a lot and healed a lot through living with AIDS. He was grateful, and still he would rather not have had AIDS. He also said that he had met many wonderful people because of having AIDS. And, yes, he would have chosen never to meet those people if he could have avoided AIDS. That gave me pause and irrational pain. I might not have known him. I might not have known many people who enriched my life if AIDS had never existed. They would have been much happier without AIDS and without knowing me (since the two events went together).

Jack had a circle of volunteers. One was from the NW AIDS Foundation. Another was from Shanti. One was from Multifaith Works (whatever it was called then). Others had met him through his volunteer speaking about living with AIDS. All of us learned and grew from knowing him. All of us felt fortunate to have been able to spend time with him.

He also saw a doctor who took care of many people with AIDS. If AIDS disappeared, half of that doctor's practice would have also disappeared. He would have still had a practice (and still does twenty-six years later). Jack died at Rosehedge, which existed because of AIDS. Many people had careers because of Rosehedge (now closed). They became part of a caring community.

Many families disowned or at least distanced themselves from family members who were living with AIDS. Friends often backed away. Partners also often disappeared. People who were living with AIDS usually couldn't continue working. Other times, employers who found out about the AIDS diagnosis fired the person who was living with AIDS. Jack, like many people with AIDS, lost family, friends, and work. However, he had the AIDS community. He had all those people who stepped up to support him (and others). He also reconnected with some family members over time.

Jack's father and his sister were with him at the end. His brother (who also had AIDS) was also around. Other family members stayed away. I don't remember him ever mentioning any friends from before AIDS. No, that isn't completely true. He had me take a photo, and he sent it to friends in California. I don't know whether he ever heard back from them. At the end, the people around him (besides his father and sister) were people he knew from AIDS organizations.

Many gay and lesbian people were horrified by the way families and friends abandoned people who were living with AIDS. Many straight people felt the same way. It seemed to me that at least half the caregivers for people with AIDS were gay or lesbian. Many others were older straight people. There was a concerted effort to meet the needs of people who were living with and dying of AIDS to make up for the stigma and the abandonment.

Rick once made a cynical comment about "AIDS junkies." This felt like a slap in the face. He didn't say he meant me, but I took it that way. I decided to think about my reasons for being involved in the AIDS community. AIDS was a way to connect with the gay community. It was also a way to offer support to those who faced a lot of rejection. I had supported those who were rejected as a special education teacher earlier in my life. Volunteering in the AIDS community was a way to be part of a caring community (with other caregivers). This was true of being a special education teacher and also (later) when I became a hospice volunteer. Connecting with people who were living with AIDS usually meant loving someone who was going to die soon. This was true in my life later when I became a hospice volunteer. Now, I think that Rick hated being pitied and was angry.

Medications, doctor's offices, hospitals, and hospices all depend on the continuing need for health care. This is true when we talk about people with AIDS and also true in general. (We could also argue that money spent on the military depends on the continuation of hostilities between various nations.) Does this mean that all doctors, pharmaceutical companies, and other companies connected with health care would prefer that people continue to get sick? I don't think so. Aging, illness, and death are inevitable. Working to help people heal physically and emotionally will always be an available path and one that will be satisfying to some people.

I hope we have learned from AIDS that support can and should be offered to all people who are living with life-threatening illness (cancer, ALS, and other diseases). I think this should also be true for people who live for years with multiple sclerosis, muscular dystrophy, and other diseases.

Bailey Boushay taught us about hospice rooms where visitors can comfortably spend the night. The rooms allow patients to bring their own possessions in. Bailey Boushay also taught us about places where patient privacy and autonomy is protected (unlike nursing homes and hospitals where anyone can walk in). People who are facing death or even experiencing pain and limitations may greatly benefit from massage, spiritual support, acupuncture, and other treatments—all of which were offered to people living with AIDS. Caregivers need training. People who are disabled greatly benefit from food services, as well as having someone come by with the food and in the process check on welfare. I wish that all the AIDS organizations had changed to offer support to people with other diseases, as well as continuing to serve those who are living with AIDS in 2019.

==========

Ghosts Walk

> Walking to hospice training
> memories beckon along the way
>
> A small plain building
> once a thrift store
> Kelly soberly sorted clothing
> some to sell, some to pass on, some to dump
> Shawn checked their donation barrel at night
> kept an eye out for police
>
> On another corner
> a chiropractor
> where I drove John
> watched his treatment once
> Kelly sometimes worked there
> traded filing and gossip for adjustments
>
> The apartment on Summit
> beyond Hamburger Mary's
> late at night
> we heard the shouts of drug dealers
> I helped Shawn to move
> after he was evicted
>
> Denny Terrace looms
> twelve stories above the freeway
> I brought groceries
> to Shawn's friend

Visited Marty in his place
promised sweatpants from J-M

Along with what I see
the unseen presence of other days

==========

That AIDS Look

you would always know
when you saw a young old man
leaning on his cane as he walked
his complexion gray
all skin and bones
you knew it had to be true
along Broadway
or on the streets near my house

AIDS Framed Ten Years of My Life

When I began working in the AIDS community, I was still married. My family schedule affected how much time and when I could spend on various things like giving rides. And then my life changed. The circumstances of my life were different at the end of those years. And I like to think I was different. I learned a lot through all the people and experiences.

In late 1990, when I began volunteering for Chicken Soup Brigade, I was working at my husband's wholesale business in the mornings, but had so little to do that I often went home early or ran errands. (I didn't have to keep track of inventory once it was on the computer. I was processing returns, but it didn't take much time.) Both kids were in school. Rebecca was a senior in high school. She drove my old car. Jacob was in eighth grade. He rode the bus or his bike to get around. They both had many activities and less need for my attention.

I was still responsible for shopping, cooking, and cleaning at home, but had lots of time in the afternoons to drive people to appointments. I had free time to visit people in hospitals or other places. In the fall, I got into the habit of stopping at Rosehedge (to see Michael) as I was driving home from work at lunchtime. Mostly, I made sure my various errands with people with AIDS didn't impact others in the family. And they accepted my choices. For instance, no one questioned when I went out in the middle of the night to be with Jack (plus his father, sister, and friends) when he was dying at Rosehedge (August 1991).

I brought Michael over to our house once after giving him a ride somewhere. We lived in Madison Park. He met the cat Pokey who thought he was interesting (though she was usually afraid of strangers). We stood in the dining room chatting for a few minutes. I don't recall whether that was before or after he showed me his condo.

Once during that time, I realized I had double booked myself. Rebecca (aged sixteen) helped by driving Jack to his acupuncture appointment. I don't remember discussing it with Mike. He was not enthusiastic about my volunteering to drive people with AIDS (worried, I think), but didn't try to stop me.

Even though we had been reassured (during Chicken Soup Brigade volunteer training) about the ease of keeping ourselves safe from HIV, I was nervous when I was visiting Albert at his apartment and needed to use the bathroom. I was embarrassed by my fear and decided the best thing was to just go ahead. I felt better then and less afraid in the future.

Michael got a blood transfusion one day when I was at Rosehedge. He had several and each time had more energy afterward. The transfusions stopped working after a few months. This particular day, the nurse giving the transfusion asked me to help by holding something down. I don't remember what it was. The nurse wasn't wearing gloves, and neither was I. However, the blood didn't come near me, and it was all over quickly. I trusted the nurse.

I began massage school about nine months after I began volunteering for Chicken Soup Brigade. I wanted different work (since I felt unnecessary at Mike's business). I wanted to help people, and I especially wanted something I could do with people who were living with AIDS and caregivers for people with AIDs. Human touch seemed so important and often lacking for people with AIDS. Once I began massage school, I stopped working at Mike's business.

Completing massage school took a year. During that time, I practiced doing massage at school and on friends. Mostly I found ways to practice on people with AIDs. I worked on Albert's feet to help with neuropathy. I studied for school and did practice massages on Jack when I was hanging out at his house after he got out of the hospital. Jack gave me feedback on massage. He also gave me feedback on touch in general. He warned that a big hug felt scary for him since he was fragile. He didn't like to be rubbed continuously on one place. He preferred hands that kept moving. Sudden movements could be frightening. His suggestions became part of how I did massage on everyone.

One requirement of massage school was a course on AIDS. We learned about precautions to take. We were told to always use universal precautions on all clients. That way, it didn't matter if we knew whether the person was HIV positive. We couldn't know for sure about everyone, so it made sense to simply build the precautions into our way of doing massage. We also learned about precautions to protect the person with AIDS, who had an impaired immune system. The school made it clear that the person with AIDS was far more at risk than the massage therapist.

The massage school knew that Terry was HIV positive. They didn't make an announcement, but he told a few people he trusted. The school had the same expectations of him, to do massage and to be a practice subject for other students, as they had for all students. Eventually, he couldn't keep up with the homework and didn't have the stamina to do massage and had to drop out.

John was a huge part of my learning to do massage. He always wanted more massages. He was generous with feedback. He wanted to experience any new techniques I learned. I turned in notes on a series of ten massages on John. The school required us to have a project. He was my project.

One of the last classes at massage school was about the business end and the necessity for planning how to get new clients. I decided to volunteer at Harborview's AIDS clinic as a way to meet potential clients. I went to talk to the nurse manager. He agreed that I could try it. I got a massage chair and gradually learned how to practice in that situation. Some of the people I met that way decided to hire me to do Swedish massage, and I gradually built a practice.

I volunteered to do massage on many people while I was in school. Eventually, it seemed to me that giving free massages to individuals wasn't really a healthy relationship. It felt like I was doing something for someone, and on some level, it seemed (to them and to me) they should give something back. Lee taught me about that when he insisted that he pay me for massage once I was licensed. Chair massage at Madison Clinic and the AIDS Clinical Trial Unit was different. I was giving my time (and efforts) to the clinic and not to individuals. I didn't expect anything from them.

I wasn't worried about money, so when I began charging for massage (spring 1992) after getting my license, I deliberately charged very low amounts for people in the AIDS community (people living with AIDS, caregivers, and family). Eventually, I extended that to anyone who even knew someone with AIDS. Plus, I made the low price available for anyone who signed up for ten massages, even if they had no connection with the AIDS community.

My husband worried about infection and wanted me to wash massage sheets separately from the rest of our laundry if used for someone with AIDS. (Yet he rented the apartment on Greenwood to my friend Kelly, who was HIV positive, which Mike knew. I guess Mike didn't tell the other tenants about Kelly's HIV status. I don't know if he was aware that Kelly took over cleaning the common bathroom and shower.) He didn't want me to do any massages at our house, even though it would have been easy to convert the downstairs guest room into a massage room (helpful having the bathroom right next to it). He thought I should charge more money for massage. Better yet, he thought the real money was in the massage schools and I should start one.

Then I moved out from the marriage (fall of 1993) and could decide for myself. Now I had a room to do massage. Before that, all I did was outcalls. Now I was the only one who had to think about laundry being mixed together. Plus, I could do laundry in the middle of the night. I could have anyone I wanted in my house, including when Eric stayed in the guest room a couple of times. We didn't share food with Eric, only because he'd had all his teeth out (to get rid of heavy metals) and had to cook his own food. He cooked it long enough that it could easily be pureed. I was able to decide for myself about money and about ways to protect myself from any possible infection.

I did worry a little when I was doing massage on Lee, who had many Kaposi's sarcoma. He assured me that they didn't hurt and I should just massage over them. More recently, I've seen the suggestion that touching KS can be a source of contagion, but only for people with compromised immune systems. (Maybe it would be an issue now that I am old?)

Once I got past the fear of being infected by people living with AIDS, I became a missionary. Anyone who mentioned the subject heard about universal precautions and why I wasn't at risk, even when giving massage to a person with AIDS. In fact, one of my clients didn't have HIV (although his partner had died of AIDS) but did have hepatitis B, which is far more contagious.

I guess I was also influenced by what Jack told me. When he had pneumocystis pneumonia in San Francisco, caregivers came into his room with double masks and gloves, plus full-length protective coats. He felt rejected and contaminated because of this behavior. I didn't ever want to act the way he had observed in those people. I was much more comfortable with the attitude of caregivers at Rosehedge, Madison Clinic, and the ACTU.

Albert also influenced me. He was sure that his family would never come near him again if they knew he had AIDS. He was especially sure they would keep the children away from him. He didn't think they would allow him to come to see them or eat with them. He chose to stay alone in his apartment rather than going into Rosehedge at the end of his life. He was more afraid of family rejection than he was of dying by himself (as he did). I wanted to let everyone know that there was no need for this level of fear. I hoped that others wouldn't face rejection.

Now that I wasn't in the marriage, I felt free to introduce people who were living with AIDS to family members. I invited Steve to one of our family meals, downstairs at Mom's, when he wasn't getting along with his family. He brought a salad. Steve had KS on his face, and everyone knew that he had AIDS. I didn't notice any apprehension among any of the people at the Thanksgiving table about Steve or about eating the food he brought. Everyone seemed to welcome him.

Mom met John at least a couple of times. She came with me to meet him at his apartment or at Bailey-Boushay (I don't remember which). John and I were at Mom's house (on Dibble) once, but he was too weak to go into the house, so we sat in the backyard on the grass. Mom brought brownies and tea out to us. Getting John back up off the grass and into his wheelchair was really challenging. Gigi came with me once to Bailey-Boushay and met John.

Things began to change in the AIDS world not long after John died in February 1994. All the work by the ACTU and clinical trial units produced protease inhibitors (1995–'96). In a short time, AIDS deaths dropped by about 2/3. Living with AIDS was (is) still challenging because of the side effects of the new medications. Still, it was a different world.

By 2000, lots had changed in the world of AIDS. I still saw patients and caregivers at Madison Clinic and the ACTU, but few people were dying. Some had recovered after nearly dying and were going about normal lives. Some had serious side effects from medications. Others seemed to be completely healthy.

In the meantime, I was struggling to continue doing massage. I looked for ways to ease pain in my hands with various kinds of self-massage. The pain was often intense by the end of the day, but minimal the next morning, so I could cope. And then came a day, in late 2000, when my hands were just as painful in the morning as they had been at night. I canceled my plans for the day and went into the doctor. X-rays showed arthritic deterioration of the joint. I was given a brace, but no promises were made that I could ever get back to my busy massage schedule. I completely canceled all massages, including chair massage at Madison Clinic. This part of my life was done.

One thing that seems important to me is to plan ahead what you can do and still have time and energy for the rest of your life. I learned as a hospice volunteer to stay with the hours I was supposed to give. I might do less sometimes, but never more.

Shawn taught me that even before I was a hospice volunteer. There was no end to what he would demand. He especially always had reasons to need money. During the last part of our relationship, when he came back into my life after a few years of no contact, he had come to realize that I wasn't going to give him any more money. That is, he believed me finally when I told him. He worked in the garden quite a few hours to earn some money and never asked me to give him any more.

John's sister and I had to enforce boundaries with John also. He did not want to move out of his apartment and into Bailey Boushay. He accepted that he couldn't be alone. He proposed that his sister and I take turns being with him at his apartment so he would never be alone. We refused. Then he was finally willing to move.

One thing I enforced with Jack (but failed with others) was expecting him to pay for anything he asked me to buy. I didn't allow him to pay for items that were my idea. He fully agreed with that position. It was easier with him since I knew he had more money than Shawn or John.

Boundaries were a lot easier to maintain as a hospice volunteer, where I could cite the rules of the organization and not have to admit I was saying what I wanted. I realized that it is good to be part of a team and to think of the needs of the team. I should have known that earlier (for instance, as a Chicken Soup Brigade volunteer), but it didn't sink in then.

I guess I did feel like part of the team at the Harborview clinics. Volunteering to individuals often seemed awkward. The situation at Madison Clinic and ACTU was much easier. I didn't have anything to do with the sign-up sheet. I obeyed the rules and worked within the time frame I set up. I didn't attempt to build friendships with patients or staff. I had a more difficult time with people who came to my house for massage or if I went to theirs. I know I often gave them too much unsolicited advice. I didn't really learn to listen until practicing as a therapist.

I finally learned to say "I'm going to leave now" rather than something feeble like "I need to leave." No one has ever had a problem with that statement.

When I stopped doing massage, I continued to hear from a few of the people I knew from the AIDS community (and still do), but my life was much different in 2000 than it was in 1990. I had moved from Madison

Park to Capitol Hill. My daughter was married and done with law school. My son had finished college and was building his life. My ex-husband had died. I had to figure out what to do next with my life now that I couldn't do massage anymore.

==========

To the Rescue (John)

complaining of pain he hobbled to the table
asked me to put my hands
here and there
no, stay, don't move on
now a couple of inches further
or on the other leg
return to the low back and the hip

incense burned on the side table below a candle
the pain left for a moment and then returned
low voices chanted, droned in the background

an hour passed and another
still he groaned in agony
begged me to keep working
I couldn't stop while he still suffered
must fix him for a while
if not for ever
my efforts meant nothing, the pain remained

==========

The Look

Thinning hair, hollow cheeks, big eyes, passing by
unknown. Only presumption, still pulls at my heart,
reminds me of men known, held close and loved,
or known less well. I miss them and long to comfort
another on the path. I know nothing, yet think I know.

==========

Michael

a sunny spring afternoon on the weekend
not the best time to head to the garden store
two blocks away, I send a message

to my parking angel
my friend dead now almost twenty years

close to the driveway
first one and then another car leaves
not just a parking place he provided two

==========

Free from the Hospice (Michael)

a day like this with trees hanging low
still laden with golden leaves
driving on the winding road through the arboretum

takes me back seventeen years
my new friend sat beside me
for a few minutes thought only of the season

Made in the USA
San Bernardino,
CA